DESERT LANDSCAPING

DESERT LANDSCAPING

HOW TO START AND MAINTAIN A HEALTHY LANDSCAPE IN THE SOUTHWEST

GEORGE BROOKBANK

The University of Arizona Press Tucson & London

The University of Arizona Press

♾ This book is printed on acid-free, archival-quality paper.
Manufactured in the United States of America

97 96 95 6 4 3 2

Library of Congress Cataloging-in-Publication Data

Brookbank, George. 1925–
Desert landscaping : how to start and maintain a healthy landscape in the Southwest / George Brookbank.
p. cm.
Includes index.
ISBN 0-8165-1201-9 (pbk. : alk. paper)
1. Desert gardening—Southwest, New. 2. Landscape gardening—Southwest, New. I. Title.
SB427.5.B76 1991
635.9′52—dc20 91-21559
CIP

British Library Cataloguing-in-Publication Data
A catalogue record of this book is available from the British Library.

Contents

Introduction

Good landscape maintenance results in less work, which leaves more time for enjoying the outdoor living that attracted so many of us to the Southwest in the first place. If you maintain your landscape yourself, this book will help you find ways to make the work more satisfying and productive. If you hire someone else to tend your little corner of the desert, this book will help you make sure the work is done effectively and economically.

Teachers of ornamental horticulture in high schools and junior colleges, as well as those who earn their livings by landscaping and maintaining other people's yards, also will find the down-to-earth information in these pages useful and instructive.

You'll find all kinds of books in the shops and at the library on desert landscape design and materials, irrigation system design, and landscape installation. Garden clubs, native plant societies, and government agencies throughout the low and intermediate deserts of the Southwest have published descriptive lists of recommended plants for local conditions. So far as I know, however, this is the only book that tells you what to do with what you've got and how to keep it growing.

As I compiled this encyclopedic guide to desert landscape maintenance, my seventeen years' experience as an extension agent in urban horticulture with the University of Arizona proved invaluable. All those years of playing detective in preparation for answering the urgent questions of homeowners and professional landscapers faced with incipient horticultural catastrophe gave me a very definite idea not only of what can go wrong in the home landscape, but also of how to avoid problems before they occur and of how to fix those that turn up anyway.

My book is divided into two parts. The first, *How to Start and Maintain a Desert Landscape*, addresses concerns ranging from how to start a wildflower garden to how to cope with Texas root rot in easy-to-use, single-topic chapters. The second, *A Month-by-Month Maintenance Guide*, distills advice from Part I into a calendar of maintenance tasks by season. Whether you are cultivating citrus trees, growing a container garden of colorful annuals on your patio, or overseeing a sprawling collection of desert succulents, you'll find Part II a handy index to the more extensive discussions contained in the first twenty-eight chapters.

I hope you'll take as much pleasure in using this book as I took in writing it.

George Brookbank
Tucson, Arizona

PART I

How to Start and Maintain a Desert Landscape

1 How They Are "Different" DESERT CONDITIONS

Visitors to the American Southwest often get their first look at the desert in winter. The weather is beautiful and inviting. Bright sunny days are the rule, and temperatures are comfortable day and night. During a "cold" winter, even the few nights of frost are not an inconvenience; the next morning the sun shines warm and friendly. Desert vegetation and yard plants are green. When it rains, the showers are gentle and kind. Winters in the desert are like summer "back home."

As those of us who live here could tell our winter visitors, it's not like that all through the year. The desert offers landscape gardeners some thorny challenges.

DESERT SOILS

Desert soils are short of organic matter. They are sandy and gritty and gravelly. With a sparse vegetation, no leaf litter is formed, and so organic material doesn't accumulate. It either burns up or is blown away before it dries into dust. Because of the low organic matter, desert soils are bright reds and yellows instead of dark browns and black.

Desert soils are low in nitrogen, the stuff that makes plants grow. Nitrogen usually comes from decaying organisms, both animal and plant, and is preserved by dampness. Deserts don't have the same abundance of animals or vegetation that wetter regions do, so nothing gets started. Any little beginning dries up and blows away.

Desert soils usually are low in phosphorus. Phosphorus comes mainly from rocks, but desert rocks are low in phosphates. The result: no beginning, no accumulation, no plant nutrients.

Desert soils contain potash in adequate amounts, largely because the rocks contained it; as they were broken by the heat, the nutrient became available and, because of the lack of rain, it wasn't washed away.

Leaves mottled like this one might mean that the soil is short of iron, or that the soil is too wet. Check soil moisture content and drainage before applying an iron fertilizer.

Desert soils contain a great deal of calcium, which can become an impediment to landscaping. First, a soil with too much calcium causes alkalinity, which makes plants—especially those from "back home," like azaleas, camellias, and gardenias—so uncomfortable they can't cope. Second, an excess of calcium in the soil interferes with the uptake of other plant nutrients, such as iron, copper, zinc, and manganese, even if they are present. In the midst of plenty, the plant starves for lack of the essential minor nutrients.

There's another handicap caused by calcium abundance that you learn to recognize early on—as soon as you dig a planting hole, in fact. Calcium dissolves in water; as the water dries, the calcium reforms as a solid. Stalactites and stalagmites are formed this way. In some soils, the reformed calcium looks like nodules of gravel. This doesn't matter too much, because roots can grow around the nodules and water can drain past them.

But sometimes it is a solid layer of a concrete-like, pinkish material three feet thick. That's serious because roots can't grow through it; they "bottom-out" on it. When abundant rains fall or when heavy irrigations are applied, the water can't drain away. Roots are drowned in this collected water, and the plant suffers. We call this stuff caliche, and it's a real nuisance. You have to physically get rid of caliche by digging it out. There's no way to remove it by adding chemicals.

Desert soils often contain sodium, and when they do the problems increase. First, sodium is a plant poison and, second, it destroys the structure of soils, making them greasy and impervious. Fortunately, sodium is water-soluble and can be washed out of the soil as long as there is good drainage.

Desert soils usually are sandy, which helps ensure good drainage. Once in a while, however, there are localized patches of heavy silt or clay. You usually find these in low-lying flat-

Most desert soils are so hard it's impossible to use a shovel to dig a hole without first loosening the soil with a pickaxe.

lands where flooded rivers poured their salt-laden waters. Nothing much grows in soils that have bad drainage.

DESERT CLIMATE

Anyone who has spent as little as a year in the desert realizes what great extremes it embraces.

Summer is very hot, with the thermometer standing at 100 degrees for days at a time and peaking as high as 115. For an hour or two in the same place, however, a nighttime winter temperature can be as low as 12 degrees.

Most of the time it's very dry, yet heavy summer rains quickly run off because they come down too quickly for the soil to absorb them. These sudden summer storms are so localized that they often leave one side of a street dry. Winter rains are softer and fall over a more widespread area.

Just before the rains the humidity climbs, but for most of the year the relative humidity reads 12 percent (or less!), dry enough to curl up sheets of paper—or leaves. And the sun has an intense heat, brilliant and burning.

Seasonal spring winds come moist from the west and then dry from the east in the same week, making new shoots—and humans—miserable. Storm winds in the summer can reach 70 miles an hour and break tree limbs. Lightning bolts kill palms and other tall trees.

(Above) Somewhere under the surface there's often a solid concretelike material called caliche. It must be removed, and that may require power equipment.

(Below) In the low-lying land along floodplains you'll find heavy silt soils and even heavier clays, like the soil pictured here, that shrink when dry and expand when wet.

Winter snows come as a surprise and don't last long in the desert. Arid-land plants can stand only a few hours of this.

In recent years the desert has beaten all records, not only for summer heat but also for dramatic winter weather. Snow, however, is not as hard on desert plants as are consistently cold nights with frost.

Day length also influences plant growth. There isn't a lot of difference between a midsummer day in Tucson, with fourteen hours of daylight, and a midwinter day, with ten hours, but lengthening spring days, culminating in the spring equinox of twelve hours of daylight and twelve hours of dark. These changing hours influence the growth of new leaves and flowers on trees and shrubs. The shortening fall days stimulate the same plants to put out new leaves and to flower at the fall equinox. Newcomers find this a strange occurrence.

These extremes determine which plants can be grown and which can't. Some plants, such as the saguaros, acacias, agaves, and many others native to the area, can take these extremes and the stresses they cause. Roses, camellias, chrysanthemums, and others from different soil types and from gentler climates don't manage nearly so well.

Plants that are compatible with desert conditions require much less fussing over (which is called maintenance) than do the introduced exotics. Maintenance is either time (if you do the work yourself) or money (if you have someone else do the work). You can save on both if you go native. (For more, see Chapter 3.) It's taken landscape architects a few decades to realize this, and some haven't learned it yet. We still see new plantings of trees and shrubs that may do well at the head office in coastal California, but that simply are not in tune with local conditions. As a result, landscape and maintenance crews struggle with a situation not of their own making, and one that could easily be avoided. What's more, someone has to pay them for their unproductive efforts.

LANDSCAPE MAINTENANCE SHOULD GO HAND-IN-HAND WITH NATURAL CONDITIONS

Soils

It's a prerequisite for any landscaping development that you first remove caliche. You must dig through it so that water drains freely; that is the key to success. If there's poor drainage, there's poor growth. You can't change that by any other cultural operation—not by a different irrigation schedule, or a changed fertilizer program, or pruning, or spraying, or anything. If the caliche is too thick to remove, you have to give up the idea of growing a tree or a shrub in that part of the yard. Otherwise, it's folly. (For more, see Chapter 6.)

Because desert soils are low in nutrients, apply fertilizers to desert trees and shrubs in small amounts, if at all. They don't normally get a lot of fertility, and they can survive without a lot of help. Frequent fertilizer applications only force growth, making new growth soft and vulnerable to pests and diseases. Restrain yourself when you get the urge to make desert plants grow more rapidly. (For more, see Chapter 7.)

Climate

Summer heat causes many plants to go dormant in the same way that winter cold makes plants go dormant. We are used to leaves changing color in November when it gets cold, and at first we don't understand why leaves turn yellow and drop during a hot desert summer.

Newcomers rush to the nursery and buy an iron fertilizer to correct the situation, the salesperson having told them that our soils are short of this element and that yellow leaves mean iron chlorosis. Quite often it's simply old inside leaves dying of heat exhaustion. Besides, with the whole leaf a uniform yellow, it's not iron chlorosis. The iron chlorosis symptom is a yellow color between green veins on young leaves. If you see this, it's often the result of a soil that is too wet because of poor drainage—a caliche syndrome. Try to improve things by not watering so often. If that doesn't work, go for the iron. (For more, see Chapter 8.)

We have cool seasons and a hot season, and annual plants to go with each. Most of our natural wildflowers are cool season growers and there also is a long list of ornamental annual flowers that thrive in cool weather. In the summer there are fewer kinds in both categories. We must remember not to get our wires crossed. Pansies won't grow in July, nor can we grow portulaca in the winter. (For more, see Chapters 16, 17, and 18.) Ryegrass dies of the heat in June. It's a lawngrass for the winter, when Bermudagrass is dormant and brown. (For more, see Chapter 19.)

Air temperatures fluctuate with alarming irregularity in the spring, but the soil warms slowly. Then, all of a sudden, both air temperature and soil temperature become unbearably hot for a newly planted tree. Spring is the conventional time in milder climates to plant shrubs and trees, but in the desert it's not as good a time as the fall, when air temperatures steadily decline and the soil remains warm enough to stimulate new root growth. Remember, too, that plants grow better during rainy periods. If you can, plant—and transplant—during these times. Desert plants are opportunists: they are static during bad times but show a spurt of activity as soon as good conditions present themselves. (For more, see Chapters 6 and 15.)

It should be obvious that there's little need to irrigate during a wet period, yet automatic sprinklers turn themselves on even during a rainshower. On the other hand, soil may still be dry after a summer storm if the storm was localized and the deluge ran off the soil surface. You may have to augment that elusive rainfall with a good deep irrigation. Even when rain doesn't fall, the universal humidity of the summer rainy season encourages plants to put out new leaves. If they do so and receive no irrigation, they have to use moisture reserves from within the plant—a risky thing if the expected rain fails to materialize. By the same token, don't stimulate growth in semi-dormant trees during warm winters by liberal irrigations. (For more, see Chapters 4 and 5.)

Rain stimulates growth, which brings us naturally to pruning. There are two basic kinds: (1) trimming for appearance and (2) cutting to train the plant's framework.

Trimming for appearance should be done lightly and frequently during growth periods. Otherwise, hedges quickly become untidy and you have to remove a lot of wasted growth if the job is left too long. Training cuts need to be done before growth spurts start. That's why it's best to prune roses at the end of a dormant period: in January for spring flowers and in August for fall blooms. (For more, see Chapters 20 and 21.)

Prune your woody trees while the sap is down; in other words, prune while they are dor-

Low-lying desert areas collect more cold and more moisture during the winter months than do higher areas, as evinced by the ground-hugging fog in the middle ground of this photo. If you live in such an area and choose frost-tender plants, you'll be doing a lot of repair work at spring pruning time.

mant. If you make large cuts during a growth period, a lot of sap comes out the cut ends. This sap is sugary and nourishes slime flux bacteria and sooty canker fungus, whose spores are blown on the wind. Once they get into a tree's system, they destroy the tissues and can kill. Always seal pruning cuts with a spray of pruning paint, especially during a warm winter that won't allow trees to go fully dormant. (For more, see Chapter 21.)

Weed seeds germinate after a good rain. Apply pre-emergent weed-killing chemicals (provided your gardening philosophy allows for such) before the autumn showers and before the summer storms of July. You'll save yourself a lot of weeding later on if you get the timing right. Otherwise, the best way to control weeds is to pull the complete plant up. You can do this when the soil is soft after a good rain. If you try it during the dry season, the stalk snaps off and the plant keeps growing. (For more, see Chapter 10.)

Texas root rot is a summertime pest. Don't let people frighten you into buying a lot of expensive stuff for treatment during the winter; your tree's poor appearance could be due to something else, requiring some other kind of attention. (For more, see Chapter 12.)

Finally, be observant of desert conditions, but also be aware that one year of watching is not enough. Each year is different from the last. To get information quickly, talk with your neighbors, join a garden club, and read the local writers in your newspaper (not the syndicated stuff from Chicago; it doesn't work in the desert).

Ocotillo responds dramatically to summer rains by leafing out like this. If the leaves drop off in a week or two because the rain abandons your neighborhood, there's nothing wrong with your ocotillo. Some people keep their ocotillos greener longer by irrigating, but that's tampering with Mother Nature.

2 They're Not Alike
PLANTS ARE LIKE PEOPLE

It's strange how many people have a short-sighted view of plants. They think that all mesquites are the same, all ocotillos, all privets. Oh, they recognize that roses come in different colors, but, even then, all rose plants are expected to perform the same.

We look at plants in the nurseries, row on row, and they all look alike. They are so alike that it's hard to pick the best one. This is a tribute to mass production by the giant nurseries. They have developed a factory-style production, complete with quality control that stresses uniformity. We unthinkingly accept uniformity when we plant to rigid specifications—ten one-gallon size and seven five-gallon size—from an architect's plan. A design for our little plot is made from a book of standards and a plant list without considering the interesting variations of a particular plant. Every juniper, we think, must look like all the others. It isn't so. You've heard people say, usually about a delinquent relative, "Thank goodness we're not all alike!" This thought applies just as well to plants. There's merit in variability.

If our first contact with plants is with those that have been grown in the mass-production nurseries and displayed in large retail garden centers for our inspection, it's natural to assume that all plants are the same. When we get them home and find out that they don't perform uniformly, we feel let down. We have come to consider any irregularity in our landscape plants to be "wrong." When they don't all behave in exactly the same way we get upset, especially if next door's plants seem to be better.

PLANTS ARE DIFFERENT BECAUSE OF GENETICS

Even a beginning gardener knows that geraniums are different from roses, and that roses come in different colors. He or she soon learns that there are less obvious differences among plants of the same species. These differences are due to genetic make-up. Some roses are bigger than others, some don't freeze as much as others, and some take the desert sun better. Some roses grow better in a sandy soil, while others prefer a heavy soil. Some get mildew more than others, some attract more aphids, some appear to get crown gall all too easily. The list is endless.

These individual characteristics—some visible and some hidden from us because they are performance characteristics—aren't confined to roses. They are present all through the plant kingdom. In fact, all plants have their own personalities. As in humans, character is often hidden, waiting for something to happen to reveal it.

PLANTS GROWN FROM SEED VARY IN THEIR CHARACTERISTICS

Let's say you want to grow a lot of desert willow trees from seed. You gather ripe pods from the trees in August and strip out the small flat seeds. You put them, one by one, into foam coffee cups filled with a mixture of perlite and vermiculite, add water, put them in a warm sunny place, and wait. Even though all these seeds came from one tree—even from one pod—you'll notice that they don't all germinate at the same time. The seedlings vary in size, too, and you'll find that they grow at different rates. Some will be leafier than others, some will have darker leaves or broader leaves. Some will drop their leaves in the fall more readily than will others. Some will branch early and others will be single-stemmed for a while. When they flower, some will be a deep purple and some will be almost white. All these differences in seeds from the same tree!

Their physical personalities are showing, but their physiological personalities won't show until later, when they meet drought, bright sunshine, dry wind, diseases, pests, and freezes. Different seedlings from the same tree will react in different ways to these influences.

The total characteristics of a desert willow seedling come from both of the parent trees—from the tree that flowered and developed the seed, and from the tree that produced the pollen that was carried by an insect to the flower. It's a matter of chance which of the parents' characteristics are jumbled together to form the personality of the seedling. This means that each and every seed provides us with a slightly different plant, different from the other seedlings and different from the mother tree.

Raising plants from seed gives us variety and change, and this can be interesting. It's the way plant breeders get new varieties. But it becomes exasperating if we get nothing but a mixture of plants when we want uniformity. We like our hedges to be uniform, we like our lawns to be even and regular, we like a row of repetitive trees to be identical. Further, we like them all to perform the same and to respond to various influences in the same way.

UNIFORMITY CAN BE OBTAINED BY TAKING CUTTINGS

Let's say we want to have a uniform hedge of oleanders. We want identical height and spread, identical resistance to frost, and an even rate of growth among plants. We want foliage color and flower color to be the same, too. It is possible to have all this uniformity, and one of the better ways to get it is to take cuttings from a single oleander plant.

A cutting is a piece of the plant, about 6 inches long, that is placed in a moist planting mix and watered until it grows roots from its base. Take ten cuttings or a thousand cuttings from one plant and they will all be the same. They will all grow to look alike—just like the parent plant from which you took the cuttings—and they will all respond alike to various influences. They are identical clones.

As soon as you collect seed from your uniform oleander hedge, however, you lose the uniformity. Instead of clones, the seedlings will be new plants with a jumble of characteristics inherited from their parents. You may get some wildly interesting new plants, or you may not. There's no telling.

PLANTS' SURROUNDINGS OFTEN VARY

Plants' personalities show up when you treat them differently. It's the same with people: personality differences show up as the result of experiences and because of different surroundings. Some of the treatments may be deliberate, some accidental. The results are often delayed—maybe by as much as a year or two—and so we don't always connect cause and effect.

Your neighbor's lawn may be better than yours, yet your management seems to be just as good. Even in your own lawn there may be better and worse patches that are hard to explain. Your lawn is flat, it is treated the same all over, and the irrigation is evenly done. So, why the differences?

Here's a possible answer. A few years ago, during a building boom, it was common practice to throw broken plaster, surplus concrete, and construction sweepings into convenient holes around a building site. Then the dirt was spread evenly to level everything. It was only later, when the new homeowner tried to grow things, that these mini-dumps showed their poisonous presence.

Here's another possibility. Perhaps a previous owner brought in topsoil to a part of the yard. Any differences in topsoil from the original means differences in water penetration, in fertilizer absorption, in drainage, in root development (which we don't see), and in plant growth (which we do).

There could be differences in soil preparation

A tree planted in a large hole invariably will do better than one planted in a small hole, or so I've found. Still, one hole could have caliche that was not smashed through; as a result, there is poor drainage and poor top growth. One of the two holes could have received a different backfill; one might have more sand or more peat moss than the other. If the contractor ran out of manure and substituted "forest mulch" in one, each tree's roots will be growing in different conditions and it will show, sooner or later. And trees planted by a landscape crew close to quitting time on a Friday afternoon generally have a poorer chance of survival than do those planted during a brisk morning at the beginning of the week!

Size at planting time is important

A nursery tree in a five-gallon container usually is the best size to plant. A smaller plant with fewer roots is less able to cope with hot soil, irregular irrigation, a blasting sun, and dry desert winds. A smaller tree will take longer to get established as an independent plant, and it will be vulnerable during that time.

On the other hand, a tree growing in a larger container usually is out of balance with itself; its foliage may be full, but in order to make the plant transportable many of its roots had to be cut. The thick support roots that remain don't have the space or the time to grow new feeder roots.

Then there is the common problem of a plant that has been left too long in its container. Instead of developing a strong downward taproot, it grows a rope of several roots that curl round and round inside the can. Such a plant will show a lazy personality for many years, and you won't know why until you dig it up. This problem is especially common among plants sold in one-gallon containers.

There's an even more severe instance of personality repression: a plant is put into the ground still in its container! After someone hurriedly threw it in the ground it struggled for years and was sworn at, but it simply was unable to mend its ways.

A B C

D E F

The six photos grouped here show the great variation in form, branch habit, openness of foliage, and general appearance of the Aleppo pine, a species that does well in the desert. Aleppo pine is grown only from seed and the lack of uniformity of character is typical. A: dense center but widely spaced branches. B: a very open tree. C: an open tree with full branches. D: a dense, billowy, round-topped tree. E: a "starburst" tree. F: a full silhouette with open branches.

Different fertilizer treatments lead to different growth rates

If a plant gets its fertilizer in small amounts during growth periods, it will develop better than one that gets its annual requirement in one application during the dormant season. You can "burn" plant roots with too heavy an application of fertilizer, and so cause leaves to drop. Don't blame the plant if this happens. Even if the leaves stay on, the killed roots cause a check in foliage growth, and you never see the cause of it. It's not the plant's fault.

Different irrigation practices lead to different growth rates

This is particularly true during the early establishment months. If growth spurts occur when the soil is dry, growth will be minimal. Too wet a soil is bad news, too. Drowning roots can't function properly and wet ground encourages soil diseases that weaken a plant, even kill it.

Different locations lead to different plant performances

This becomes very clear when you see a hedge

Can you spot the "odd man out" among these palm trees? It's easy to tell now that one is a different species, but in the nursery it was indistinguishable from the others.

planted all around a building. Those plants on the north side don't get enough sunshine and are spindly. Those on the west side get too much sun in the summer and their foliage blisters. Plants on the east side look best because they get good morning light and are protected from the fierce afternoon sun.

Even if all the plants started out the same (as a clonal propagation, say), received equal irrigation from a drip system, and were equally well cared for, they will perform differently because of their situation. It's largely a matter of light, but there's winter cold to consider, too.

Plants placed around a parking lot have to put up with exhaust fumes that a human being wouldn't tolerate. Plants don't like it, either. Don't criticize them if they're not as happy as those on the golf course; it's not their fault.

Micro-climates make a difference

A parking lot is a micro-climate, and a pretty nasty one. There are micro-climates all around us, some obvious and some quite subtle. As far as plants are concerned, your front yard is different from your back yard, and plants will express their personalities differently in each place.

Any shrub growing near a wall that gets a lot of sunshine will have to put up with a double dose of heat and a double dose of light. During summer either could be too much for it, but during a freezing winter the additional heat might save its life. Away from the wall, the same kind of plant will grow differently. A white wall affects plants differently than does a dark wall, owing to the differing levels of reflected light.

Plants growing too closely to a sidewalk, a blacktop area, or a brick wall will be hot in summer. Plants out in the wind will have a different shape than will the same kind growing in a sheltered place. Both plant shape and form are influenced by too much shade. A normally compact rose bush is drawn out by the shade of a tree and becomes spindly.

PLANTS ARE LIKE PEOPLE: THEY'RE DIFFERENT

Next time you compare your neighbor's plants with yours—or those in the front yard with those in the back—don't begin by criticizing them. Think. Discover the reasons for the differences. If maintenance practices are the cause, you can easily change them. If differences are caused by the plant's personality or by the way it was brought up, change is not so easy, but you probably can make some adjustment.

But don't take the analogy too far

Plants are like people, but sometimes you hear people talking about their plants as if they *really were* people: "Should I give him a little more water?" "Does she need feeding this month?" "He's all over the place; what shall I do with him?" "I don't think she looks very strong."

It's understandable. What's more human than black-eyed Susan, sweet William, violet, daisy, and rosemary? Don't fall for it, though. It's better not to give your plant a name for fear of giving it too much milk of human kindness. Plants don't think. They simply do what they have to do. You can't change their personalities, but you can provide them with the best possible conditions. Then they will give their best performance—for themselves, not for you.

ENJOY THE DIFFERENCES YOU FIND IN PLANTS

It should be comforting to realize that plants aren't all the same, that a compact shrub is just

Why aren't all the oleanders in this hedge flowering? The answer is simple: Although they are all oleanders, each is a separate plant with its own personality.

as acceptable as an open, rangy one. There is as much delight in an early bloomer as in another that blooms later.

A landscape that is installed to do its thing in a regular, consistent, predictable, and reliable way is awfully dull. A landscaped area made up of a variety of plants that give us pleasant surprises is interesting. *Vive la difference!*

3 USE ARID-LAND PLANTS TO SAVE WATER

Long ago, when people first began to settle down and build houses, there was no such word as landscaping. People simply chopped down plants that were in their way and saved a few that appeared to be useful. Trees provided shade, thorny plants kept wild animals out, others gave a little fruit, some medicine, leaves for thatching, rope for binding, and so on.

Even in today's emerging countries of the world, where life is more of a struggle, plants are not valued for their appearance. There's something astounding to a native of such a place in watching foreigners dig the ground, make it smooth, plant grass and water it, fertilize it to make it grow, cut it to keep it short, and then throw the grass away!

In a similar way, new arrivals in the desert have always brought conflict with them. It's a resource issue here: we can't afford to use plants that need a great deal of water.

A great variety of plants makes up a natural desert landscape. Try to emulate this diversity in your home landscape.

ALL LANDSCAPES HAVE BASIC COMPONENTS

Every landscape is made up of components in several categories, some more prominent than others. First, there are specimens: the eye-catching plants, usually trees. Then there are foundation plants: the shrubs and hedges. Groundcovers and lawns, together with colorful bedding plants, complete the list.

The function of combining these different categories is to give a pleasing appearance, remembering always that beauty is in the eye of the beholder. Landscape plants provide shade, screening, color, and boundary markers; they soften the hard edges of structures, and they offer a recreational surface.

Any number of plants fit these categories

One professor of desert landscape architecture, deliberately trying to get his students to forget plants they knew only by name instead of by function, talked about "big green things," "little round bushes," "low spreading greenies," and "space fillers." This horrified people in the more conventional nurseries, who expected graduates to know long lists of plant names, Latin as well as common.

If you think of plants as being the bits and pieces of a landscape, you'll have little difficulty in accepting the use of unfamiliar desert plants in place of those you grew up with in another environment. Desert plants don't need a lot of

There is a great saving in water and in maintenance when parks are planted to native trees. In summer this tree provides ample shade.

This may be someone's idea of a desert landscape, but it more nearly resembles a moonscape. It lacks an understory of desert grasses and small flowering plants, rendering it artificial and unappealing.

water; that's the big difference. What's more, they don't call for a lot of maintenance.

A matter of nomenclature

Excuse the long word, but we need to sort things out a bit. You'll read, and hear, a bunch of names for plants that can be used in desert landscape. The names are similar, yet they express differences. Some people say it's nit-picking, while others say there's a need to be precise. It's always good to know whereof you—and they—speak.

A *native plant* is one that grows naturally in a particular locality. Roses are native to China. Firs are native to North America. Every plant is a native of somewhere, but gardenias are not native to the desert.

A *desert plant* is one that grows naturally in a desert somewhere in the world. There are deserts in Australia, in Africa, in South America, and so on. People who like to split hairs will tell you that a desert is a very dry place, with its quota of specialized plants. On the edges of these deserts are zones that are not quite so dry, although they still are arid, and so support a wider variety of plants.

Arid-land plants, then, include both highly specialized desert plants and the more generalized plants that grow in transitional zones at desert margins. Even this title changes from book to book. There are *dry country plants, drought-tolerant plants, low-water-use plants,* and so on. Recently, they have all achieved a degree of respectability by forming themselves into a union; they call themselves *xeriscape plants.*

Xeriscape is pronounced something like zero-scape, which is unfortunate. Arid-land plants ought not to be considered leafless, lifeless, colorless objects in an empty moonscape. A xeriscape is simply a landscape of low-water-use plants.

As homeowners trying to save on water bills by planting low-water-use plants, we don't care which desert the plants come from. One desert is as good as another, for our purposes. In the same way, the other names are as interchangeable as the plants themselves.

ON THE IMPORTANCE OF MATCHING PLANTS TO THE ENVIRONMENT

The important thing to remember, as far as ease of landscape maintenance is concerned, is that the further a plant has come from its natural environment the more maintenance it will need. A gardenia, which likes acid soil, cloudy weather, cool temperatures, constant humidity, and quite a lot of rain, finds itself far from home when it is planted in a desert. If we plant a gardenia in the desert, we have to help it adjust by changing soil alkalinity, finding a shady place, abating the heat, supplying extra humidity, and giving careful irrigations. And that means constant work; even then, the plant may not perform well.

The way to avoid unnecessary and unrewarding work is obvious: use only those plants that like local conditions.

If you want a challenge in growing something, try orchids and bananas, or sweet peas and tulips, even roses and chrysanthemums. It can be done. But is it worth it?

The bird-of-paradise is not a true native of the desert Southwest, but it does very well here. Seeds are thrown out of the pods when they dry and in this way the plant colonizes. These seeds are on the point of scattering themselves about the countryside.

CHOOSE YOUR LANDSCAPE STYLE, THEN CHOOSE THE ARID-LAND PLANTS THAT SUIT THAT STYLE

Get your "low spreading thingies," your accent plants, or your "tall space fillers" from any old desert, arid land, or xeriplace. They are guaranteed to thrive with minimum attention. More important, they will give you the effect you desire: shade, screening, showing-off, and general property enhancement.

After you have determined the general effect you want, start selecting plants by their names and individual characteristics. Many local lists have been developed by knowledgeable enthusiasts, such as those in your local native plant society. Society members make group decisions on such qualities as attractive appearance, low water needs, hardiness to both heat and cold (remember the extremes of a desert), resistance to pests and diseases, and a satisfactory rate of growth. Sometimes they even consider the availability of their recommendations in local nurseries. You might want to consider, too, whether the plants have thorns or not, flowers or not, a messy litter habit or not.

A notable feature of desert plant communities is the way one plant will "nurse" a number of others in its shade. Even the ribs of a saguaro funnel rainwater to seedlings at its base.

Be sure you understand what your source means by "low water use." With luck, it means that a mature plant won't need supplemental irrigations except in extreme drought years. "Moderate water use" might mean that a mature plant needs to be irrigated once a month to keep its foliage looking good.

Arid-land plants need good drainage

Plants need a soil that is free of caliche. If this is present, it must be removed. Dig down 4 or 5 feet for trees, 3 feet for shrubs, and 18 inches for groundcovers to make sure there is good drainage. You want trees' roots to grow down as easily as possible; a deep digging, even if the soil is good, will loosen it and let this happen. It's better to have your planting site slightly raised than slightly depressed.

Arid-land plants don't need an improved soil

Steer manure or fertilizer may be added if you want your plants to get a quick start, but don't overdo it. For a five-foot hole, two or three bags of manure and three pounds of ammonium phosphate is enough. There's no benefit in adding sulphur, because most arid-land plants grow naturally in alkaline soils.

Arid-land plants prefer a sunny place

After all, they grow naturally in a desert. They won't do well in the shadow of a building or under a tree with dense canopy, although some arid-land plants grow better in light shade. In the desert, you'll see plants in groups, shading one another.

Arid-land plants need to be generously irrigated the first year

This is important. It also is contrary to the widely held belief that desert plants can take harsh conditions from the day they are set out; otherwise, we reason, why call them drought-tolerant?

For the first year, treat these plants as if they were thirsty chinaberry trees or roses or periwinkle groundcovers. Watering twice a week is advisable, especially during the first summer, but use your soil probe—a simple metal rod, not a tensiometer—to make sure you are not wasting water. Irrigate trees down to 3 feet and shrubs to 2 feet, in order to encourage deep rooting.

This first-year investment in water will pay off later, when you may not need to water at all. If you skimp during the first year you won't get strong roots and your plants will forever need frequent waterings simply to keep them alive, let alone produce good foliage.

Stake your trees, especially if you irrigate by a drip system

Drive two stout stakes into firm, undisturbed soil on either side of your tree. Loosely tie the trunk to these stakes with soft rope. A slight bending from gentle winds is good for the tree, as a little flexing strengthens the trunk, but you don't want a storm to blow it over.

As the tree grows, trim up and remove suckers

If you want your native tree to look natural, don't chop it about. Just let it grow the way it wants to. Give yourself room to walk under a tree by cutting the lower of two branches before they get too heavy. Take out suckers that grow from the trunk at ground level. Avoid the temptation to create a lollipop on a stick by uniform trimming.

Normally, arid-land plants grow slowly. Try to keep it that way

You can speed up the growth of arid-land plants by giving them lots of irrigations after the first critical year, but you'll defeat the purpose of economizing on your water bills. You can increase their size by fertilizing during spring and fall growth spurts too, but this will develop soft growth that invites attack by insects and diseases.

A judicious combination of irrigating and fertilizing during the spring and fall growth spurts is the best policy. Avoid a vigorous program during winter and summer dormancies.

Native trees have a natural beauty that should be left alone. Too many people try to improve their appearance by unnecessary pruning.

(Left) If you *must* prune a desert tree, don't overdo it. Its natural response will be to produce suckers at its base.

(Right) A tree like this requires a little water from time to time, and nothing else. No pruning. No spraying. Nothing.

Here's an attempt to make a native tree look like an orchard tree on an eastern parkway. Removal of the lower branches destroys the tree's natural good looks.

Arid-land plants survive on little water, but they grow more luxuriantly when they get a little more. This oleander hedge shows a dramatic "water gradient," from more watering at left to less watering at right.

There are rewards in growing arid-land plants, if you treat them right

First, there is no need to spend money amending the desert soil. And arid-land plants have few pests or diseases, which means there is no need to spray them. They grow slowly, so that little or no pruning is required. They don't need irrigating after they have become established. They tolerate both summer's heat and winter's cold, and their leaves withstand bright sunshine. What more could you want?

4 HOW TO IRRIGATE IN THE DESERT

The desert, as we all know, is a dry place. Certainly it rains, but rainfall is unreliable and unpredictable. If we want our plants to grow, we have to irrigate them.

Irrigating is one of the more obvious gardening chores, even if we use desert vegetation in our landscapes. It's an absolute necessity if we plant flowers and lawns and exotic plants.

We might have to irrigate even during the rainy season if rains are inadequate. Rain and the attendant humidity tease our plants into a little growth. If the rain stops or goes somewhere else, that growth will not be sustained, which means we have to supply the water necessary for growth.

DORMANT PLANTS DON'T NEED IRRIGATING

You can save water—and your dollars, since water is becoming more expensive each year—by not watering plants until they need it.

During the desert winters most plants stop growing. Obviously, those trees that have dropped their leaves don't need a lot of water, nor do brown Bermudagrass lawns. Desert trees, whether native or imported from Australia or Africa, won't come out of dormancy until warm weather arrives.

With the return of warm weather, shrubs and trees start new growth; it's one of the joys of spring. Everything suddenly turns fresh green. Bermudagrass lawns green up, too, but more gradually.

There's no regularity to the awakening. It depends on how each plant is affected by the warming temperatures, more than on the lengthening days. Sometimes the desert spring is early.

When to apply the first spring irrigation

As soon as you see the buds swelling, give your plants a good deep soaking. A thorough watering sustains that important first spurt of growth, which determines the plant's appearance for the next few months.

If you don't water at this time, your plants will have only their own moisture reserves to fall back on; this means that leaves come out small and twigs may die back. A few years of this kind of treatment means that your plants simply don't grow any bigger.

Irrigating new transplants

In the spring and in the fall you can safely and easily transplant trees and shrubs, even large ones. You cannot avoid cutting—and losing—most of the plant's roots in the process; the roots left to put into the new hole are barely adequate for the plant's survival.

Take care of these few roots by liberal irrigations. Try to prevent leaves at the soft ends of twigs from wilting. If the days are warm or windy, you may have to irrigate twice a day for a week. The next week you may be able to preserve the strength of those end shoots with a daily watering. Then the following week you may find that watering every other day will be enough. In any event, try to prevent a lot of leaf loss. You'll get some; it's unavoidable.

Because you lose a lot of roots in the transplanting process, it's usual to balance up the ra-

Too often a tree gets this treatment: a neat little circle where water is poured. What these trees need is a shallow basin that extends beyond the tips of the branches, where the new feeder roots are.

As a tree grows, give it a larger basin. Use a stick on a string to mark the new basin boundary.

Scrape soil toward the trunk from outside the root area to make a low bank. Digging deeply near the trunk is likely to cut feeder roots.

The resulting circumference of the watering basin may appear excessive, but it will "draw out" new roots. Roots will not grow from a moist area to a dry area, which means the tree will not grow.

tio of roots to leaves by cutting out a lot of branches before you dig up the plant. Sometimes you may cut everything back. Sometimes you can keep the natural form of the plant by judicious thinning. Either method gives your plant less leaf surface to dry out.

Irrigate in summer between rainstorms

Summer rains can pour down buckets of water in a few minutes. Unfortunately, much of that rain runs off the surface—gullywashers, these storms are called—and the soil remains dry 2 or 3 feet down. That's where a lot of tree roots are, and they don't get the moisture they need from a gullywasher.

Meanwhile, the air becomes humid because of cloud build-up and the foliage of plants reacts to that humidity; the leaves open their stomates and the plants actually lose moisture. If the building clouds fail to deliver the rain they seem to promise, your plant could run a moisture deficit.

It appears to be contradictory to water your trees and shrubs between summer storms that give abundant water, but it is helpful, especially to those that have been newly planted.

There's a case for deep winter watering

Salts build up in desert soils because of high evaporation and because we don't water thoroughly enough. Repeated shallow irrigations during the summer months simply dissolve the salts in the soil, as well as those added in fertilizers. If these salts are not washed through the soil by heavy rainfall or deep irrigations, they build up over the years to the point where they damage plant roots.

A deep irrigation during the cool winter months is more effective in getting rid of salts than is a similar irrigation in midsummer; there's less evaporation because the sun is less fierce in winter.

HOW TO TELL WHEN TO IRRIGATE YOUR PLANTS

The leaves of broadleaved plants, such as roses and mulberry trees, get hot when they are short of water. (It's the same with humans; if you can't sweat, you get hot.) If the leaves feel hot, the plant needs water.

Another sign is that young leaves at the ends of the branches droop, or wilt. If you catch this condition early on, the wilt is reversible; if you wait too long to irrigate your plants, the leaves won't take up water, and so they scorch and die.

Desert trees and shrubs have learned to adapt to temporary shortages of water. They go through the same routine, but it's hard to see the signs. When they drop their leaves, there's less damage done and recovery is quicker. The next step is that the ends of the twigs die back. If the drought continues, the smaller branches die, and then even the larger ones follow suit.

The dead branches stay in the tree without attracting harmful bacteria, but wood-boring beetles usually get to them. Otherwise, the tree survives the ordeal, and when sufficient rain fails—maybe the following year—the tree starts growing again.

Prickly pear plants and saguaros are hardier still. They can live, though not happily, several years on light rainfall. When a prickly pear is dry, its pads shrivel, wrinkle, and look dull. When saguaros are short of water, they lose their fat round trunks and become deeply corrugated as they shrink.

Flowers, of course, droop their heads when they are dry. Lawn grasses look dull and bluish.

A definition of good watering

"Keep the soil around the roots of a plant moist at all times."

Very few plants tolerate absolutely dry soil for very long, nor can their roots function properly in a soil that is always wet. There needs to be a happy medium most of the time, with extremes being tolerated for only a few days.

THE SEVERAL WAYS TO DELIVER WATER TO A PLANT

There are many ways to deliver water to a plant. Some are better than others.

The old fashioned way

The most commmon way to water plants is to sprinkle them by hand. There's a personal satisfaction in holding the hose and putting water on the plant, around it, and into the soil.

Unfortunately, it's an unsatisfactory way of doing things. First, you seldom stay at one plant

Sprinkler systems are wasteful because they throw water high into the air to evaporate.

Water from a sprinkler can be blown off target by even a light wind.

long enough to get sufficient water to the roots. Second, most water contains salts, which evaporate on the leaves after an hour's sunshine; for this reason, you should never spray leaves.

Basin flooding is the best way to irrigate

Make a basin under the spread of the branches by scraping soil from *outside* and bringing it *toward* the tree. As the tree grows and its branches spread, increase the size of the basin. This allows for root growth, which corresponds to the growth of the branches.

Don't dig a deep well just around the trunk of the tree. If you dig deeply, you are likely to cut the tree's roots. Roots never leave a wet soil to grow into dry soil outside the well. A tree needs a wide basin, just deep enough to prevent the water from running away and being wasted.

To irrigate properly, first quickly fill the basin. Then turn the faucet down to the point where the soil absorbs the water as quickly as it comes out of the hose. Keep a head of water in the basin until the water reaches down to the roots; use your soil probe (see below) to be sure.

This method puts a lot of water down deep, where it is stored for several days, even for weeks. It won't evaporate as a shallow sprinkling does. A deep watering encourages roots to grow deeply, and this gives the tree strength, especially during hot summers. A deep watering carries down unwanted salts, whereas a shallow sprinkling collects them at the soil surface.

Bubblers are automated flooding

A tree basin can be served by a bubbler; all nearby trees can be bubbled at the same time, each with its own bubbler on a single delivery system controlled by a single faucet. Remember to provide each tree with a wide, shallow basin and make sure the water reaches to the roots.

A drip system is the ultimate in controlled delivery

Unlike a quick-delivery bubbler, a drip system uses small apertures that take much longer to deliver the same amount of water. To cover a wide area, you'll need several emmitters. To water deeply, you'll have to leave the system running for a long time. It's a good, but not perfect, way to put water on plants. (Chapter 5 deals with drip irrigation systems in detail.)

An improperly adjusted sprinkler head compounds the waste and makes the sidewalk a hazardous place to boot.

If a sprinkler head is not cleaned periodically, water distribution becomes inefficient and dry brown spots will appear in your lawn.

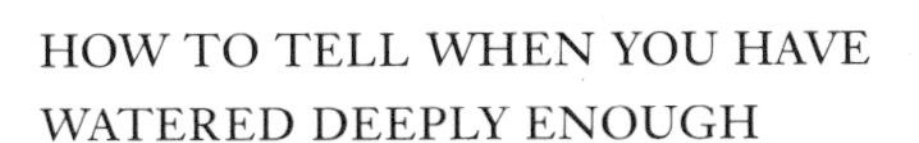

HOW TO TELL WHEN YOU HAVE WATERED DEEPLY ENOUGH

It's necessary to get water down to the roots, and even a bit further, if you want to wash salts away from the root zone.

Flower beds should be irrigated down to 12 inches. The roots of most flower plants grow to that depth. Shrubs, such as roses and junipers, should be irrigated down to 2 feet. Trees should be irrigated to 3 feet. Grass lawns should be irrigated to 2 feet, and dichondra, which is a shallow-rooted plant, should be irrigated to 9 inches.

These are arbitrary measurements. Bermudagrass lawns can have roots 10 feet deep, St. Augustine grass roots are almost as shallow as those of dichondra, most trees have deeper roots than 3 feet, and so on. However, if you water to these recommendations your plants will do well.

How do you know the water has gone as far as it should? You can't tell by looking at the surface. You can't tell by timing the period the water runs. Putting out coffee cans to collect water from the lawn sprinklers won't tell you, either. If you dug into the soil after each irrigation to see how well you'd irrigated, you'd chop a lot of roots. But there is an easy way, and one that won't do any damage.

Everyone should have a soil probe

Find someone who is good at working with metal. Ask that person to make a 3-foot-long piece of 5/8-inch rebar with a handle at one end and a sharp point at the other. Make file marks at 12 inches and 2 feet. Keep it handy.

A stick like this will slide easily into moist soil. There's no need to hit it with a hammer or to strain to poke it into the soil. If it won't go into the soil, the reason is simple: the soil is dry. Even better, when it stops slipping through moist soil you've reached dry soil. That's how far the irrigation—or the rain—went.

Of course, a soil probe will stop when it hits a rock, or a pipe, or anything solid. Just to be sure, bring it up again and probe nearby to see whether you've hit a rock. If you keep hitting "bottom" at the same depth all through your yard, the probe is giving you bad news: there's caliche underneath. (See page 44.)

A caution for probe users

Don't hammer a soil probe when you hit a solid object under the soil surface. It may be a plastic water pipe; if the point is sitting exactly on top of the pipe and you bang it too hard, you will discover water. It will be all over the place!

There's no risk with metal pipes, for water and for gas, or with electrical wires encased in conduit, as they should be. Around old houses, however, there may be underground electrical or telephone wires that are not properly protected.

DO YOU IRRIGATE IN THE MORNING OR IN THE EVENING?

You don't want to sprinkle any plant while the sun is shining on its leaves.

Since you can't avoid sprinkling leaves of lawn grasses, irrigate your lawn in early morning. If you irrigate a lawn at night—perhaps to gain water pressure because few people are drawing on the city supplies at that time—there's a danger of keeping the leaf surface too wet for too long, long enough to allow fungus diseases to develop by crawling over the leaf surface and into the plant through those natural openings in the leaves called stomates. This is a hazard during summer months, when continuous high humidity accompanies summer rains.

Water flower beds and irrigate newly planted trees and shrubs in the early morning. This prepares them for the rigors of the day. An evening watering simply repairs the damage caused by a day of hot sun and drying winds; the suffering plant is merely back where it started from twelve hours earlier. A plant doesn't grow under such a regime; it just exists.

There are salts in the water here—that's what these deposits on a drained evaporative cooler are—and some sources are worse than others. Avoid sprinkling plants while the sun is shining if you want to prevent leaf burn. And *never* use "overflow" water from the cooler for irrigation!

In the case of well-established shrubs and trees that are irrigated by a good soak, it doesn't matter what time of day you irrigate them. The deep watering will last a long time.

(For details on when and how to water container plants, see Chapter 17.)

A caution about garden hoses in the summertime

A garden hose lying out all day in the hot sun holds very hot water—too hot to handle and too hot for plants. Empty this water where it won't do any harm. The best place might be the edge of the large irrigation basin around a tree that is going to get a lot of cool water from underground pipes. The worst places to put it would be on the foliage of any plant, near any plant that has been recently set out, or near any shallow-rooted plant.

It's more than being tidy to hang up a garden hose. You can't trip over it when it's hanging up, and it won't kink. It's in the shade, protected from the sun, so it will last longer. And it's not full of hot water that, in the summer, can burn your plants.

HOW OFTEN DO I WATER?

This may be the most common question people ask me. Most of us like to have a schedule for our landscaping activities—the X on the calendar hanging on the kitchen wall that tells us what to do each day.

The fact is that there is no schedule; you have to use good judgment. The reason for this unhelpful comment is that each soil is different: depth, sand or clay content, and amount of organic matter all vary. Each day is different: some are hot and dry, others are windy, and it might even rain. Each plant is different: cactus don't need much water but lawns do, pines don't need a lot of water but mulberries do, and so on. Each location is different: a southern sunny slope needs more water than does a northern slope, and a plant inside a courtyard needs less water than does one out in the wind.

You need a soil probe to help you irrigate properly. Use it to tell you when you've got water down to the roots of your plants. Then, over the next few days, watch the condition of the plants you watered. When the leaves feel hot, when the foliage is dull and bluish, or when the new leaves wilt, the plant is short of water. Check these observations with an investigation of the soil around the roots, using your soil probe.

Remember the golden rule: "Keep the soil around the roots of your plants moist—but not wet—all the time."

Obviously, you'll be irrigating more frequently during the summer months, more often around newly planted trees and shrubs than around established ones, more often around smaller plants than around bigger ones. You'll be doing less irrigating of dormant plants than of those in spurts of growth, less of arid-land plants than of imported exotics, and less during rainy periods.

All of which is to say that there is no clear answer to that frequently asked question, "How often do I water?"

If you irrigate on a rigid interval you'll be right only some of the time. And that brings us to the shortcomings of sprinkler and drip irrigation systems operated by time clocks. They don't know when to irrigate; they do it automatically, without thinking.

5 HOW TO DESIGN AND INSTALL A DRIP IRRIGATION SYSTEM

A drip system is a way of taking water through tubing to a plant, where it slowly drips out of an emitter.

Drip irrigation systems are becoming the rage, and for good reason. They are appropriate for desert landscaping, where plants are set out separate from one another in a non-grass area. By watering only desired plants, weeds are discouraged. Drip systems are economical of labor, since several plants are watered at the same time. That labor is further reduced if the system is operated by a time clock; while you are away on a vacation the plants get watered and you return to a full landscape. Drip systems are economical of water when compared with flooding, which spreads water everywhere over a wide area, and with sprinkling, which throws water high in the air to evaporate.

DON'T FORGET THE BASIC RULE OF IRRIGATION WHEN YOU USE A DRIP SYSTEM

You must get water to the roots of your plants, both downwards and sideways. You'll need your

Use your soil probe to measure water penetration at the edge of a watering basin or of the circle of moisture spread by a drip system.

Before installing a drip irrigation system, find out how your soil accepts a slow drip. Put out a single emitter of your choice on dry soil. Turn on the faucet so that you get a drip per second. Count the minutes needed to achieve an adequate depth and spread of moisture.

The way to tell when water has penetrated to the proper depth is by plunging your soil probe into the moist earth. Surface appearances can be deceiving: On a heavy soil you'll get a wide circle with little depth, while on a sandy soil you'll get a small circle with greater depth.

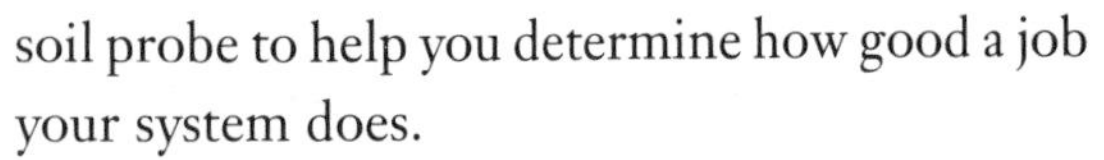

soil probe to help you determine how good a job your system does.

Most people install a drip system after a summer of high water bills. As a consequence, they become *very* economical when irrigating their plants. A drip system will save water, especially if you have been wasteful in flooding or sprinkling, but it won't allow good plant growth unless the plant gets the water it needs. Don't expect a drip system to give you a good-looking landscape all by itself. It can be too efficient and save *too much* water if you don't monitor it properly.

Don't use arithmetic to irrigate your plants

Unfortunately, drip irrigation systems were not devised by plant people. They were invented by technicians, engineers, and the like. That's why the catalog descriptions emphasize gallons per minute, flow rates, pounds of pressure, and other hydraulic stuff. Home landscapers, even those good at figures, don't need to pay a lot of attention to the technical specifications.

An irrigation balance sheet starts off with a false premise: that someone knows how many gallons of water every plant in the landscape consumes every day of the year.

We can safely say that roses need more water than does a prickly pear, but we don't know how much more water a large Queen Elizabeth rose needs than does a small Love rose. Most landscapes are made up of plants of different kinds and different sizes, each with different management requirements. As we have seen, soils differ from one another and climate differs from day to day, from place to place, and from season to season. In short, there's such a bewildering variety of factors that the equation doesn't add up.

Find out how much water your soil "takes"

It's of prime importance to know how your soil absorbs water. Set up the following test before you get involved in designing your system.

Go to the irrigation supply house and ask for a piece of half-inch tubing about 3 feet long.

Buy an emitter that delivers maximum flow (likely more than a drip), an end cap, and a hose-bib fitting. Ask for the emitter to be installed on the tubing. (We'll talk about these bits and pieces later, but they'll know what you mean.) Take this "investigative assembly" out to a bare patch of ground, attach the garden hose to it, and turn on the faucet until you get a drip a second. Now you can turn into a scientist. You'll need a clock, your soil probe, a measuring tape, and the back of an envelope.

Come back after twelve hours and measure how wide an area of soil has been wetted. Poke the soil probe in to see how far down the water went. Write it down. Come back after another twelve hours and repeat your tests. You're going to use this information when you create your system.

The size of the investigative circle tells you how many plants you can irrigate from one emitter. You can add emitters to make more circles, but make sure they overlap; in this way you can make flower beds of different shapes.

One emitter will be sufficient for a newly planted shrub or tree for the first two years of its life. If you want to landscape with clumps of plants, then you'll know how many emitters should go on the line to adequately provide water to the roots of your chosen number of plants.

To irrigate a large tree with a drip system, make a circle of tubing just outside the tree's drip line. Insert emitters into that tubing so you'll have a series of circles of moisture that overlap one another all around your tree. All the roots will be served with moisture by this circle of circles, and they will be encouraged to grow outward because the moisture is a little beyond their present needs.

So much for your lateral spread of water.

Different manufacturers of drip systems make different kinds of punches. Be sure all your parts and tools belong to the same system, and stick with one brand throughout your installation.

Now you need to know how long to leave your system running. You know how far down the water went in a twelve-hour period; your soil probe told you. Armed with this information, leave the system on long enough to get water down to the roots. (The rule of 3 feet for trees, 2 for shrubs, and 1 for flowers dictates separate drip systems for each category of plant.) Keep coming back with your soil probe to reassure yourself that you are getting water down deep enough, but turn off your system before it begins to waste water.

Try to avoid lots of isolated circles of wetness

A drip system is a slow-delivery system. Water from an emitter dissolves salts in the soil and gathers them to the wettest part of the circle, but allows them to evaporate at the dry edges of the circle. During summer, the delivery rate may not keep up with the evaporation rate. Salts will appear at the edges of the circles all around your plant. There'll be more edges if your circles don't touch—and more salt.

One standpipe with four hose bibs gives you flexibility. The glass jug contains liquid fertilizer, which is being syphoned automatically into a garden hose.

An anti-syphon valve, like the one pictured here, is required by most cities and towns, in order to prevent chemicals or dirty water from being backflushed into the common water supply.

Salt build-up can be corrected by leaching

It doesn't seem to be a problem during the cooler winter months, but during summers without normal heavy rains and when evaporative rates are high it's advisable to give a supplemental irrigation the old-fashioned way. Once or twice a summer, make a retaining bank around your trees and give them a good flooding to wash the salts down. This is especially important for non-native plants, which usually are sensitive to salts, but do it for the natives, too. They don't like the extra salts that an emitter collects.

YOU CAN INSTALL YOUR OWN DRIP SYSTEM

It's easy to install your own system. No special skills, experience, or tools are required. All you need is a measure of common sense and a liking for putting things together. You buy all the pieces and fit them into one another without messy glue, exact measurements, or difficulty. You will need a sharp knife or a hacksaw to cut the tubing and a special punch to make the holes for the emitters.

The punch has a squared end, not a point, because you want a well-defined hole that won't leak. The punch makes a satisfying "pop" when it goes through the tubing wall and then it stops. If you make a hole with an ice pick it will be an expanded hole that shrinks when you take the pick out. Besides, there's the danger of pushing the point right through the opposite wall of the tubing.

The components of some systems require a punch that actually cuts out its hole. Don't mix up punches and systems.

An optional filter basket traps flakes of rust and sand that might otherwise enter your drip system from old pipes.

An end cap lets you drain your drip system in a cold winter or flush dirt out of the system in summer.

The two tubes of Bi-wall make it a useful tubing for drip-watering long straight lines of plants like hedges.

If you punch a hole in the wrong place or want to move an emitter, simply fill the unwanted hole with a "goof" plug.

THE BIG QUESTION: DO YOU BUY A KIT, OR DO YOU BUY ONLY THE PIECES YOU NEED AND MAKE YOUR OWN SYSTEM?

There isn't a kit that exactly fits your landscape. If you buy one, you'll find yourself short of some pieces and with others left over. This is both irritating and wasteful. You'll have to go back to the store and buy extra items of that particular make. Kitmakers are notoriously proprietary; you can't add in someone else's components because they won't fit.

When you want to run your drip line at a right angle, just cut the line and install a T. When you want to turn a corner, use an elbow.

It's better to make a list of what you need and to buy just those pieces from a well-established supply house. Sooner or later you're going to have to expand your system, and you'll want to add in parts that are interchangeable.

Before you start, make some helpful changes to the plumbing

Usually, there's only one faucet coming out of the wall of your house. If you use this for a drip irrigation system, you'll not have a hose to wash the car or to hand-water your plants.

Remove the faucet and install a shut-off valve. This will enable you to turn off the outside water while you work on the new system, without interrupting the water supply to the inside of the house. You'll find this a great convenience later on, when you have to make outdoor repairs or modifications.

Instead of replacing the single faucet, add in a couple of T's, which will enable you to add a couple of extra faucets. Now you've got room for the drip irrigation system and for a couple of extra hoses.

You'll need these components to install a drip irrigation system

Starting at the faucet, you must install an *anti-syphon valve.* This device prevents water that might be contaminated by fertilizers and insecticides from being sucked back into the city supply. In most municipalities, it's the law.

You'll need a *control valve.* This turns the water on and off. It can be manually or electrically controlled, or it may have both options.

Continue the installation with a *filter.* This is

a basket in a tube that collects any foreign matter in the water and prevents it from plugging the emitters. Rusty pipes in old houses are a real handicap when you have water flowing through the small holes of emitters. Remove and clean the basket periodically to keep the system working efficiently.

Put in a *pressure regulator* at this point, even though a control valve partially adjusts the pressure when it is turned one way or the other. Variations in city water pressure can blow out your soft plastic system; the components are not glued, remember. Play it safe; control the pressure.

Now you needs lots of soft plastic *irrigation tubing,* usually of a half-inch diameter. Cut it with a knife and push it into the pressure regulator outlet. Take the tubing to the first plant, gently bending it if the curves are gradual but using an *elbow* of 90 degrees wherever you have to make a sharp turn.

Don't pull the tubing tight, but let it lie slack. A certain amount of looseness and flexibility will be useful later. If you need to go to another group of plants, cut the tubing and push in a *T* to provide a second line to go in the new direction. Keep adding T's every time there is a need to reach other plants.

Every time you start a "branch line" to another group of plants, it's a good idea to install an *in-line valve* or *shut-off valve.* Each valve lets you close down that "branch line" without affecting the rest of the system. It gives you local control, and that's always useful.

Install an *end cap* at the end of the line. The end cap unscrews to let water out of the system

Don't forget this basic principle of drip irrigation: Widen the watering circle as the tree grows bigger. The emitters in this photo are too close to the trunk for such a big tree. As a result, irrigation failed to encourage the spread of roots out of the limited circle of wetness and the tree toppled in a windstorm.

(Above) BiWall has tiny holes in the smaller tubing every 12 inches. The water comes out to make small circles of wetness.

(Middle) The circles gradually spread until they touch, eventually forming a solid band of moisture.

(Bottom) You may have to let the water run as much as a full day on a heavy soil.

when you want to flush sediment out of it or drain it during a cold winter.

Now you're ready to install the *emitters.* There are any number of different designs, but the most effective ones are those with large openings. Large openings don't get plugged with invasive roots or clogged with salt deposits. The best kind is one that is adjustable from a slow drip to a full flow simply by twisting its cap.

You'll know from your initial "investigative assembly" how large a circle of moisture one emitter makes on your particular soil. Just make sure that the roots of your plants get the water they need; use your soil probe regularly.

If you wish to water containers on a patio, you can use *spaghetti tubing* with a lead weight on the end. (See Chapter 17 for more about container gardening.)

How to use different emitters with different delivery rates

It's advisable to standardize your system by using just one kind of emitter. It makes repair work easier and it gives uniformity in water delivery. Larger amounts of water can be supplied to larger plants simply by inserting more emitters, all of the same kind and delivery rate. You'll need to do this as plants grow bigger over the years.

Another way to add capacity to your system (but not a very good way, because you don't increase the spread of water) is to replace a small-delivery emitter with one with a higher flow rate; emitters are made in half-gallon per hour, one-gallon-per-hour, and two-gallons-per-hour rates. Outwardly, they look the same; read the fine print stamped on them to find out which are which.

Adjustable emitters are a better alternative. Drips from their eight apertures can be increased to a steady flow by twisting the cap and counting the clicks. A few more clicks and the emitter throws jets of water further out. A reverse twist turns the emitter off. If a plant is too wet, turn off the emitter. If a plant needs more water than others on the system, open the emitter more.

An alternative to emitters

When you have a straight line of plants, as in a hedge, you can give a more even delivery of water to all the plants if you use special tubing that has a small hole every so many inches along its length. This tubing is called *Bi-wall.* Each opening starts by wetting a small circle, but the circles soon join up to make a continuous length of moisture, the width of which varies according to the kind of soil you have. A sandy soil drains straight down, whereas a clay soil spreads the drips.

Bi-wall cannot go around sharp corners, so you'll have to insert an elbow whenever you want to make an abrupt turn. Use an end cap that lets you flush the line, or drain it during freezing weather. *Bi-wall* also will leak at all connections, so you'll have to clamp each connection to close the little secondary tubing that gets its water from the main tubing.

Another kind of tubing is a perforated soaker that sweats out small beads of water along its length. It's not very satisfactory. If you bury it, the small pores soon become crusted with salts that are in the soil or in the water—or both—and the tubing stops working. Because it is underground and out of sight, you don't realize it is failing until plants begin to die. If you lay it on top of the ground where you can keep an eye on it, the pores just as quickly fill with algae and it just as quickly stops working.

Another big question: Do you lay the system on the ground, or do you bury it?

If you lay the system on the ground, you can easily tell where it stops working and you can quickly repair it. It's easy to add on and to replace faulty emitters. If the system lies loosely on the surface, you can pull the tubing and its emitters toward a plant group or away from it to vary the wetting pattern. The hot sun will not make the water at the emitters too hot for plants, nor will ultraviolet light damage the tubing. However, rabbits, packrats, squirrels, javelinas, and dogs will chew the tubing to get more water out of an emitter; they are impatient at a slow drip on a hot summer afternoon.

If you want to have a natural-looking desert landscape, you will have to bury the system. Lengths of tubing trailing over the ground between your plants look messy. Don't bury the emitters, though. Use a small piece of tubing extending from the buried tubing to raise the emitter a few inches above soil level. The whole delivery system is out of sight; all you see is a number of little spiky tubes near your plants. You will easily know whether they are working properly.

A buried system will have to be dug up when it's time to enlarge it or when you have to carry out repairs. Against this eventuality, you should make a map of the underground layout—and don't lose the map!

A drip system can be changed, added on to, and expanded

Provided you can get to the tubing—that's where the map comes in handy—you can change a system as your plants increase in size. In fact, you must. The feeder roots of a plant are under the ends of the branches, at the drip line. Initially, the emitters should be set around the plant, halfway between the trunk and the drip line. The circles of wetness should overlap.

As the drip line expands outward, it's advisable to move the emitters outward. Cut the line around the tree, spread the circle, and add in an extra length of tubing, with an emitter or two, to close the gap.

If you decide to remove a plant, you'll want to shut off the emitters or remove them. Leave the tubing there; you may want to use it later when you change your mind again. If you take the emitters out, fill the hole with a "goof plug."

It's a good idea to buy a lot of these goof plugs—not to admit your fallibility, but to anticipate changing the system at a later date. After all, when it becomes necessary to move emitters outward from a tree you planted a few years ago, the larger tree tells you that you've been a good irrigator.

At any point in your system, no matter how complicated it is, you can cut the tubing, insert a T, and give yourself a branch line to a new planting. Don't forget the in-line shut-off valve.

Consider your plants' water needs when you design a system

Put your plants into one of three broad categories: high, medium, and low water use. Try to get all the plants of one category on one delivery line. Use another delivery line for another category. Don't agonize over the sorting; you'll never get it exactly right. Besides, you don't need to be exact if you use adjustable emitters. Each line should have its own in-line shut-off valve to give you line control.

It's easier to do this if you are beginning your landscape, since you can group your plants in their different categories. It gets tricky if you are converting to a drip irrigation system with different established plants all over the yard. You'll most likely end up with a monstrous spider of a system that you'll want to bury. A way out of this predicament is to take out the heavy water users—and save even more water!

Finally, the time clock

It's a great convenience to have your system turned on and off by a time clock. You'll appreciate this refinement when you go away on an extended vacation. The danger in a time clock is that you soon get lazy and forget to look at your plants to see whether they need water. A time clock does not think, or make allowances, or change things when needed. You are supposed to do all that.

If you choose to include a time clock, buy one that allows the system to deliver water for twenty-four hours or more. It can take a whole day for an emitter to deliver enough water to reach a tree's roots 3 feet down in a heavy soil. There's no point in buying a time clock that turns a system on for only a half-hour. Good watering develops deep roots, and you can't water adequately by spoonfuls. You should also be able to turn your timer off completely, just in case we get a year of "normal" rains.

6 How to Plant in the Desert
SOILS AND THEIR IMPROVEMENT I

Although desert soils lack almost every plant nutrient, they usually contain more calcium, and sometimes more sodium, than we want. And they are always short of organic matter because there isn't much plant litter in the desert and what little there is blows away in the dry winds.

When we set about improving a desert soil we must bear two things in mind. First, soil improvement is absolutely necessary when we include non-native plants, such as annual flowers, lawns, roses, pyracantha, and ash trees, in our landscapes. They are fast growers and need lots of nutrients. Second, local desert trees and shrubs require less improvement of the soil because they are slow growers and are tuned into a lower level of nutrients. In fact, a conventional improvement might alter the soil too drastically for them.

FIRST, FIND AND REMOVE CALICHE

If you are a newcomer to the desert, the foregoing will be a mystery statement. What does it mean?

In many of our soils there is a layer of hard material somewhere underneath the surface. It may be 6 inches down (in which case gardening becomes almost impossible) or it may be hiding

Away from flat alluvial areas, the obvious thing about desert soils is that they are shallow and rocky. This roadside cut reveals a shallow layer of dark soil on the surface, underlain by rock and caliche. Each square of the reinforcing metal grid measures 18 inches.

The soil probe, a 3-foot length of rebar marked off in feet and inches and fitted with a handle, will tell you how deep your soil is. If caliche shows up too near the surface, you may want to hire a backhoe to dig your planting holes.

4 feet down. This layer is called caliche. It is a concretelike material, whitish and hard. Chemically, it's calcium carbonate with, perhaps, some iron mixed in to give it a pinkish color. The characteristic that's most important to you is its hardness. Roots can't grow through it, nor can water pass through it. A soil with caliche underneath doesn't drain; water accumulates, causing roots to drown for lack of oxygen. If water doesn't drain through the soil, chemical residues are not carried away from the root area and salts build up, to the detriment of plant growth.

When roots are confined in standing water, the plant suffers. Leaves wilt and even fall. Twigs die back. Often, we misread the symptoms and give the plant more water. This is an easy mistake to make during hot summer days, but the plant already is under stress from the heat and watering under these conditions simply makes things worse.

Caliche may be only half an inch thick or 6 feet thick. You won't know until you've actually got through it. And you must get through it. There are no half measures with caliche. If you don't remove caliche, even if you want to plant only shallow-rooted flowers, the outcome will be dead plants.

How to discover caliche

Knowing that caliche is there will suggest, among other things, contracting out the digging of tree-planting holes rather than doing it yourself. To find out, use a metal rod—your soil probe will do nicely—to explore the underground of your property. Provided the soil is moist, the probe will slide easily through it. It will stop when it hits something hard. You may have hit a rock, or a water pipe, or Spanish treasure—or caliche. If the probe stops at the same depth at many places on your property, it's caliche you have, not any of the others.

Of course, the probe doesn't tell you how thick the stuff is. It just gives you the unhappy message that it's there.

HOW TO PREPARE THE SOIL FOR LAWNS AND FLOWERS

First, wet the soil to a depth of 12 inches. Pull out any weeds and clear the area of trash and debris. Then spread 3 inches of steer manure or compost over the area. You can use bagged or-

You give tree roots the best chance to grow strongly by digging a *really* big hole.

Neither a shallow soil nor a hard soil allows proper root development. Plants grow poorly and are easy prey to strong winds.

(Right) A tree handicapped by a shallow soil will grow reasonably well if it is given a lot of water, which usually is the case if it grows on a lawn.

ganic matter from a nursery—forest mulch, peat moss, or fir bark—but it's not as good. Now scatter ammonium phosphate—16:20:0—on top of the organic matter at the rate of three pounds to every hundred square feet. Then spread soil sulphur at the rate of five pounds to every hundred square feet. (Chapter 7 discusses fertilizers in detail.)

Dig these materials into the soil down to 12 inches, mixing thoroughly. That's why you wet the soil in the first place; you can't dig dry soil.

Plant after a week of settling and mellowing.

Useful microbes exist in steer manure and compost

One of the values of steer manure and compost is that they both contain useful microbes. You won't find the same usefulness in peat moss or forest products.

Don't be frightened out of using steer manure. A lot of salespeople will tell you that it contains salts, and that it will poison your soil. These people are eager to sell you something more expensive.

Make sure that tree roots have the best chance of growing strongly by digging a big hole and punching through any barrier underneath. Here are the tools to do the job: a pickaxe and a "caliche bar." Note the heavy boots.

There was nothing on the soil surface to warn of problems to come. Hidden hard soil layers like those exposed in this pit are a severe handicap for a tree. You must dig through these layers to get drainage and to give roots the chance to grow properly.

HOW TO PREPARE YOUR SOIL WHEN PLANTING A ROSE OR AN ASH TREE

For a shrub, dig a hole 3 feet down and 3 feet square. For a tree, dig 5 feet down and 5 feet square. If you're planting from a five-gallon can, a hole of these dimensions seems unnecessarily large. It's not.

If there's caliche at 6 feet, you won't know about it and you won't worry; there's enough room for roots to grow strongly in 5 feet. On the other hand, if you discover caliche at 4 feet you'll have to use chisel and crowbar to remove it.

After you've dug the hole, set aside the poorest soil with its rocks and boulders. Keep the better soil for putting back into the hole, along with soil amendments. Use the same proportions of amendments as in digging the ground for bedding plants. Here's a formula to help you buy the right amounts: Calculate the cubic content of the hole you have dug by multiplying depth times length times breadth. A hole for a rose or juniper measuring 3ft × 3ft × 3ft would contain 27 cubic feet of soil. Divide this volume by 5 to get the *cubic feet* of steer manure to buy. Divide by 16 to get the *pounds* of ammonium phosphate to buy. Divide by 4 to get the *pounds* of sulphur to buy. In this example, you would need 5.5 cubic feet of steer manure, 1.7 pounds of ammonium phosphate, and 6.75 pounds of sulphur.

Thoroughly mix the better soil you dug out of the hole with these amendments as you refill the hole; don't make layers. There'll be some soil left over and the hole will be mounded up, but it will settle in a day or two. Settling can be hastened with a stomping as you backfill, followed by a good watering.

If roots don't have enough room to spread out they go 'round and 'round and eventually choke themselves. Although the damage pictured here happened while the tree was still in a nursery container, it's the sort of thing that happens when a tree is planted in too small a hole.

HOW TO PREPARE YOUR SOIL WHEN PLANTING A DESERT TREE

Most desert trees are deep-rooted plants, and this means that you should dig deeply. You might discover caliche, in which case you would remove it to the appropriate depth. Your hard work in digging such a big hole—5ft × 5ft × 5ft—ensures easy root growth down to great depths, which is just what a desert tree requires. If you dig deeply, the tree will become established easily during its first year of growth.

When it comes to soil amendments, however, add only one-third to one-fourth the amounts of steer manure and ammonium phosphate prescribed for non-natives and omit the sulphur; desert plants have evolved to succeed in alkaline soils of low fertility, and changing those conditions too drastically is bad for them.

HOW TO PREPARE YOUR SOIL WHEN PLANTING SHALLOW-ROOTED CACTI

Use even smaller amounts of organic matter and ammonium phosphate, and, again, omit the sulphur. Roots of agave, ocotillo, barrel cacti, saguaro, prickly pear, and cholla tend to spread rather than to go downward. Provided you know there is good drainage—your soil probe will tell you—you can trade off digging deeply for digging widely. For a single plant, you might dig 2 feet down and 6 feet across. (For more on succulents, see Chapter 23.)

This is still a lot of soil to work over, but you can recoup some of the energy you spend by sowing wildflower seeds in the area of disturbed soil; September and March are good times for this. (For more on wildflowers, see Chapter 18.)

But what about old-timers who add in sulphur?

Some landscape installers automatically mix in sulphur when they set out desert plants. Why? They probably are confusing this practice with two legitimate uses of sulphur.

The first is the customary soil treatment for backfilling a hole when fruit trees are planted, which is an attempt to change the alkalinity of the soil. A liberal amount of sulphur counteracts the spread of Texas root rot, and it's a good precaution to take when planting fruit trees. The second is an attempt to prevent soil organisms from entering the succulent root tissue of an agave or barrel cactus. The usual quick treatment for this is to dust the cut ends of the roots with sulphur.

Remember, desert plants are adapted to grow well in alkaline soil. There's no point in making the soil less alkaline with lots of sulphur. Neither will a little sulphur scattered throughout the soil protect exposed succulent root ends.

THE LEGACY OF HASTY BUILDING

During a building boom, construction crews were in a hurry to finish one house and move on to the next. It happened too often that they sped things up by burying scraps of wallboard, cement and plaster instead of hauling it off the site. Much later, the new homeowner finds it difficult to grow things in certain parts of her property.

Practically all building lots get a rough treatment; a slope is scraped away or a hollow is filled in. This rearrangement of the soil's surface seldom employs similar soil; it's brought in from elsewhere. "Elsewhere" can include holes made for swimming pools, where rocks and gravel and caliche were smashed out of the ground.

The surface of the graded plot after a house is built looks nice and even. Underneath, there could be a mix of material that would frighten you if you knew about it. You'll find out—albeit too late—when you dig a hole for planting a tree. You might discover it when you plant a rose, but you might never know about it if you start a lawn without a deep digging.

Isolated pits full of plasterboard and cement can be dug up, although it's irritating work. Large areas of rocky burden covered with a thin layer of soil are a particular handicap. They can be left to turn into a "natural" landscape after going through a period of weed growth, or you can import better material for isolated plantings and go with that. Digging tree-planting holes calls for changing the soil into something better; this means importing material.

TOPSOIL: WHAT IS IT?

First, we need to sort out the term "topsoil." You see it advertised in newspapers and it's supposed to be something really valuable. True, it's often the answer to soil problems, but topsoil is a term that doesn't tell you anything about the material other than it came from the top; from the top of what?

This is a test bed in which a soil suitable for growing annuals is being developed. The "new" soil is lumpy and full of clods. There is a great need for organic matter, but these crop residues will need several weeks before they contribute much to soil improvement. It's better to use compost or steer manure.

In the foreground of this test bed is a modest layer of steer manure. In the middle distance are broken-up clods of dirt with the steer manure mixed in. In the background the clods have been worked with a hoe to make them smaller and to more thoroughly mix the manure. If a soil is very heavy, it's better to dig it with a fork than with a spade.

To improve soil for flower beds and lawns, dig to a depth of 12 inches and mix in organic matter, ammonium phosphate as a fertilizer, and soil sulphur to make the soil less alkaline. Be sure to dig deeply. Merely scratching the surface won't give good results.

Usually, soil from the upper layers of a meadow or a farmer's field or a wood is good stuff. So, topsoil should be good stuff, right? Before deciding that it is, ask some questions: Does the seller of the material you are thinking of buying know where his topsoil came from? Will he tell you? Can you go and see for yourself? You want to know that it's a good "somewhere" and that the soil is not contaminated with weeds or chemicals. Go take a look.

Often, however, topsoil doesn't even come from the top of anywhere. It's something nobody else wants. Find out before you buy.

How to be sure of what you need

If you want to fill a planter or a half barrel with good soil that will grow fine flowers, simply find a material that is somewhere between free-draining sand and heavy clay. Its color should be dark brown, showing that there is old organic matter in it. When you break it up in your hands it should fall easily into crumbs, like breadcrumbs.

If you want topsoil to improve a heavy clay soil, then you should look for something sandy. If you want to give a gravel or a sandy soil some body, you should buy topsoil that is heavier with clay or silt.

Any soil that is high in organic matter is going to be useful to a gardener, and that's where topsoil from a farmer's field usually comes in—unless, of course, that farmer used a lot of weedkillers or grew cotton in that field. In the latter case, the soil may be infected with Texas root rot (see Chapter 12).

HOW TO BUY TOPSOIL

First, determine whether you need to lighten a heavy soil or give body to a sandy soil. Take a bucketful of your soil to the soil yard. Ask whether the seller has a soil that will improve yours; mix them together to see what happens. If you are satisfied, then buy as much as you can afford. Take a sample of his soil home with you.

When the delivery truck arrives, don't let the driver dump the soil until you are sure he has brought what you ordered. Compare the sample with the truckload. Show it to the driver. Once the stuff is on the ground it's yours and you'll have to pay for it.

WHAT TO DO WITH THE TOPSOIL YOU BOUGHT

Spread about three inches of it over the poor ground and rototill it in as deeply as possible. Then spread another three inches and rototill that into the ground. Repeat the process until you have finished the pile.

The purpose of this slow, hard work is gradually to change the poor soil underneath into good soil on top for the benefit of your lawn, or flowers, or groundcover. There will be a gradient of improvement from the bottom up. The wrong way to use topsoil is to spread it on top of the underlying soil in an attempt to hide it. The resulting drastic change from good to bad will interfere with root growth, water penetration, fertilizer uptake—and everything.

7 How to Use Fertilizers
SOILS AND THEIR IMPROVEMENT II

It's unfortunate, in a way, that people tend to call fertilizers "plant food." It's an idea we get from the advertising branch of the fertilizer industry. They want us to give our plants some fertilizer to make them happy, just as the dog food people urge us to feed Fido with their particular product to make him wag his tail. Plants are supposed to look bright and cheerful after a feeding of *Brand X.*

Plants get their nutrients from the soil. They usually find enough, because their roots spread far and wide. If a soil is short of the necessary nutrients, we should bolster that soil so that it can nourish the plants that grow in it. Only when we spray the fresh foliage of growing plants (more on that later) are we actually feeding our leafy friends.

The message from the fertilizer industry is right, however, when it comes to houseplants. Plants growing in a container of sterile soil mix have no resources to fall back on. Their roots are confined and they are entirely dependent on what you give them in the way of fertilizer. Most house plant fertilizers contain a quick-acting form of nitrogen; because most houseplants are foliage plants that need a lot of nitrogen, the plant's response is quick and obvious. It's almost as if the plant *does* wag its tail.

In the ground, plants with wide-ranging roots are able to extract nutrients from the soil, provided there is enough moisture available. It's important to know that plants "drink their food." They are about 90 percent water themselves, and they can't handle solid stuff.

It's a mistake to think that fertilizers make plants grow. Fertilizers support growth; they don't cause it. By the same token, it's folly to apply fertilizers to dormant plants, unless they are on the point of growing, as in the case of deciduous trees in January. Such an application anticipates growth; it doesn't start it. Once a tree has started to grow, you can push it along with fertilizers containing nitrogen and thereby get faster, more luxuriant growth.

Beginning gardeners like to think that a fertilizer high in phosphorous will make a plant produce flowers, or that a fertilizer high in potash will make oranges taste sweeter. It's not so. Admittedly, phosphorous aids flower production and potash is required for sugar synthesis, but you can't expect these nutrients to turn on a plant function in the same way that a wall switch lights up a bulb. A fertilizer, by itself, won't make a plant produce flowers.

Another common misunderstanding is that a "sick" plant can be cured by giving it "food." Don't make the mistake of heaping a lot of dry fertilizer around a plant that is not doing well. It won't work the same as reviving an invalid with chicken soup.

Know what you are buying: Read the label on the bag

There are sixteen chemical elements that plants need for growth and survival. Three of these—carbon, oxygen, and hydrogen—are found in either air or water, and the rest are found in the soil. When the soil fails to provide its share of some of these elements, we turn to fertilizers for help. It is important to know just what help a given fertilizer has to offer.

Most fertilizers—as you buy them in the nursery, in a bag—are made up largely of clay or an inert filler. This is necessary, owing to manufacturing and handling considerations.

All manufacturers are required by law to declare on the bag what their products contain. This safeguards the consumer. Ammonium sulphate is a chemical fertilizer that is consistently the same, no matter who manufactures it. On the other hand, citrus food, pecan food, rose food, African violet food, camellia food (there we go again!) can contain anything, and often do, but the manufacturer is required by law to tell us what the ingredients are.

Under the name of the product, you'll see three numbers; for example 16:20:0 or 30:15:15. These are percentages, by weight, of nitrogen (N), phosphate (P), and potash (K), always in that order. These are the main plant nutrients. In smaller print, you'll find other nutrients listed with their percentages. The amounts usually are just as small as the print.

Calculate how many nutrients a fertilizer contains, and the cost

Let's say you are comparing costs of ammonium phosphate, a standard fertilizer, with *Wonder Boy*, a highly advertised lawn food offered at a "super" price. Is the lawn food a good buy?

To find out, first add all the numbers to find the total percentage of nutrients versus clay filler. The total number of nutrient units in ammonium phosphate is $16+20+0=36$. (In passing, you may notice that some manufacturers sneak in a fourth number, sulphur, at perhaps 25. Disregard this number; we'll mention it later. It's simply a ploy to make you think you are getting something extra.)

If 36 percent of the bag's contents are nutrients, 64 percent must be filler. You're not interested in the filler; it's the 36 percent that you want. Let's say a 40-pound bag of ammonium phosphate costs $8. You'll be buying 36 percent of 40 pounds, which equals 14.4 pounds of nutrients. One pound of nutrients will cost $8 divided by 14.4, which comes to 55 cents per pound.

You do the same calculations with the lawn food, which has a total of 32 units of nutrients (15 percent N, 5 percent P, 10 percent K, plus 2 percent iron). It is priced at $8 for 20 pounds. Multiply the weight of the bag by the percentage of the nutrients: 32 percent $\times$ 20 pounds $=$ 6.4 pounds of nutrients. Divide the $8 by 6.4 to get the price of one pound of nutrients, which comes to $1.25 per pound. Clearly, *Wonder Boy* is not such a good buy.

Now you know the dollar value of the two fertilizers, but money isn't everything. You still have some thinking to do.

Which is the right fertilizer for your purpose?

There's no point in paying a lot of money for something you don't need. That's what your mother told you, a long time ago.

Lawn food implies that it will make the lawn grow green. Usually, all that is needed for this to happen are water and nitrogen in one form or another. Lawn food, in addition to nitrogen, contains phosphate, potash, and iron, which, in most cases, are not necessary. Even the cheaper ammonium phosphate is a luxury fertilizer for a lawn if all that lawn needs is nitrogen. In this case, buy ammonium sulphate, which contains 21 percent nitrogen.

If a 20-pound bag of ammonium sulphate (21:0:0) costs $1.79, what's the cost of a unit of nitrogen? Did you get 42 cents? Good. Clearly, ammonium sulphate is the best buy for your nitrogen-loving lawn.

A SOIL ANALYSIS GIVES YOU A BALANCE SHEET OF NUTRIENTS

If you take a bucket of your soil to a soil chemist, he can tell you what elements, and how much of each, it contains. Then he looks up the chemical needs of the plants you are trying to grow in that soil. If there is a shortfall in any category he can calculate how many pounds of this and that—in the form of fertilizer—you should put on the ground to make everything right.

You should be aware, however, that soil analysis is not without its drawbacks and limitations.

First, did your bucket of soil truly represent the conditions all over your property? You will have gotten off to a bad beginning if you collected your sample just outside the kitchen door or in a corner where there used to be a compost pile. Your sample was not representative at all.

Second, soil analysis tells you what is in the soil, not how difficult it is for plants to get it. Desert soils are notorious for not letting go of their minor plant nutrients (such as iron, copper, zinc, and molybdenum), owing to an overabundance of calcium. If you hear learned folk talking of "lime-induced chlorosis," that's what they mean. The stuff is there but the plant can't get it.

Third, soil scientists may know a lot about the nutrient needs of cotton, soybeans, alfalfa, and other farm crops, but they don't know much about landscaping plants.

All this makes the cost of soil analysis of doubtful value.

When to invest in the cost of a soil analysis

It may be worthwhile to look for chemical reasons for your plants' sluggishness, provided you're sure they are watered properly, that there's good drainage, and that no diseases are in evidence. And don't forget to suit your plants to their environment.

Excess sodium and excess calcium prevent plants from growing vigorously. An analysis for these chemicals is routine and is not expensive. You might also want to turn to soil analysis if you suspect that weedkiller residues or a chemical spill are to blame for your problems. This is a complex undertaking and, therefore, more expensive.

As an alternative, learn to recognize the signs of nutrient shortages

Plants themselves tell you what is happening. The signs are not infallible, but, provided all other needs are being met, you can use them as indications of some nutrient shortages:

- Small leaves, slow growth, and a pale color (in normally dark-colored leaves) indicate a shortage of nitrogen.
- Leaves with brown tips and edges indicate a shortage of potash.
- Leaves with red or purple colors indicate phosphorus is lacking.
- Distorted leaves, generally curled or small and close together, tell of a shortage of zinc.
- Leaves with dark green veins surrounded by pale green indicate that the plant is lacking iron.

HOW ARE THE NITROGEN FERTILIZERS BEST APPLIED?

Desert soils commonly can't provide enough nitrogen or phosphorus (and sometimes iron and

Never apply fertilizer to dry soil. First, irrigate to a depth of 18 inches (use your soil probe to be sure). Scatter fertilizer on the moist soil. Resume irrigation until you can sink your soil probe to a depth of 3 feet for a tree, 2 feet for shrubs.

zinc) for healthy plant growth, so we apply fertilizers to supply the deficit. With nitrogen fertilizers, timing is important. Apply them just before, or at the beginning of, a growth spurt. This usually is in the spring when temperatures warm, but many plants go dormant during the heat of summer and show a secondary growth spurt in the fall; fertilize in the fall, too.

Nitrogen fertilizers are best applied in frequent small amounts rather than in a single heavy application. This is especially true if plants are irrigated heavily. Such irrigations carry the fertilizers out of reach of the roots and they are lost.

Lawns give us a good example of this situation. Bermudagrass lawns don't begin to grow until the weather warms up, so it would be wasteful to apply ammonium sulphate until green leaves replace the brown ones of winter. Because we irrigate lawns heavily in summer, one heavy application of fertilizer would either be washed out of the soil or used up by plant growth early in the season. Instead, apply small amounts of ammonium sulphate throughout the summer, at every other irrigation, until the lawn goes dormant again in the fall. In this way you will fertilize the growth.

Nitrogen fertilizers are applied with irrigation

Never put dry fertilizers on dry soil and then water them in. You'll burn tender roots that way because high concentrations of salts—good ones, in this case—are corrosive. Applying a lot of fertilizer with a little water will cause leaves and flowers to drop off a citrus tree, a flower

To effectively fertilize a growing tree, first extend its irrigation basin far enough to water the new feeder roots found at the ends of root branches. Nutrients are carried down to the roots by water. Never apply fertilizer to dry soil. Before applying fertilizer, moisten the soil to a depth of 18 inches, then stop.

plant to curl up and die, and a lawn to show dead spots.

When you want to apply ammonium sulphate to a shrub or tree, first apply water out to a line even with the ends of the branches; that's where the active feeder roots are. Stop when you can easily poke your soil probe 18 inches deep. Scatter ammonium sulphate over the wet surface at the rate of two pounds to every hundred square feet of soil under the tree. (If you do this more than once a year, use smaller ammounts each time.) Continue the irrigation until you can poke your probe down 3 feet. The first half of the irrigation prepared the soil; the second half dissolved the fertilizer and carried it down through wet soil. In this way you supplied nutrients to the feeder roots, which are all over beneath the spread of the branches.

Don't figure fertilizer needs by measuring tree trunk diameter

You often see a fertilizing method described that relies on measured tree diameter. It's a method that supposedly relates tree size to the amount of fertilizer needed, which in itself is a good idea. In desert soils, however, it can lead to trouble, owing to the dryness of the soil and to our reluctance to water properly.

The recommendation, according to this method, is that you apply a pound of nitrogen for every inch of trunk diameter. The implication is that you throw the fertilizer at the trunk and leave it there, which is what beginning gardeners often do—to their subsequent sorrow. When the fertilizer is dissolved by "filling the well" you get a strong corrosive solution that

Next, scatter ammonium sulfate—or ammonium nitrate if your tree is a winter grower—onto the surface of the wet soil. Don't dig it in, or you will cut the new roots and do more harm than good. Now, continue the irrigation until you can poke your soil probe 3 feet into the soil. At that point the soil will have been supplied with nutrients all around the roots.

damages plant roots; this happens even if you fill the well two or three times. In any case, a little circle of bricks around a tree deludes you into bad watering habits; feeder roots are—or should be—all under the spread of the branches, not just near the trunk.

Don't work to a timetable; look at the state of your plants

It's a mistake to apply nitrogen fertilizers on certain dates of the year. You read that February, May and August are "magic dates" for this gardening chore because those dates commonly—but not always—coincide with growth spurts.

If the leaves on your plants are dark green, you can skip an application—or two, or three, or more—until the leaves begin to pale out.

The results of overfertilization with nitrogen

If you keep applying nitrogenous fertilizer to a plant that doesn't need it, you'll get a large plant that is dark green, that has soft tissues attractive to insect pests and fungus diseases, that is tender to frost, that doesn't flower freely, and, in the case of citrus, that has an unduly thick fruit skin.

Again, don't overfertilize desert plants

Remember that desert plants have become adapted over thousands of years to a spartan existence; for this reason, they should not be "pushed along" in their growth by heavy watering and heavy fertilizing. It's safe to encourage a little faster-than-usual growth by giving young desert trees and shrubs small amounts of nitrogen—about a quarter the amount you'd give to mulberry trees or roses will be enough—but it's probably better not to fertilize mature plants. It certainly is better not to fertilize cactus plants.

WHEN TO USE PHOSPHATIC FERTILIZERS

Phosphate does not move easily through the soil. It tends to be held by minute soil particles until plant roots find it. The provision of this plant nutrient can be likened to putting money in a bank account in preparation for future needs. You also have to place it ahead of root growth. This means that you apply it at digging time, before you set the plant in the soil.

When digging a planting hole for a shrub or a tree, mix phosphate fertilizer at the rate of one ounce for every cubic foot with the other soil amendments as you backfill the hole. If there are a number of holes to be dug, some people will rent a concrete mixer to make sure the soil and amendments are thoroughly mixed.

Before planting a lawn or flower bed, dig in the phosphate. The usual rate is 3 pounds to each hundred square feet.

SOME OF THE MORE COMMON FERTILIZERS FOR THE DESERT

Nitrogen fertilizers

Ammonium sulphate: 21 percent — has an acid reaction with the soil because of its sulphate residue. "Residue" is a bad word, implying something we don't want, so salespeople have added in the sulphur number on the bag analysis statement to make you think that you are buying something extra. Sulphur is good for our soils, though; it's not a bad ploy. Ammonium sulphate is soluble in water. It needs to be changed by soil organisms into the nitrate form before plants can use the nitrogen it contains, however, and this occurs only when the soil is warm.

Ammonium nitrate: 33 percent — does not have an acid reaction because there is no residue. It is very soluble in water, and is doubly valuable because the nitrate component is immediately available to a growing plant. The other, ammonium component, is stored on soil particles and becomes available later. The nitrate part is available to plants growing in cold soil, but it will be lost through drainage if the plant is dormant.

Urea: 45 percent — is a strong fertilizer with no acidic reaction; there is no residue. Bacterial action, which requires a warm soil, changes it to nitrate, making it simultaneously available and subject to loss through drainage. It is, therefore, a summertime fertilizer and should be used in small amounts.

Calcium nitrate: 15 percent — is useful during the winter months because of its nitrate component, but the calcium component simply adds more of an elment that already is in excess in desert soils.

Blood meal, cottonseed meal, seaweed, and other organic fertilizers — are available in nurseries from time to time, usually at a higher cost. Read the figures and the fine print to discover what you are buying. Organic fertilizers are low in nutrients.

Complete, or composite, or balanced, or formulated fertilizers — often contain nitrogen. Read the figures and the fine print, and you'll discover that you may be paying extra for some nutrient you don't need.

Phosphatic fertilizers

Ammonium phosphate 16:20:0 — has an acidic reaction because it contains some sulphur in its formulation. The ammonium part needs to be changed into nitrate before plants can use it. It's wasteful to scatter it on the ground and water it in for growing plants, because the phosphate part will stay near the surface and not reach the deeper roots. Dig it in before planting.

Single (18%), double (36%), and triple (42%) superphosphates — are different strengths of basically the same stuff. Read the fine print to make sure what you are paying for when the label simply says "superphosphate."

Bone meal, bone dust, and other organic fertilizers — are available from time to time, usually at a higher cost. Read the figures and the fine print to discover what you are buying.

Complete, or composite, or balanced, or formulated fertilizers — often contain phosphates. Read the figures and the fine print, and you may discover that you are paying extra for something you don't need.

Potassium fertilizers

Because desert soils have adequate amounts of potash, there's no need to supply it; most nurseries don't stock potassium fertilizers. You can order sulphate of potash or nitrate of potash for special occasions.

Compound, balanced, blended, and special needs fertilizers

There are any number of compound fertilizers—those that have several elements in them—and they usually are more expensive than the straight ones. Most houseplant foods contain a number of nutrients, but you may not need them all. It's the same with special formulations for azaleas, citrus, roses, and pecans.

All of these fertilizers will provide nutrients to the soil surrounding any plant, and the plant will benefit. However, it's an expensive way to improve your soil.

Look at the percentage numbers and see what it is you are buying. The ratio of nitrogen to phosphorus to potash is important. For leafy plants, you want a ratio of 2:1:0, or maybe 2:1:1; in other words, more nitrogen. For other plants,

Ammonium phosphate is used when you prepare the soil by digging; it's pelleted and gray. Ammonium sulfate is scattered on the surface and washed into the soil before spurts of growth; it looks like sugar.

you need a ratio of 1:2:1 or 1:2:0; more phosphate. Seldom is it economical to buy a fertilizer with a ratio of 1:1:1. Potash often is not needed, and it's always expensive.

Compound fertilizers often give us some interesting information in the fine print. They define the source of the nitrogen portion by telling us how much is ammoniacal and how much is nitrate. Ammonia works more slowly than does nitrate, so if you want a quick response you'll buy your "plant food" on the basis of its nitrate content.

Don't buy a separate special needs fertilizer for every plant. Specific plants are not so specific in their fertilizer requirements as special needs fertilizer manufacturers would have us believe. Rose food can be used on lawns, camellia food can be used on roses, pecan food can be used on pyracantha, citrus food can be used on a flower bed, lawn food can be used on citrus, and so on.

We generally expect such plants to grow quickly for our pleasure. It's the nitrogen portion of the fertilizer that does this, particularly if it's in the nitrate form. The other ingredients may be needed, but the determining factor is whether those nutrients already are in the soil and available to the plant. Nitrogen usually is missing because it's the one that's used most quickly and because it is, in a nitrate form, easily washed through the soil with irrigation. Nitrogen gives the most dramatic result.

The "special" case of iron

Salespeople have brainwashed us well on a plant's need of iron. We now ask ourselves, "Will it get better if we give it iron?"

The signs of iron deficiency are pale new leaves with dark green veins in them. The cause of iron deficiency is the plant's inability to take up enough iron. The question is, "Why not?"

First, it may be a simple case of there being no iron in the soil; in that case, you should add some. The second reason may be that the characteristic abundance of calcium in desert soils prevents the plant from using what iron is there; this is the "lime-induced chlorosis" mentioned earlier. The remedy is to add iron. Since many forms of iron fertilizers are acidic in nature, you do two things at once: you supply the nutrient and you acidify the soil. In this case, adding iron is good.

The third reason could be that you have created conditions under which the plant can't use the iron that is in the soil. If you overwater a plant you drown the roots—they need oxygen, just as the leaves do—and the stresses on the plant lead to an iron deficiency. In such a case—and it's very common—you can "cure the disease" by watering less frequently, not by adding expensive iron.

HOW TO APPLY FERTILIZERS WHEN PREPARING THE SOIL

Simply scatter ammonium phosphate on the ground and then dig it in as deeply as you can. For flowers and lawns, 3 pounds to every hundred square feet will be needed, together with organic amendment, usually steer manure.

If preparing the soil means digging a planting hole for a shrub or tree, use ammonium phosphate at the rate of one-sixteenth (in pounds) of the volume of the hole (in cubic feet). Mix the phosphate thoroughly into the backfill soil; don't make layers.

HOW TO APPLY DRY FERTILIZER TO GROWING PLANTS

Always scatter dry fertilizer on wet soil. This is important because you want fertilizer chemicals to be as dilute as possible when they reach the roots of plants. Never put dry fertilizer on dry soil, even if you water it in liberally afterwards.

First, irrigate the soil to the half-way point. Use your soil probe to tell you when you have watered down to 6 inches for flowers, 12 inches for lawns and shrubs, and 18 inches for trees. Stop. Scatter the fertilizer on top of the wet ground and, in the case of shrubs and trees, out to a line even with the ends of the branches. Continue watering until the soil probe indicates you have gone the full depth.

Remember (1) that plants have their growth spurts (that's when you apply the fertilizer) and their dormant times (that's when you don't), and (2) that it's better to apply small amounts frequently than to apply a large dose all at once; in this way you avoid burning tender roots.

The standard is to scatter 2 pounds of ammonium sulphate per hundred square feet twice a year, usually in spring and fall. If you spread the spring and fall applications over a period of one month in each season, use a pound each time. If you use a stronger fertilizer, such as ammonium nitrate, go for two-thirds of the rate. If you use urea, a much stronger fertilizer, apply at half the rate.

HOW TO USE DRY FERTILIZER STAKES

These come in various sizes of hard, bulletlike spikes and deliver different nutrients. You hammer them into the ground around your plants and let the irrigation water dissolve them. They may last three or four months.

If you like this labor-saving idea, make sure you surround your tree with plenty of spikes. A mere half-dozen provide nutrients in just a few spots, leaving the intervening soil as poor as ever it was.

HOW TO USE SLOW-RELEASE FERTILIZERS

These are pelleted fertilizers that commercial nurseries like to use because it saves them labor. You find them in the soil of plants you buy at your retail nursery; if they are spent, you think they are the empty egg cases of some pesky nuisance.

The pellets come in various formulations—often with a lot of expensive potash, which you don't need—and they usually last about three months. They are good to use in containers because they don't release a lot of chemicals at one time and so don't burn the roots. (For more about container gardening, see Chapter 17.) You can use them in the flower bed, too, but most people consider them too expensive to put in a tree-planting hole.

PLANTS "DRINK THEIR FOOD," SO APPLY FERTILIZERS IN SOLUTION

It's a good idea to provide nutrients in the water when you irrigate plants, especially exotic trees, shrubs, lawns, and flowers.

It's tiresome to work in terms of one tablespoon per gallon, but that's the normal proportion to use. If you buy a hose-end proportioner and install it at the faucet, you can save yourself a lot of trouble and time. It's a brass gadget with a side tube that sits in a bucket of dissolved fertilizer. When the faucet is turned on, the fertilizer solution (usually at the strength of one cup to a gallon) is sucked from the bucket into the hose where the flow of water carries it to your plants (at the rate of one tablespoon to a gallon). Every time you water, you automatically give the plants their nutrients at the right strength—until you remove the gadget or let the fertilizer bucket run dry. (See page 36.)

SPRAY PLANTS' LEAVES WITH FERTILIZER AND THEY'LL ABSORB IT

Fertilizer companies have created solutions to spray on such commercial crops as pecans, citrus, and grapes, and there's no reason homeowners can't use them on their landscape plants. The young leaves of trees have a thin skin that is absorptive; furthermore, that's where the growth is and where the need for nutrients is greatest.

Besides being an easy thing to do, there are two arguments in favor of foliar feeding (nutrient spraying). First, it takes too long for any fertilizer applied to the soil to get down to the roots, be changed into the nitrate form, be taken into the roots, and then be carried up the trunk and out along the branches to the leaf buds that are breaking out in the warming weather. By the time this happens, the party is over. Foliar feeding gets there at opening time. It is used right away, when it is most needed.

Second, desert soils that are high in calcium swallow up any application of nutrients such as iron, zinc, copper, manganese, and magnesium. They never become available to plant roots; they combine with calcium and remain locked in the soil.

Foliar feeding is best done as new leaves appear, and it is done with a very dilute solution. It may not be easy to do on a really big tree, but you can try it with pressure equipment. Several weekly applications will be necessary, since leaf buds open and remain absorptive over a period of time.

FOR PROBLEMS WITH LIME-INDUCED CHLOROSIS, USE CHELATED FERTILIZERS

If your plants show deficiencies of the minor elements—iron, zinc, copper, manganese, and so on—and you are unable to use foliar feeding for one reason or another, there's another trick to try. Specially formulated fertilizers called chelated iron, chelated zinc, and so on, can be mixed in the soil or sprayed onto the leaves. Spraying seems to give better results.

Chelated fertilizers are expensive, and they don't always work as well as you'd like, but they are worth a try. They are particularly helpful where an excess of calcium in the soil prevents the plant from using the fertilizer you put there.

FERTILIZING WITH TREE TRUNK IMPLANTS

A few years ago, there was a lot of interest in providing large trees with soluble iron or zinc or copper solutions in little gelatin capsules. These were hammered into holes drilled in the trunks, and the flow of sap was supposed to carry the nutrients up the tree.

Up to a point, it was a nice idea—in some ways, it made good sense—but it's not used very much these days. With this method you have to drill a lot of holes, and tree experts nowadays frown on the concept, saying that the holes do more harm than the fertilizer does good.

You may remember your grandfather curing his orchard trees of sickness by hammering galvanized nails into the trunks. That gave the tree some zinc. Copper nails gave it copper, and ordinary nails gave it iron. But all that was in the olden days.

8 A Troubleshooter's Guide
WHAT TO DO WHEN THINGS GO WRONG

Don't get too excited or worried when little things go wrong. Plants don't mind a few yellow leaves, wind scratches from thorns, or twig damage caused by cicadas. Besides, in the nature of things, the missing leaf on your rose bush means a happy grasshopper somewhere in the world.

Those "ancient immemorial lawns" of Oxford are full of dandelions and daisies, and no harm done either. Don't be dismayed if your landscape is not picture perfect. Take a look at your nearest "best" highly maintained commercial landscape; in its perfection you'll see a sterile scene.

"A garden is a lovesome thing, God wot!" If we accept plants for what they are, instead of expecting a lot from them, there will be peace and quiet in the garden, and more contentment.

There's a danger in trying too hard when we care for a landscape. There's merit in letting it develop on its own.

Very often it's our fault that things go wrong. We think that our plants grow too slowly, they don't flower enough, or they take up too much room. We attack their unacceptable ways with more water, or doses of fertilizer, or vigorous chopping, all of which often are unnecessary and damaging.

Some plants we don't tolerate—we call them weeds—and blast them with chemical poisons. Any little thing that flies or crawls causes the same knee-jerk reaction: a squirt, a spray, a dousing with chemicals. Overkill is easy; it's sad that we don't realize how we upset nature's balance and subsequently spoil things for ourselves. In a landscape, most problems don't require the urgent measures we use to eliminate pests and diseases in a vegetable garden. Take it easy.

POOR SITUATIONS CAUSE LANDSCAPE PROBLEMS

An infertile soil won't grow good roses and one that has poor drainage won't grow good trees. You can't grow a lawn on a shallow soil. Magnolia trees won't grow where dry desert winds blow.

However, a poor situation for some plants is quite acceptable to others. In a desert region, the local plants, the arid-land plants, the desert plants—call them what you will—are the ones that are best adapted to desert conditions. Jungle plants are not adapted. That should be obvious enough, but there are finer degrees of suitability. Jojoba plants, native to low deserts with summer rains and where it doesn't freeze, won't thrive in the high desert, where there is summer dryness and winter snow.

Those plants that we bring to the desert from more gentle climates don't do well in full sun. A good example is the commonly used hedge plant euonymus. We soon learn that it won't take full sun, so we plant it in the shade. Then it succumbs to mildew. Euonymus, a useful plant in other climes, is a problem plant in the desert.

In the same way, we discover that plants such as azaleas and camellias don't grow well in an alkaline soil, in the bright sunshine, with low humidity, and at high temperatures. Contrariwise, if we put desert plants, which need full sun, in a shady place, they don't grow or don't flower the way we'd like them to.

An effective way to avoid plant problems is to match your plants with the conditions in your yard.

POOR MANAGEMENT CAUSES LANDSCAPE PROBLEMS

It's no surprise that plants in the desert must be watered. Proper watering means giving them enough, but not too much. Arid-land plants frequently are killed by overwatering from automatic drip irrigation systems.

Overfertilizing is another common mistake. You should not "feed" your plants on a schedule in the same way you feed the cat. Desert plants are tuned to poor fertility and it harms them to force their growth; they develop soft wood that is inviting to diseases and insect invasion. It's a good rule of thumb, as we have seen, to apply fertilizers in small amounts during periods of plant growth. Even the exotic plants we bring to the desert should be allowed to grow slowly.

Weedkiller chemicals need to be used with discretion. The use of sterilants on stubborn weeds affects underlying roots of nearby trees and shrubs. Signs of distress soon appear on the leaves and twigs of trees you didn't mean to harm.

A simple operation like spraying foliage with chemicals, or even with plain water, in the noonday sun causes distressing symptoms. The desert sun is too fierce for that kind of carelessness.

Wrong timing wreaks havoc with plants. For example, a heavy pruning of a tree or a hedge during the summer months exposes inner branches that before pruning were shaded by

This pattern on growing leaves indicates the past use of soil sterilants somewhere nearby. Never use soil sterilants. They work *too* well.

top foliage. The result is severe blistering of framework branches, which, instead of putting out new growth, die back even further.

During the winter months the soil is too cold for planting desert plants, and during the summer it's too hot for the temperate plants. You have to choose the right time for each plant; otherwise, problems develop.

Even at the very beginning of a landscape, you must properly dig the ground to make sure of adequate drainage and make sure that the roots of your new plants are not bundled up in a knot. When distress signs appear later, prompting you to mistakenly identify them and mistakenly treat them, you compound the situation.

PLANT PROBLEMS ARE INHERENT IN NATURE

We can include pests and diseases in this category. Our management practices won't stop caterpillars or grasshoppers or rabbits or gophers.

We simply supply the food for them and, if conditions are right, here they are. They've come to enjoy the feast.

Of course, we need to do something about them. We can surround an area with chicken wire to keep rabbits out. We can cover young plants with sheets to hide and protect them from insect pests. We can reduce gopher populations by a determined trapping program, and we can, as a last resort, spray the roses until there are no aphids left.

Note that pests and diseases are closely associated with seasons. Aphids need tender new growth on which to feed. We should expect their attacks in the spring and fall when mild temperatures encourage fresh shoot development. Harvester ants get busy after the soil has been softened by rain, which itself encourages new leaf growth, which becomes their food. Rabbits are not a problem until the hot summer dries out their varied diet of desert plants. Summer continues, their food gets short, they get bolder, and they eat almost everything in our landscape, even prickly pear pads.

We have no control over drought, though we compensate for it by increasing our irrigations. We can't do anything about flooding, either. A waterlogged soil handicaps our plants, and it behooves us to remember this when we plant them. Don't put desert plants in a depression,

This tree *looked* healthy for years, but a storm revealed the truth: the tree planter failed to punch through caliche when digging the planting hole, and the tree's roots never grew deeply enough to anchor it.

A

This trio of photos illustrates three common management mistakes. A: Apart from making a beautiful tree into something ugly, this sort of ill-considered pruning invites the entry of bacteria and ensures a mass of bushy growth that weakens the tree. B: This sort of mutilation does nothing for the tree, except to turn its natural architecture into a mass of congested shoots that struggle with one another for light. This tree will never recover its former beauty. C: Someone forgot to remove a string, probably originally holding a price tag or label, from the base of this rose bush and it strangled itself as it grew. The damage could easily have been avoided.

B

C

but set them on a mound of well-drained soil. Don't put a lot of moisture-retaining peat moss or manure in the planting hole, either.

The desert has a lot of poor soil with underlying layers of rock-hard caliche. We can, and must, improve the soil, but improvements alone will have little benefit unless we first remove the caliche. If we don't, our plants will develop problems caused by poor drainage.

Lightning and summer storms bring plant problems, and there's not much we can do about the weather. However, branches won't be torn off nor trees blown over if good pruning, to open up the tree, enables wind to blow through the foliage. By placing drip system emitters far out from tree trunks, roots will grow out to anchor young trees against storms and they won't blow over.

Desert sun kills the foliage of some kinds of plants, and so we should not grow them. Winter freezes do the same to other plants, and we should not grown them, either. We should be selective when making our plant lists and match plants to our conditions. It will save us a lot of worry and work later. Unless we match our plants with conditions, we inherit a bunch of problems whose symptoms we don't recognize and whose causes we don't know. As a result, we spend a lot of time and money on ineffective methods trying to put things right.

POOR DECISIONS CAUSE THINGS TO GO WRONG

Management is, after all, a series of decisions. A single poor decision, such as applying too much fertilizer, will damage a plant. You might confuse the results with salt build-up, frost damage, sunburn, or loss of roots due to insects or diseases. Had you done the right thing, there wouldn't be any problem.

Planting at the wrong time of the year can have disastrous results, causing problems that linger and confuse a proper diagnosis.

Planting petunias or any other annual flower in the same bed year after year is a poor decision. You'll build up soilborne diseases that weaken and can kill your plants.

Mowing grass too short during the hot summer is a poor decision. Soil and grass roots will get too hot and you won't have a nice-looking lawn because of it.

Planting a sun-loving plant in a shady place, and vice-versa, is a poor decision. Things are sure to go wrong if you do either.

It's a poor decision to irrigate when the soil is wet. It might have been a poor decision in the first place to rely on a time clock to do your irrigating for you.

It's a poor decision to spray insecticides when you want to control a fungus disease.

It's a poor decision to top a tree, to severely prune a mulberry tree every spring, to use soil sterilants, to dig in gypsum (unless you have a sodium soil), to dig up a native tree and expect it to live in its new place, to apply fertilizer to an ailing plant in the hope of "curing it with chicken soup."

AVOID PLANT PROBLEMS BY BEING A GOOD CARETAKER

Be observant all the time. Make a good diagnosis, then take action quickly. The longer you wait, the worse things will be.

Get into the habit of watching your plants. Appreciate their good health and you quickly will recognize when something goes wrong. It won't take a lot of your time if you look at your plants as you drive in your driveway, when you take out the garbage, when you glance out the window, as you feed the dog, and so on.

Look at the leaves

Actually, it will be the leaves that look at you. Leaves display the first, obvious sign that something is wrong with your plant.

Drooping, wilting leaves — tell you that the plant is short of water. There are many possible reasons for this. One that often is overlooked, paradoxically, is that the roots are drowning in too wet a soil. More commonly, however, the soil is dry. Apart from the extremes of wet and dry, you might find the roots have been damaged by gophers, grubs, fungus diseases, nematodes, stem borers, too much fertilizer, weedkillers, even carelessly discarded engine oil or carpet cleaner.

Pale green leaves — starting with the older ones, indicate that the plant is short of nitrogen; new leaves that are pale with dark green veins indicate a shortage of iron. The iron deficiency symptom can be confusing. It happens when the soil is too wet, in which case it can easily be corrected simply by letting the soil dry out. A wet soil has lost its oxygen, which roots need to function properly. Always examine the soil before you apply iron fertilizer.

Blotchy leaves — brown and green and yellow, indicate an uptake of weedkilling chemicals, the sterilants.

Leaves with brown dead edges — suggest the presence of excess salts in the soil; these often are associated with poor drainage. Either there's not enough water to drain the salts away or the soil won't allow drainage because of compaction.

Small leaves that are dull or bluish — tell you that the plant is chronically short of water.

Small, pale leaves — indicate a low level of nutrition, which has retarded the plant's growth for a time.

Deformed, puckered leaves — can be caused by weedkilling chemicals, by virus diseases, and by tiny insects called thrips. Thrips damage is common on citrus leaves, but you see it several weeks after the damage was done and the insects have moved on. Thrips rasp on the leaf tissue when it is very small and tender. The irritation causes uneven growth in the leaf, which is magnified as the leaf gets bigger. It looks bad, but the leaf functions normally and the actual damage is negligible.

Bunched, twisted needles — on Aleppo pines are caused by a very small mite. Another causes "witches'-broom" on palo verde trees.

Dead leaves — can be caused by frost in winter and by sun in summer, but don't overlook what a hot, dry desert wind can do. Dead leaves also can mean that the roots aren't functioning because of Texas root rot (see Chapter 12), nematodes, fungus diseases, gophers, grubs, stem borers, and so on.

Dead spots on leaf centers — especially on the upper surfaces of exposed leaves, are caused by sunburn. This happens in summer when, just for a moment, a plant is short of moisture.

Bronze-colored leaves — especially on pyracantha, tell you that a red spider mite has been rasping on the upper surfaces. The older leaves feel gritty and have a covering of webbing, which shows up dramatically when you mist it.

Dying leaves on inside stems, twigs, and branches — are quite natural. They are not getting enough light; they are aging and giving up their nitrogen to the younger leaves. This natural process is hastened by adverse conditions. You'll see more yellow leaves of this kind after a frost, during a flush of spring growth, after a period of drought, after transplanting, and as the tree grows older and bigger.

Isolated clusters of dead leaves — scattered throughout an otherwise green foliage can be the result of stem borers (in the case of euonymus hedges) or of cicada damage, which is shown by serrated twigs where the insect laid her eggs.

These furled bits of leaves might have come from roses or grapes or hibiscus or peppers. Now they're the nest of the leaf-cutter bee, which builds its home in any snug little round space, such as this length of metal tubing. Don't be upset; the damage to the donor plant is negligible.

Tattered leaves with scratch marks — are the result of wind banging the leaves about, sometimes against the plant's thorns, its branches, or a nearby building.

Leaves with ragged edges — have had grasshoppers or caterpillars eating them. Sometimes birds will leave the same damage.

Leaves with neat round holes on their edges — have been visited by the leaf-cutter bee. The bee works very quickly—it's a marvel to watch—and carries the piece away to build its nest in a small opening, such as a keyhole. Tender leaves are preferred. Although the damage looks unsightly, it's not significant.

Leaves with serpentine lines — on them are being tunneled by a small maggot of the leaf miner fly. The damage is superficial, and you don't have to worry about it.

Leaves with light-colored spots — show that water (from a sprinkler head, perhaps, or from a careless spraying) fell on the leaf while the sun was shining on it. Water spots magnify the strength of the sun, so they actually are burn spots. Chemicals add strength to the droplets.

Small black leaves — usually are the result of a freeze early in the fall or late in the spring, when a growth spurt is vulnerable.

Disappeared leaves — perhaps lying on the ground, have been taken by ants, usually during the night. You often can follow a trail of leaf pieces back to their nest, which may be quite distant. Desert trees and shrubs (ocotillo is an example) naturally drop their leaves to save water when summer becomes hot and dry. If the drought is severe, there will be an overall twig and branch die-back.

Brightly colored leaves — appear after a sharp cold spell in the fall. It's surprising how many newcomers think something is wrong with their plants when the leaves start turning a fall color. Surprisingly, those people are from New York, where the trees make a point of putting on a display in the fall. Desert colors are not so intense, but it's the same story.

Falling leaves in November — are a natural phenomenon. This causes city folk, newly arrived in the desert, to worry. Perhaps the gradually falling temperatures take newcomers by surprise, and they reason that if the sun is shining the leaves ought to stay on the trees. Come to think of it, have you ever seen a picture postcard from sunny California that shows a tree without its leaves?

Then check twigs, branches, and bark

Don't forget that leaves, although showing signs of a direct attack, more often are indicators of an attack somewhere else, at the stems or at the roots.

The serrated twig behind a bunch of dead leaves — on a tree has been damaged by an egg-laying cicada. This is a summertime event and is not serious enough to call for any counter action.

A regular series of small holes — running horizontally around a tree trunk is the work of a small bird, the sapsucker. The small holes exude sticky sap that traps curious insects. The bird, a sparrow-sized sort of woodpecker, returns after a day or two to collect the insects. Smart bird.

Regular, small holes running along the branches — of a tree are the breathing holes of borers inside. The borers need to be removed—by cutting off the whole branch—before they work their way down to a limb and do more serious damage.

A hole at the end of a rose branch — tells you that a borer has entered at a pruning cut and is working its way down to the main stem. Prune it out and, this time, protect the cut end with a spray of pruning paint.

Brown sap running out of the branches — of a tree and both staining and corroding the bark is caused by a bacteria in the tree. It gained entrance through unprotected pruning cuts. The disease is called slime-flux, and it can be a killer. Sometimes the tree recovers on its own—the problem simply goes away—but you can help by drilling quarter-inch holes into the center of the limb and inserting pieces of copper tubing to drain off the fluid. You want the corrosive fluid away from the bark; let it drip directly on the ground, where it won't hurt.

Dead bark along the branches, with black sooty areas inside — is caused by a fungus that enters through unprotected pruning cuts. The nearby twigs die and so do the leaves. This is sooty canker, and it can be a killer. Prune out the dead limbs and spray pruning paint on the cut ends.

Dead bark without the soot areas — is caused by frost damage in winter or by sunburn

Here's an interesting case. A jade plant wilted as if it were short of water, but additional water didn't help. The wilt actually was caused by the grubs seen here, which were destroying the plant's roots. When things go wrong with a plant, take a look at its roots.

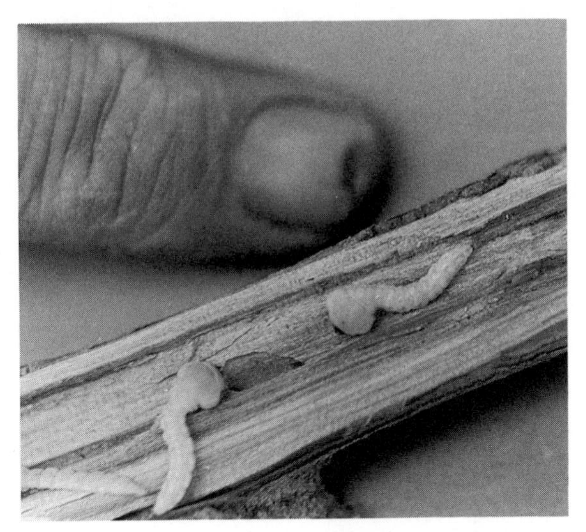

The flat-headed stem borer attacks many plants, including roses, pyracantha, and ocotillo. There is no chemical means of destroying this pest. Instead, cut out the infested branch and seal the cut with a spray of pruning paint.

in summer. Of course, the nearby twigs and leaves also die. Prune out the dead wood and protect with a spray of pruning paint.

A bunch of dead leaves in an otherwise green foliage — on olive trees in particular, suggests that a bacterium is at work. Slice the twigs to see whether there are brown stains in the conducting vessels of the twig. They can be followed right down to the roots, where verticillium gained entry through physical damage caused by a gopher, a grub, or careless use of a spade.

Citrus trees that exude gum from a discolored part on the trunk — usually at ground level, also show a dark streaking of the conducting vessels. This time it's a fungus, Phytophthora, that is obstructing the flow of water to the leaves. Yellowing and falling leaves are the first signs of attack. The fungus lives in wet soil, so don't overwater. The damaged parts should be cut out and the trunk should be painted with Bordeaux mixture.

Landscape trees growing on lawns show a gumming at ground level — also often show swelling and scarring of the bark, but with no discoloration inside. This is caused by careless use of gas or electric string grass trimmers, whose nylon strings bruise and cut the tender bark of a young tree. The first sign of something wrong is poor leaf growth.

An agave with all of its leaves on the ground — except the pencil-point upright ones, is short of water. Watering doesn't help, however, because the stem has been damaged. The first indications of this incurable condition are small gum exudates near the leaf bases. They're hard to see, but when you see wilted leaves it's too late; the stem has been consumed

When you see your agaves looking like this, it's too late for treatment. Dig them up and get rid of them, along with the grubs in the plant and in the soil.

This is the culprit that destroyed your agaves: the agave snout-nosed weevil. Both grubs and adults work their way into the succulent tissue at the base of the agave, bringing in bacteria that rot the heart of the plant.

by grubs and weevils. Yuccas sometimes suffer the same fate.

Poor top growth — can have many causes, but an easily avoided one is tree support ties that have been left too long on a branch. As the branch grows thicker, it chokes itself. Another cause of poor top growth is to be found on the bark of a tree trunk. Rabbits, squirrels, and deer sometimes eat bark and interrupt the flow of water and nutrients up and down the tree. If they eat right around the trunk, girdling it, the tree will die; at best, it will grow sprouts below the damage. Don't overlook the same sort of damage done by horses and dogs—or by little hatchets on cherry trees.

And don't overlook root damage

Root damage is not so easy to see. Because of this, we often overlook the root cause of distress in our landscape plants, from little annual flowers to tall permanent trees. When something goes wrong with your plants and you can't see any obvious reason for it, think of roots. Dig down and find some. Whenever a plant dies, the first thing you should look at is the roots. They tell you a lot.

Roots that are twisted around one another — can never function properly. If they are not spread out at planting time, they grow so tightly that they strangle themselves. This is a surprisingly common occurrence. It starts in the nursery with a small plant that is kept too long in its container. Instead of being thrown away, which is what should happen, it is moved to a larger container, where it again stays too long and develops a second congestion. This might be repeated a third time. The apparently healthy plant, with its invisible twisted roots, never grows well. Always examine the roots of plants—preferably in the nursery, *before* you pay

The roots of this young tree, which has fallen victim to the wind, were restricted in the nursery container and never had a chance to develop. The tree shouldn't have been planted, even if it was bargain-priced.

for them. Such a potbound plant hasn't a chance. All you can do is to pull it out and start again with a new plant. You find plants in large containers suffering from the same sort of confinement.

Roots travel sideways — when they are prevented from going down any further. If the obstructive layer, which can be caliche or clay, collects water, the roots will rot and cease to function.

Rotted roots — are caused by bacteria that thrive in poorly oxygenated soil. Such roots retain their central core and outer bark, but the soft tissue in between is gone. The loose bark slides along the core as you grasp it. (This condition is not to be confused with Texas root rot; for more on that deadly disease, see Chapter 12.)

Chewed roots — mean that some animals—gophers, rats, insect grubs—have been working on the roots, actually removing them.

Swollen bumpy roots — have been internally damaged by nematodes. Eventually the plant dies, but it takes a long time.

Large corky knobs — on the roots and on the stem at ground level also take a year or two to kill a tree. This is crown gall, a bacterial disease that you sometimes inadvertently buy with the tree at the nursery. After you have dug up the dead tree, use *Vapam* to sterilize the soil, so that the next tree you plant won't be infected.

ELEMENTARY, MY DEAR WATSON

There's another way to look at plant problems that will lead you, by the process of elimination, to the cause. It's based on plant growth. Use this system in conjunction with the list above. Use as many systems of diagnosis as you can to lead you to the real cause. If the situation weren't so serious, you might think of it as a detective game that challenges your powers of observation and deduction.

Let's use this method to examine the possible causes of slow growth in plants. Disregard the items on the following list that obviously don't apply; use those that do to make a composite sketch of the villain.

- Slow growth can be caused simply by falling air temperatures. Plants go dormant in winter, so there's nothing wrong with a plant that is slowing down in the fall.

- Growth also slows during the heat of summer, especially in the case of imported temperate plants. Any plant not in tune with its environment is uncomfortable and so stops growing, at least temporarily.
- Sunburn, an extra ration of heat, stops plants from growing.
- A poorly raised plant, such as one with congested roots, grows slowly.
- A plant with poor root development owing to underlying caliche grows slowly.
- A plant diseased by a virus, bacteria, or fungus grows slowly.
- Pests, such as aphids or nematodes, cause plants to grow slowly.
- Poor management, such as too little or too much watering, poor drainage, mowing grass too short, or the careless use of sterilants to kill weeds, makes landscape plants grow slowly.

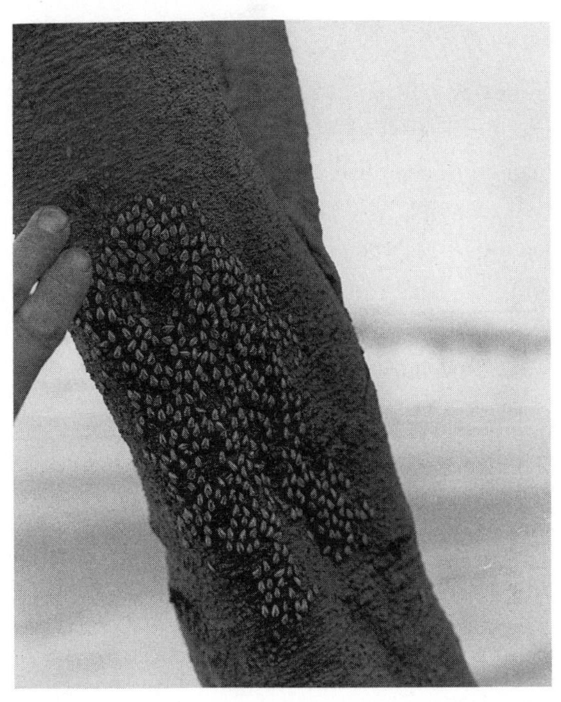

Biological control of garden pests is a sensible and effective alternative to chemical control. Seen here are old egg cases left over from a large hatch of ladybugs, one of the landscape gardener's best allies. It's getting easier to order ladybugs and other insect predators through the mail. Gardening magazines often run ads for outfits that sell the critters.

FINALLY, A QUICK REVIEW AND A DASH OF COMMON SENSE

Item 1:

It's better to avoid problems through good management. Don't overwater, go easy with fertilizers, prune carefully, and so on. Relax rather than fuss. To a large extent, plants manage things better when you leave them alone.

If you need to do battle with natural events, try the simple method first: fence off plants against rabbits, trap gophers, pick off insects, dig out caliche, add soil amendments, and so on.

Item 2:

Practice good sanitation. Protect each pruning cut with a spray of pruning paint. Don't leave infected material, such as oleander prunings with gall on them, lying about. Remove plants that have died of disease. Pick up damaged fruit; it attracts insects. Prevent weeds from going to seed by pulling them. Don't plant the same kind of flowers every year in the same bed; you build up soil-borne diseases that way. Repair storm-damaged branches quickly.

Item 3:

Be alert. Pick off insects before they increase in numbers and do a lot of damage. Don't allow plants to wilt. Remember to remove tie-wires from young shoots before their own growth strangles them. Watch the weather; it determines when you should—and shouldn't—plant, irrigate, fertilize, mow, prune, sow seed, and control weeds.

Item 4:

When all else fails, use spray chemicals—but use them wisely. There's a useful but bewildering armory of chemicals at the nurseries for the control of weeds, insects, and diseases. Before you use them, read the complete label. The best example of what can go wrong if you don't is to be found in the misuse of that dreadful weedkiller *Triox Vegetation Killer.* Very few people read the entire set of instructions, which tell you not to use the stuff near trees. Improper use enables the chemical to live up to its name: vegetation killer. It kills everything and contaminates the soil for years.

Item 5:

Don't forget that weeds can be controlled by hoeing and pulling, that insects can be picked off or shaken off, and that many diseases can be pruned out. There's no need to blast the environment with poisons whenever you see an insect crawling over a leaf. Most insects don't do any harm, and they shouldn't bother us. Many insects, such as the ladybug and the praying mantis, are beneficial, and we should encourage them. Only a few are harmful, and we should control them before they become a nuisance. It pays to know which are which.

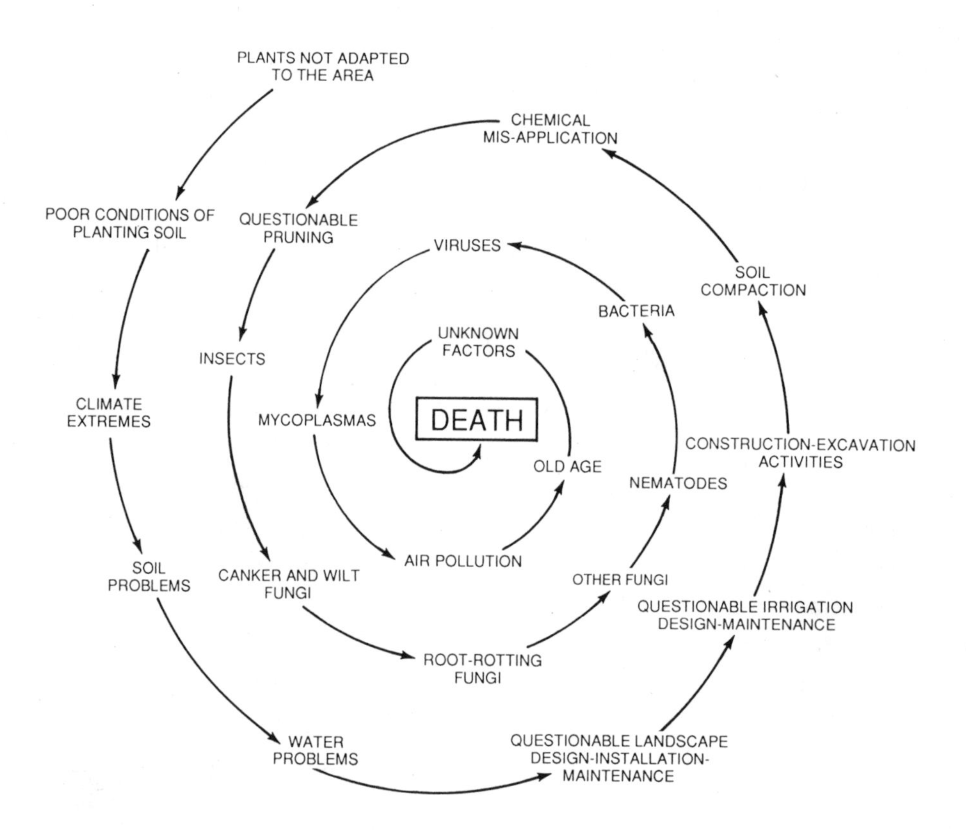

Why plants don't do well and why maintenance can be so costly. Situational problems are more common than pests and diseases. A spray gun full of chemicals has limited value—yet, for many people, it is the first thought that comes to mind. (From Paul D. Manion, *Tree Disease Concepts*, 2e, © 1991, p. 333. Adapted by permission of Prentice Hall, Englewood Cliffs, New Jersey.)

Guide to Diagnosing Plant Problems

by George Brookbank and Master Gardeners

Plant Part	Overall Condition	Particular Condition	Possible Causes
Leaves	A. normal shape	1. green, small	a. nitrogen deficiency b. zinc deficiency c. nematodes on roots d. dry soil
	A. normal shape	1. green, wilting	a. soil wet from poor drainage b. soil moist; grubs; chemical spill; excess fertilizer; Texas root rot; other root rots; nematodes c. soil dry from lack of rain or faulty irrigation system
	A. normal shape	2. all yellow	a. old age b. nitrogen deficiency
	A. normal shape, pale	3. green veins on new leaves 3. green veins on old leaves 3. green veins on all leaves	iron deficiency herbicides wet soil
	A. normal shape	4. brown in center only 4. brown at edges only 4. all brown 4. brown on lower leaves only	sunburn a. excess salts b. herbicide residue c. wind-dried a. frost b. wind-dried c. terminal twig borer d. cicada damage e. Texas root rot f. lack of water g. fire blight on pears, apples normal aging process
	A. normal shape	5. mottled old leaves 5. mottled new leaves	herbicides virus disease
	A. normal shape	6. silvery appearance	leaf-hopper damage
	A. normal shape	7. bronze color	red spider mite
	A. normal shape	8. purple color	frost, phosphorus deficiency
	A. normal shape	9. gray, powdery appearance	mildew on peas, grapes

Continued on next page

Continued from page 75

Plant Part	Overall Condition	Particular Condition	Possible Causes
	B. abnormal shape	1. twisted, puckered	a. aphids b. thrips c. leaf roller d. mites e. 2, 4-D-type herbicdes f. virus diseases
	B. abnormal shape	2. bunched, small rosette	a. zinc deficiency b. mites
	B. abnormal shape	3. chewed edges, holes	a. snails b. tomato hornworm c. crickets d. cabbage loopers e. cornstalk borer f. tortoise beetle g. grasshoppers h. birds
	B. abnormal shape	4. neat-edged holes	leaf-cutter bee
	B. abnormal shape	5. ragged edges, tears	wind damage
	B. abnormal shape	6. wandering brown lines	leaf miner
	C. leaves gone or chewed	1. stalks remain	a. ants b. rabbits c. birds
	D. leaves on ground		a. frost b. drought c. fertilizer burn d. ants e. rabbits f. birds g. individual leaf drop, not widespread, is normal h. seasonal leaf fall
	E. lower leaves lost		normal aging process
	F. all leaves gone		a. ants b. tomato hornworm c. birds d. rabbits e. squirrels f. pack rats
Stem		1. soft rot (brown, mushy) on seedling	soil organisms
		2. soft rot (brown, mushy) on stem	damping-off fungus

Plant Part	Overall Condition	Particular Condition	Possible Causes
		3. streaky under bark	bacterial wilts
		4. dark, dry spots	powdery mildew on grape
		5. flaky, black, dusty	sooty canker
		6. weeping brown fluid	slime flux
		7. weeping clear gum	a. heat stress b. citrus-foot rot c. bacterial gummosis (fruit trees)
		8. chewed, wet	squash-vine borer
		9. chewed, clean, dry	a. crickets b. cutworm c. gophers d. rabbits e. squirrels
Fruit		1. dropping off	a. heat stress b. lack of water (*see* wilt, *above*) c. overbearing
		2 drying out	overbearing
		3. dry spot on side	sunburn
		4. soft rot	a. heat destruction of peach, apple b. poor squash pollination c. tomato blossom end rot d. stone fruits brown rot
		5. mottled spots	heat rash on tomato
		6. small black spots	leaf-footed plant bug
		7. holes	a. birds on citrus, tomato b. caterpillars on tomato c. BB shot in ripe grapefruit
		8. half-eaten, on the tree	birds, squirrels
		9. half-eaten, on the ground	little boys
		10. split fruit	rapid fruit growth
Roots		1. knobby, bumpy galls—small and long lumps	nematodes
		2. knobby, bumpy galls—small and round lumps	legume nodules
		3. knobby, bumpy galls—large and rough lumps	crown gall
		4. soft, brown galls	wet soil
		5. soft flesh, central thread	a. wet soil b. chemical
		6. chewed wood	a. borer beetles b. gophers

Note: This chart originally appeared in *Desert Gardening—Fruits & Vegetables*, published by Fisher Books, P.O. Box 38040, Tucson, Arizona 85740-8040. Copies of this book are available for $17.95 + $2.50 shipping and handling. Arizona residents should include 5% sales tax.

20 Questions — or How to Solve a Puzzle

1. What is the plant? ____________ Planting Date ____
2. Describe the extent of the damage ____________

3. How long has it gone on for? ____________
4. What other plants nearby are affected? ____________
5. How many hours of direct sunshine a day does the plant get? ____________
6. Is the soil: sandy ____ clay ____ loam ____ gravel ____ salty ____
7. How deep is it? ____________
8. Is caliche present? ____________ How far down? ____________
9. Is there good drainage? ____ 10. How often do you water? ____________
11. Do you fill the well: ____ or water to the drip line? ____________
12. How deep does the water go? ____ (feet) How big is the well? ____ (diameter in feet)
13. How often do you fertilize? ____________ What fertilizer? ____________
14. When did you last fertilize? ____________ How much? ____________
15. With what has the plant been sprayed? ____________
16. Has the area nearby been treated? ____________ With what chemicals? ____________
17. What insects are present? ____________
18. What other pests are present? ____________
19. Is the damage the result of sun(burn) or frost(bite)? ____________
20. After all these questions, what do you think the problem is? ____________

Date ____________

9 HOW TO AVOID—AND REPAIR—FROST DAMAGE

There's a lot of anxiety during December and January. Will it freeze? Which plants will be damaged? And how much? What shall we do? Shall we pick the fruit off the citrus trees? Before the freeze? After the freeze?

Freezes are to be expected, and frost-tender plants need to be protected on a cold night. Mature palm trees are too tall to be covered—they'll simply have to take their chances—but hibiscus, bougainvillea, lantana, and citrus deserve protection. So do tender flowers, such as beds of lobelia and pots of geraniums.

If you grow frost-tender plants in containers, you can shelter them under a tree or in the carport during cold weather. Otherwise, you'll have to cover each plant on a frosty night and uncover it the next morning.

Cold air falls like snow. This photo shows how the inside of a tree and the ground under it are covered by the tree and protected. Any kind of a covering (in this case, snow) acts like a cap on a bald man's head: It keeps the cold out and the residual warmth in.

This is an example of how *not* to protect your plants from frost. The cloth is too flimsy and doesn't cover enough of the plant. If left on during the day, it will prevent the plant from being warmed by the sun.

COVER PLANTS TO KEEP THEIR WARMTH IN

At the end of the day, cover small trees and shrubs with a heavy sheet or a light blanket. Put a large cardboard box, such as household appliances come in, over a container full of tender plants. Flower beds can be covered with old fertilizer bags or cardboard. It's not so easy to completely cover a large tree, but anything placed over the top of it is going to help. It will be like a cap on a bald man's head; warmth will be held there.

That's the basic trick: make the most of daytime warmth and hold it in during the night. Each evening, before the sun goes down, cover your plants before they lose their heat. Next morning, remove the cover to let the sun warm them up again.

All this is very unsightly, and the physical exertion of covering the plants at night and of removing the covering each morning is decidedly an unwelcome chore. But it's necessary.

To protect a frost-tender plant growing against a wall—a bougainvillea, for example—hang a large cloth on the overhanging eaves, rather like an old-fashioned shopblind. It stays rolled up during the warm winter days and is lowered by a string system as night approaches. It's easy to roll it up again in the morning as sunshine returns to warm the plants.

Don't use clear plastic as a cover

This transparent material very readily lets light and heat through. During the day, a dormant plant, such as a citrus tree, will be warmed into growth as if it were in a greenhouse. The new growth will be tender and is sure to be damaged on a cold night because clear plastic lets the heat out at night—and the cold in—just as readily as it stores heat while the sun is out.

Cloudy days mean no warmth is generated

If there are several days when the sun doesn't shine, your plants won't gather any heat; they could be in great danger if the clouds clear and you get a starry night. In that case, it becomes necessary to provide heat. If the clouds stay all night, however, it will be warm. Clouds act like a blanket over the Earth; they keep it warm, provided it was warm in the first place.

Keep plants warm at night with artificial heat

Containers can be brought into a warmer part of the patio or into a garage during freezing weather. Landscape trees are not portable, of course, but you can easily carry the warmth to them. Run an all-weather extension cord with a light bulb at its end out to each frost-tender tree. The wattage doesn't matter very much, but if it's going to be very cold you'll need more heat; in that case, use a higher wattage or two light bulbs. If the soil is wet, put the light bulb on a dry board and then cover it with an upturned bucket to keep rain or snow off the hot

Larger plants, such as citrus trees, can be tented to lighten the chore of covering and uncovering each time frost threatens. Be sure to unfurl the canvas during the day.

bulb. Any other source of heat, such as a small hot plate, a pressure lantern, or glowing charcoal, is all right, although charcoal usually doesn't last long enough to do the job.

Don't throw hot ashes under your tree; they will make the soil too hot now and too alkaline later. Orchard heaters—sometimes called smudge-pots—don't help because their heat goes straight up rather than sideways to the trees, where it's needed. They burn a lot of smelly oil and their smoke causes air pollution.

A PLANT KILLED BY FROST IS A MESSAGE FROM MOTHER NATURE

In more ways than one, there's a sort of finality to freezes. If many of your plants are killed during winter freezes, the message is that you were growing plants unsuited to that locality. When you replace them, find another kind of plant, one that takes the cold better. Otherwise, you continue to gamble on winter temperatures and you could spend a lot of money unnecessarily repairing your landscape every hard winter—as well as all that time devoted to nightly covering and morning uncovering.

If you want to reduce maintenance and anxiety, select plants entirely suited to your conditions.

WHAT TO DO IF YOUR PLANTS ARE DAMAGED

What happens after your plants are damaged by winter's freezes? The lemons, lantana, geraniums, hibiscus, and periwinkle look terrible. But don't do anything in a hurry; it's almost certain that they look worse than they really are.

An annual such as lobelia is easily killed by a light frost; if this happens, pull it up. Geraniums and pansies are tougher and are not so easily killed, although they look devastated. Inspect the base of the plant; if there's any green color

One way to protect a frost-tender plant growing close to a wall, such as this bougainvillea, is to install a blind that can be lowered on a cold night and raised the next morning. The one pictured here is plastic, but cloth would be better. If plastic is left in place during daylight hours, it will work like a greenhouse and force the dormant plant into new, tender growth, which increases the risk of frost damage. The floodlights at ground level provide heat on really cold nights.

A wall completely surrounding a landscape acts as a box and will hold cold air on a frosty night. The plants inside will be damaged.

when you scratch the stem with your fingernail, leave things alone—for the time being, anyway.

Inspect the twigs of your woody plants for green. Green is alive; brown is dead. This will give you some assurance, but the morning after is too early to take action. So is the week after, or even the month after.

A light frost that kills out only the very ends of a tree's branches is nothing to worry about. In fact, it might be a blessing in disguise; it has done a very even trimming for you. It's doubtful that you could have done any better.

Don't be in a hurry to prune out damaged foliage

Now comes the hard part. Wait until warm weather comes again—which may be six weeks away—before you do any cutting. At present, you don't know how much damage was done. You have to wait and see. It's the eventual re-growth, after warm weather returns, that tells you how much material to prune out. Another reason not to prune immediately after a freeze is that there may be other freezes later, and you'll have to go through the process again.

The "dead" color doesn't show itself all at once—it takes time—so for the time being you don't know how far to cut back. You might cut too much or too little. Some plants look terrible after a freeze, but it's only the leaves that have been damaged; the twigs are still alive. It would be a mistake to severely cut your plant if this is the case.

On the other hand, severe damage calls for strong measures, but the only sure way of knowing how much to cut back is to look for new growth.

New shoots are the signal to start pruning

Watch for buds on the sides of the damaged twigs to break out into new shoots. Cut off both the dead brown wood, where no new growth oc-

An enclosed space with holes in the sides of the box allows cold air to drain out. Moving air is not so damaging as still air on a freezing night.

curs, and a couple of inches of green wood with two new shoots on it. A cut into live wood, as shown by those two shoots, stimulates new side growth and this thickens up the appearance of your plant. If you merely cut the dead brown twigs, no new growth will be stimulated and the foliage will be slow to thicken up, showing the effect of the frost for several months.

Irrigate a recovering tree, but hold back on the fertilizer

When the weather turns warm again and new shoots appear, give the tree its usual springtime deep irrigation. It's better not to overstimulate new growth with fertilizer treatment, however. Wait until the buds are safely out and the new leaves are opened to fertilize. There's always the danger of a late spring frost, and you don't want the new growth to come out too quickly; if it does, it will be soft and frost-tender.

A frost-damaged plant loses a lot of foliage, but its root system usually is unharmed. This means there is a considerable imbalance between the two halves of the plant. When good weather returns, the undamaged roots "push out" a superabundance of shoots, which gives a tree a bushy appearance. This extra growth has to be trimmed out gradually and judiciously to return the tree to its original condition. This means thinning out, rather than cutting back. This exuberant growth reminds you that there is little need to fertilize a frost-damaged plant.

FINALLY, WATCH THE MOON SIGNS IN NOVEMBER AND DECEMBER

A reliable, longtime nurseryman in Tucson says, "Watch out for the full moon in November." It gives the first mild frost of the year as a warning. December's full moon can be a killer.

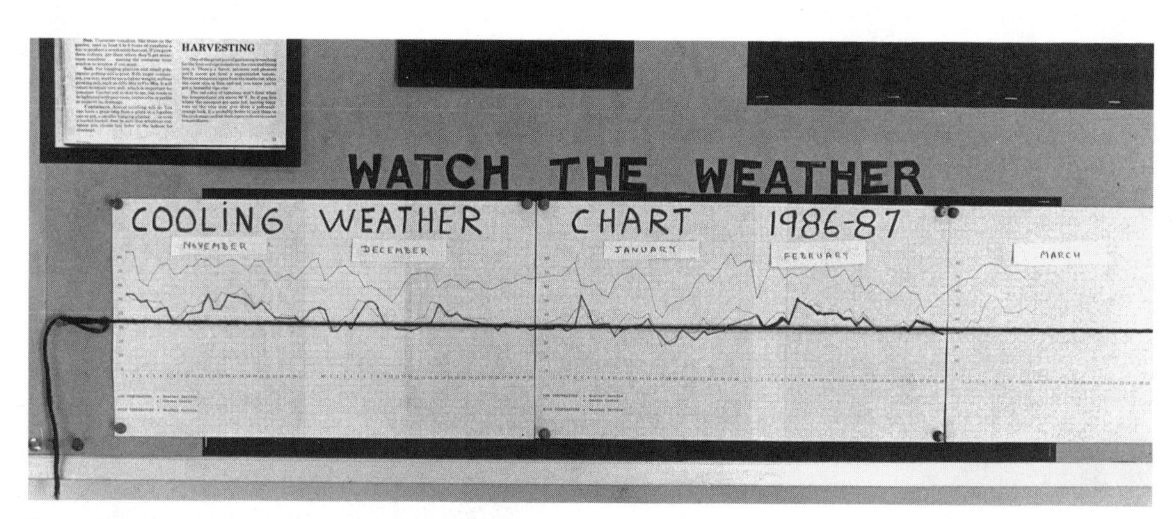

You need to know whether your landscape is in a cold part of town or a warm one. The only real way to find out is to record the temperatures at your house, using a maximum-minimum recording thermometer. Place a thermometer wherever you intend to save a plant—at the height of the plant and away from the influence of a wall. Start recording in November and keep a chart through the winter months.

10 HOW TO CONTROL "WEEDS"

It's essential to know what we mean by weeds. This is particularly true in the context of desert landscaping, where plant growth is more natural and casual. In the more disciplined styles of conventional landscaping, anything that was out of a straight line or out of color or out of season was obviously out of place, and so was called a weed.

The old definition—"a weed is a plant out of place"—reflected our standards of tidiness, uniformity, and symmetry. A plant that grew on its own was an affront to our management. In desert landscaping, there are no straight lines, no boxes of space dedicated to a particular plant, no "purity" of planting. We are delighted to have a plant grow on its own.

And here's a case in point: desert broom is the most cheerfully green plant there is. It grows by itself, with no attention and no irrigation. Pests and diseases don't bother it. It lives a long time under the harshest of conditions and livens up a landscape, even during our fiercest summers. If you want to "improve" desert broom, it responds well to a little watering and pruning. Even so, the plant has a bad reputation and is introduced to newcomers as a weed. They needlessly spend a lot of time trying to kill it, usually with little success; it's a tough plant.

A better definition of a weed is "a plant that we don't like." Such a definition allows any little "weed" that shows some color to be called a wildflower and to be treasured. It allows the rancher's poisonous jimson weed to become the nurseryman's angel's trumpet. It lets native trees grow where birds drop the seed and grass to grow on a bank that gathers water after a rain. In short, it allows Mother Nature to take over.

On the other hand, hardly anyone likes wild barley or black mustard, those annual plants that cover the ground between desert trees and shrubs during a wet winter, or puncture vine and pigweed, which thrive in the hottest summers. Then there are Bermudagrass and nutsedge, which are difficult to control and nearly

Bermudagrass turns into a weed when it creeps into flower beds or cactus plantings. One way to stop the invasion is to sink metal edging 12 inches into the soil between the lawn and adjacent areas.

A small patch of newly sprouted nutgrass can be eliminated quickly by pulling or by spraying before it becomes established. Over the course of a summer, however, the plant spreads rapidly by runners, and in winter dormancy it preserves itself by little subsurface nutlets that store food. It's not easy to get all of these pieces out of the ground.

impossible to remove. On a lesser plane, most people don't like a mesquite or an African sumac seedling—both useful and pleasing landscape trees—growing in the sheltered corner of a building where the wind happened to blow a seed.

To a large extent, you decide which are the weeds; you don't have to consult a reference book to find out.

"Weeds" are either annuals or perennials

Annuals complete their cycle in one season. Annual weeds are a nuisance because they produce thousands of seeds before they die. There's an old saying, "One year's seeding, seven years' weeding." This gives us a clue as to the best method of keeping annual weeds down: do your best to prevent them from flowering and setting seed.

Winter annual weeds start their lives with the fall rains in October and drop their seeds in January. Summer annual weeds germinate in March and drop their seeds in October.

Perennial weeds are most active during the warmer months of the year and set their seed in the fall. They go dormant in winter and come to life again when the soil warms up in the spring. Perennial weeds are persistent plants, and are hard to kill.

All "weeds" thrive when conditions are right. Their seed germinates well with the right temperature and good rains. Showers need to continue during their early growth if they are to develop strongly and produce a lot of seeds. There's a striking similarity between a good wildflower year and a bad weed year. After all, a wildflower is nothing more—nor less–than a pretty "weed."

REDUCE "WEEDS" BY A WELL-TIMED APPLICATION OF PRE-EMERGENCE CHEMICALS

There are chemicals available that we place around the seeds before they germinate. They are called pre-emergence chemicals and are sold under a number of manufacturers' names. The management trick is to anticipate the arrival of the rains—not always an easy thing to do—and to get the chemical into the ground before the seeds start to germinate. Fortunately, the chemicals are effective for several weeks, so it's better to plan an early start rather than to be late. Apply in spring to prevent the growth of summer weeds, in the fall to catch winter weeds.

Pre-emergence weedkilling chemicals are a useful tool if you wish to control summer spurge in a Bermudagrass lawn. The lawn grass is not affected, and you kill all the spurge before it can appear; the chemical kills the seedling as it starts to grow.

Apply evenly over the surface of the weedy area and water in

The chemical usually comes as a powder to be mixed in water. It often has a dye in it that lets you see where you have applied it. Follow directions on the label. Apply half of the material going north and south, then use the other half going east and west. By traveling in two directions you avoid stripes of untreated ground that would give you uncontrolled growth. You're not likely to miss if you go in both directions.

Weeds develop a resistance to chemicals, just as insects do, so it's a good idea to use a particular brand for a couple of years and then switch to another.

A word of warning

Pre-emergence chemicals have even less discrimination about plants—Is it a weed or is it a wildflower?—than you do. They remain effective in the soil for several weeks and they destroy *every* seed as it germinates.

You must not expect to be successful in killing the weed seeds without being just as efficient in killing wildflower seed or the seed of a winter lawn grass that you sow in the same area a few weeks later. Plan your operations carefully.

HOW TO KILL WEEDS WITH CONTACT WEEDKILLER

There are a number of chemicals that corrode plant tissue. Apply them in bright sunshine, and in a day or two the foliage turns brown. In many cases, especially when the plants are small, death continues into the roots—but not always.

There are a large number of contact weedkillers in the garden stores. The Environmental Protection Agency prohibits the use of all petroleum products except diesel for this purpose.

A winter-dormant Bermudagrass lawn is safe from chemicals, but growing weeds are vulnerable to sprays. This is your management opportunity!

(Left) These leaves show evidence of careless use of weedkilling chemicals applied to the soil.

(Right) Withering like this happens when a weedkilling spray is blown by the wind onto a nontarget plant (a citrus tree, in this case).

HOW TO KILL WEEDS WITH TRANSLOCATED HERBICIDES

Translocated means being moved within the plant—from leaves to stems to roots. Herbicide is a fancy name for weedkiller. The thing about all of the translocated weedkillers is that the plants must be alive and growing for the poison to be absorbed by the leaves and to be moved from there to the roots.

A good thing for a landscape manager to know is that some translocated herbicides are fatal to grasses and not to other plants, while some are fatal to broadleaved plants and not to grasses. Then there are the general-purpose translocated weedkillers that affect all plants. Your nurseryman will know which are which, and you should read the label to make sure you get what you need. The products are not mentioned here by name because environmental chemicals are subject to controls that can include their removal from the general marketplace.

Here are some examples of this weedkiller's uses. If you have spurge, a broadleaved weed, in your grass lawn, you can make the lawn weed-free by spraying the whole area with the chemical that does not affect grasses. Be careful of the flower bed and the roses on the edge of the lawn; they are broadleaved plants. If you want to kill Bermudagrass that is creeping into a cactus bed, use the grass-killing chemical; use common sense, however, and keep the spray off the cactus as best you can. If you want to kill weeds coming up through a brick patio, simply spray the leaves

When filling a sprayer, measure the correct amount of chemical (read the label instructions!) into a gallon of clean water, then pour the mixture into the tank. You can't see what you're doing if you try to mix the stuff inside the tank.

without letting excess material wash into a nearby flower bed.

If you accidently spray a plant, cut off those leaves that received the chemical before the chemical moves into the whole plant.

Soil is safe with translocated herbicides, but watch the wind

These chemicals are sprayed on foliage. Any chemical that falls on the ground will soon be changed by bacteria into something innocuous, making these chemicals "safe" when applied properly. Even a light breeze, however, can blow a fine mist away from the target plants to other nearby plants. The remedy is to spray on a calm day, preferably in the evening, because a warming day has unseen uplift currents of air. Turn the nozzle to deliver a coarse spray that drops on the target, instead of a fine mist that may be carried downwind.

HOW TO USE HERBICIDES SAFELY AND EFFECTIVELY

First, a spraying tip. You always want to get right up to the edge of an area for complete control, but in so doing there's the danger of hitting some plants beyond the target zone, especially if the wind is blowing. To prevent this from happening, call in a friend and have him hold a sheet of cardboard or plywood between you and the flower bed. Now you can work faster and your flowers will be safe. Don't let your assistant walk over a sprayed area and carry the poison on his boots into the flower bed, however.

Mix the chemicals carefully. Don't guess

Don't slop the chemical directly into the spray tank and then fill with water. That way you make a frothy mess, because a lot of spray chemicals contain a little detergent to make them

Maintain two sprayers, one exclusively for weedkilling chemicals and another only for foliar sprays. This will help keep you from accidentally applying weedkillers to the roses when you spray them for aphids.

work better. A frothy mess won't let you see the levels, and you can't be accurate unless you do see them. Instead, pour the measured amount—as stated on the label—into a glass gallon jar that is nearly full of water. Pour the mixture into your spray tank. If you need only a gallon, you have it accurately measured. Should you need more, do another gallon or a gallon and a half, but measure it; don't guess.

Don't mix more chemical than you need

Once you have added the chemical to water—indeed, once you have opened its container—the chemical starts to deteriorate. If you keep a little leftover in the tank for another day, the chemical will corrode the metal parts of the sprayer. Besides, it loses its potency in a day or two, which makes that later spraying a waste of time.

Another reason to make up only sufficient spray material is the problem of disposing of the surplus chemical. What do you do with it? It must not go down the sewer, or into the street, or on the compost pile. Surplus chemicals become a problem.

Disposing of chemical surpluses

The garden chemicals available to homeowners are relatively safe. Until some better arrangement is made, authorities say the best place for their disposal is a regulated dump. Old bottles of liquid and boxes of powder go out with the trash after you have wrapped them in several layers of newspaper and then tied or taped them. You don't want the trash collector to be contaminated by a broken box of dust or splashed when a bottle breaks.

The dangerous, restricted chemicals have to be disposed of in a more regulated way and the certified applicators who are licensed to use them should know what to do; make a point of this when you hire one. Some communities advertise a "dangerous chemicals day" and arrange collection of hazardous materials.

Store chemicals in a safe place and keep them labelled

Don't keep chemicals in the kitchen. Keep them on a high shelf away from curious children or in a locked cupboard. Should a label come loose or be unreadable, dispose of the container and its contents unless you are quite sure what is inside; in the latter case, make a new label.

When using any spray, remember that a fine mist is easily blown off target.

For that reason, always use a coarse spray for weedkillers.

The label is a legal document. Read it all

All labels start off with the caution, "It is a violation of federal law to use this product in a manner inconsistent with its labelling." If you don't follow the directions exactly, you are to blame when something goes wrong. This means you must read the complete label, not just the large print.

If you wish to kill brownleaf paspalum, for example, and the name cannot be found on the label, you are in error if you go ahead and "see if it works." You'll also be in error if you follow the advice of a friend who tells you that doubling the strength gives you better results.

Besides its function as a disclaimer to protect the manufacturer, a label is an interesting piece of information to the home landscaper. Be patient; read it and be wise.

Buy a small sprayer. Better yet, buy two

A big sprayer costs more than a small one, it is heavier, and you seldom need that much chemical. The two-gallon size is plenty big enough. Use it just for weeds, and label it so. Buy a second small sprayer, of a different color, if possible. Label this one for foliar spraying (applying nutrients or killing insects). Don't get them mixed up. Now you can keep your chemicals separate and your plants safe.

If you have only one sprayer and you use it for all kinds of chemicals, the day is sure to come when a plant that you spray for aphids dies of the residue left in the tank from the last time you used it to kill "weeds."

HOW TO USE SOIL STERILANTS TO KILL WEEDS

Never use sterilants. Don't even think of using them. When you read the label you discover they poison the soil for years. Sterilants may be okay for railroad rights-of-way, gasoline tank farms, and other places where someone doesn't want anything to grow—ever—but they have no place in the home or commercial landscape.

The label warns you, but few people read it carefully. If you use *Triox* or *Ureabor* without reading the label, you're usually satisfied with the immediate results. Those troublesome weeds that persisted after previous all-out attacks are killed. But the next time you plant a new shrub or tree, it dies. And repeated plantings die.

The next stage is realized a few months after applying the sterilant, when nearby trees show discolored leaves, often on the side where the ground was treated. Then the leaves drop off and the branches die back. In the end, the tree itself dies.

These progressive steps reflect the travel of the poison down through the soil. First, it gets the shallow-rooted weeds. Then, it gets to the trees' upper roots and, finally, to the whole root system. There's no cure for this, and the poison will last a long time—maybe six or seven years. You shouldn't have done it.

HOW TO CONVERT FROM A LAWN TO A GRAVEL LANDSCAPE

You've decided to make a radical change, from a water-consuming lawn to a water-thrifty landscape unified by a gravel groundcover. It's a forceful statement, based on a revised opinion of lawngrasses; you no longer like them, so they have become weeds.

Don't use sterilants! You'll still want drought-tolerant trees and shrubs in your landscape, and *nothing* grows in ground treated with sterilants. Instead, follow this procedure:

Step 1:

Irrigate the grass to get it growing and receptive to a translocated herbicide.

Step 2:

Apply glyphosate (sold as *Roundup* or *Doomsday*) evenly over the area. Wet the foliage, that's all.

Step 3:

Wait for the grass to turn brown and die. With enough time, the poison will reach the roots and kill the whole plant.

Step 4:

If you are going to use large gravel, simply spread it over the dead grass. If you are going to use decomposed granite or a fine material, scrape off the dead grass but don't dig too much; you might stimulate seeds to grow.

Step 5:

If little spots of grass come through the gravel, spray them with more glyphosate from time to time.

Don't try to control future weeds by laying down black plastic before you spread the gravel. Plastic soon disintegrates and shows up as black dog-ears poking through the gravel. It doesn't let rain reach the soil, which is bad news for your trees and shrubs, whose roots can't breathe. Hollows in the plastic hold water and dust, which turn to mud, and weeds grow in the hollows.

To control future weeds, spray a preemergent weedkiller through the gravel at the proper seasons.

FUMIGATION: A TEMPORARY STERILIZING AND ONE NOT TO BE TAKEN LIGHTLY

Once in a while you get a persistent weed that needs a vigorous treatment. Fumigation probably will work, but you should consider it a last resort.

Fumigants kill everything: weeds, worms, insects, tree roots. Soil microorganisms, both good and bad, also are killed. In effect, you are clearing the soil of life and starting over. For such persistent weeds as nutgrass, fumigants can be useful.

The chemical is watered into the soil to a certain depth and the area is covered with a piece of plastic. At the right temperatures, the liquid turns to vapor and rises to the top, where it is held by the plastic for a week or two. The details of the operation are printed on the label, and so are the cautions. Read both.

If there are tree roots growing in the area, your trees will be affected by the treatment. One way—albeit a drastic one—to avoid this possibility is to dig a trench 18 inches deep around each tree to cut surface roots near the trunk. The fumigant will kill the severed roots, but your tree will not be hurt—except for having had its roots cut. For this procedure to be successful, the tree must have deep roots, not just surface roots.

Fumigation is a last-ditch operation.

SOLARIZATION: ANOTHER POSSIBILITY OF LAST RESORT

This is a summertime operation, wherein you wet the ground and cover it with clear plastic for a month. It won't be effective in a shady yard; you must have plenty of sunshine, which, with the help of the plastic, cooks the soil and everything in it. At the end of the month you remove the plastic, dig the ground to bring the lower soil and its seeds up to the top, water again, and cover with plastic for a second month of sunshine.

A garden fork is a good tool for grubbing out most runners of nutgrass or Bermudagrass. If you dig with a spade, you're likely to cut the runners and leave some pieces in the ground, thereby multiplying the nuisance.

Solarization is sterilization without chemicals, but the outcome is similar. Everything in the soil is killed.

COMMON-SENSE METHODS OF WEED CONTROL

None of these requires special equipment, just a little work and good timing.

The first is called the sprinkle-sprout-spade or sprinkle-sprout-spray method. Where you know a weed problem lies lurking, give the ground a sprinkling to germinate dormant seeds. When seedlings appear and are small, simply hoe them out or spray them. It's a very effective way to clean up an area, but it takes time and some planning. If you dig rather than spray, it's a form of green manuring that enriches the soil. But don't let the weed crop mature enough to set seed.

The second method takes advantage of rainy weather that has moistened the soil to some depth. Just pull the weeds out of the ground! If you try to do this when the soil is dry, you invariably snap off the stem of the plant and it grows new shoots. Pull the weeds before they set seed.

The third method is more fun for teenagers. Drive over the weeds with a power lawnmower. Sprinkle to keep the dust down, for it can be a dirty job. It's also an incomplete job, because you only remove the top part of the problem. The roots continue to grow and the secondary growth often hugs the ground closely and sets seed under the blades of the mower. In the end, you have to pull them out, but meanwhile you have stopped the weeds from producing seed—maybe.

The fourth method is lightly to hoe weed seedlings wherever they are when they are small—the smaller the better. Do this on a dry, sunny day and they will die before lunchtime. If you hoe when the soil is wet, you're simply cultivating the next crop of weeds; dormant seeds respond to soil disturbance by germinating.

11 What to Do About PALO VERDE BORER BEETLE

The palo verde borer is a beetle peculiar to the Southwest. The adult beetle is three inches long, dark brown, clumsy, and is adorned with a pair of long antennae. It flies around at the beginning of the summer rains, having come out of the ground where it lived as a root-devouring grub for a year or so.

The grub is a soft white thing as big as a finger. It has no obvious legs. Its large jaws tell you how it spends its time: it eats roots. You probably found it when you dug up a tree that died. Its favorite food is the palo verde tree. One or two beetle grubs don't do much harm, but a dozen or more can kill a tree.

People come to know about its activity in different ways. The observant gardener notices that his trees—it's not just the palo verde, but several kinds of trees that can be affected—just aren't doing as well as they should. Oftentimes, he just lets the hot weather and stressful times account for it.

The person interested in new things around him notices recent holes, about as big around as a broomstick, in the ground under his trees.

The thoroughgoing urbanite, enjoying his evening drink on the patio, gets hit in the face by a slow-flying monster after it has clumsily crashed a few times into the porchlight.

Let's take the middle case, the holes in the ground that weren't there last week: they are the

Remember this villain from Chapter 8? At the beginning of the summer rains, you may find holes in the ground under your trees. They are palo verde borer beetle exit holes. Sometimes, the beetle that comes out of these holes goes back in to lay its eggs.

(Above) The eggs turn into grubs, which spend a year or two underground chewing on the roots of your trees.

(Below) Here's a root that has been so thoroughly chewed that it leaves the tree with no support. A summer storm toppled it.

exit holes of the beetle. In other words, that's where it came out of the ground, so there's little point in pouring chemicals down the holes in an attempt to destroy the pest.

The beetles usually don't come out until the ground has been softened by the first summer rains. The rains beat a wake-up tattoo on the soil surface, and this, too, seems to be part of the annual activation process.

By the time you notice the holes in early summer, the initial damage has been done. There could be plenty of grubs still in the soil, however, still chewing on the roots. Do something.

A simple application of an insecticide poison

(Above) The grub, after its disastrous feasting, turns into a beetle that flies around in the open air looking for a mate. The adult beetle does no damage.

(Below) Here, alas, is the end result of the palo verde borer beetle's work.

is not good enough. You should adopt a three-pronged response that also helps the tree to get over the attack. Do it as soon as you see the first beetle of summer.

First, wet the soil under the spread of the branches to a depth of 18 inches. This gets the soil ready to receive the chemicals. A good way to do this is to set a small sprinkler under the tree, halfway between the trunk and the ends of the branches. Move it around the tree until the entire area has been moistened.

Second, spread ammonium sulphate over the wet soil at the rate of two pounds to every hundred square feet. This supplies nutrients to the tree and helps it to grow new roots.

Third, scatter *Diazinon* granules, according

to the instructions on the label, over the wet ground.

Resume irrigation until your soil probe shows you that water has gone down to 3 feet. It will carry the treatments that deep, and it will give the tree a new lease on life.

Admittedly, the insecticide part of this treatment is hit-or-miss; you don't know how many grubs are under the soil or where they are, but it's the best you can do under the circumstances. The watering and the fertilizing can't help but be beneficial, so something good will come of the exercise.

To give your tree all the protection you can, repeat the treatment six weeks later. The reason for this is that a number of beetles will fly back to the place where they spent a happy childhood, and they'll lay eggs there. The tiny grubs, after they hatch, will burrow downward; you want to catch them before they reach the roots. The second treatment will get them (they're smaller and more susceptible to poisons), the fertilizer will nourish the tree, and the irrigation will make sure it grows.

12 HOW TO AVOID TEXAS ROOT ROT

It's usually summer when Texas root rot kills our trees. The disease is most active in a wet year. Some years Texas root rot makes a disappointing show, at least for people who like to start horror stories. Oldtimers enjoy frightening newcomers with the perils of this soilborne disease. It's a bad one, to be sure, but don't be distressed by such stories. Learn all you can about Texas root rot before it strikes, and you'll effectively meet its challenge.

Texas root rot thrives in warm alkaline soil, which we certainly have. It attacks trees with soft wood, and quick-growing trees grow soft roots if they are heavily fertilized. The fungus also needs a thoroughly wet soil, which can be caused by overwatering or by heavy rains. We keep hoping that Mother Nature will give us plentiful summer rains, but Texas root rot is the downside of that bounty.

Native trees are less likely to be stressed than are those that come from places with a milder climate. There's merit in landscaping with natives.

WHAT ARE THE SIGNS OF TEXAS ROOT ROT?

After summer rains have wet the soil to a depth of a foot or two, you sometimes see a mass of tan-colored stuff lying on the surface of the soil. People liken it to pancake batter. It might cover a wide area, overgrowing grass and weeds. It wasn't there yesterday. Afer a day or two it turns a darker color and becomes powdery. This is the spore matt of Texas root rot, but experts on the subject say this is not how the fungus spreads. They say it moves from tree to tree along the roots, without necessarily appearing above ground. Other fungi develop similar spore matts, so this sign is not foolproof. The copycat fungi are not killers.

I first met Texas root rot when an agitated homeowner called to tell me his yard was on fire. This was in the '60s—a hallucinogenic period of our history—and a number of science-fiction books and movies were flooding the market. He was sure he had been visited from outer space during the night.

He said that when he opened the door that morning, this "weird stuff" covered his yard 2 inches thick. It looked like volcanic ash. When he touched it with a stick, it blew off as dust; when he turned a hose on it, steam came out. He

Spore mats like this appear after summer rains have wet the ground. This is not a sure indication of Texas root rot, however; other fungi develop similar spore mats.

couldn't extinguish the layer of smoking ash. His trees had been burned, too. The leaves were just hanging there, blasted, brown, and dead.

Fascinated, I rushed to the stricken landscape. I discovered that the ground wasn't hot and that the neighborhood was in no danger of being engulfed in flames. Nevertheless, the yard was totally destroyed for the future growing of trees.

"*Phymatotrichum omnivorum* has struck again," I told the crowd that had gathered.

"Wow!" they all said.

The signs of attack shown by trees

An affected tree—and just about all trees are susceptible in varying degrees—suddenly wilts. The leaves stay on the tree and eventually turn brown. The whole tree may be affected in this way, or just one side of it, or only one branch. In the soil, under that patch of wilted leaves, the roots have been destroyed. They can no longer function, so the leaves give up. At this point, you need to take a look at the roots.

Dig down to find roots about as thick as a pencil. Carefully cut them, so that you can bring them up with the dirt still attached. Wash them gently to remove the dirt. Look for flat ribbons running along the outsides of the roots. The ribbons are about an eighth of an inch wide, and they branch. They are superficially attached and come off easily; that's why you have to be careful when getting the roots out of the soil. They disintegrate quickly, too, so you need fresh samples for diagnosis if you take them to a clinic.

This peach tree is finished, even though a few green branches appear at the base of the old trunk.

A clinical examination is needed for a positive diagnosis

It's the clinic that has the last word in identifying the fungus. If the expert, with a microscope, finds a cross-shaped fungus organism, you can be sure your tree is suffering from Texas root rot. You need to take action today. Now!

But be sure before you act.

Check out some other possible causes for dead branches

The symptom that first caught your eye—the sudden wilting of leaves that don't drop—could be caused by any one of several things: an excess of fertilizer, weedkiller chemicals, grubs chewing on the roots, overwatering, poor drainage, borers in the branches, extensive cicada damage, or sheer heat exhaustion.

Or it could be something as simple as drought, and that's the possibility you should investigate first. It's the easiest to diagnose and the easiest to do something about. Get out your

One dying plant in a row of several healthy ones *could* be suffering from Texas root rot, or perhaps the irrigation system wasn't working properly. The situation needs to be examined promptly to determine the cause.

trusty soil probe. Poke it into the ground to see how wet or dry the ground really is. If it's dry, irrigate.

WHAT TO DO WHEN YOU'RE SURE THE FUNGUS IS PRESENT

If it's certain that your soil has Texas root rot—after a root examination and a clinical test—you have few options. The treatment is simple, but it's troublesome and expensive. You use it both when you anticipate an attack and when a tree suddenly shows the symptoms. In the latter case delay is fatal, so don't promise yourself you'll do it over the weekend. You've got to do it today. Take the day off from work if you want to save your tree.

To save a sick tree, first put 2 inches of steer manure or compost—not peat moss or "mulch"—on the ground under the spread of the branches and a bit farther out. Scatter 1 pound of ammonium sulphate and 1 pound of soil sulphur for every 10 square feet of manure. Dig these into the soil without chopping the roots of the tree. Then water heavily. Use your soil probe to be sure you've watered these amendments in to a depth of 3 feet. Although there's the risk of keeping the soil too wet—and so favoring the fungus—irrigate deeply every two weeks unless it is raining heavily.

This treatment *may* be carried out on trees that appear to be healthy at the moment but that are at risk. On the other hand, you *must* do it as soon as you see the symptoms on a tree that is attacked for the first time.

This treatment makes the soil more acid. It suppresses the Texas root rot fungus, which prefers an alkaline soil, and it makes the soil more favorable for another soil fungus that parasitizes the pest. The ammonium sulphate also provides nutrients to the tree, which gives it a chance to "grow out" of the problem.

Even with several plants dying, the cause could be poor irrigation or attack by palo verde borer beetles—or Texas root rot. Examine the soil for moisture content and the roots for the tell-tale ribbons of the fungus.

Measure the amount; don't guess

The amounts of amendments necessary to kill the fungus are nearly enough to kill the tree as well. Measure everything carefully. Calculate how many square feet of ground you are going to treat, weigh out the ammonium sulphate and the sulphur, and measure the 3 feet of water penetration. If you apply too little, the treatment will not be effective. If you apply too much, you might harm those roots that were not killed by the fungus. If you overdose on amendments and use only a little water, you'll cause damage.

Help the tree recover by cutting out damaged branches

Your tree lost a lot of roots. Brown dead leaves appeared because the tree was unable to get moisture from the soil at the time of year when its water demand was highest. The branches aren't dead and they will try to put out new leaves, but this effort will exhaust the tree. Save its energy and help it recover by removing these marginally useful branches. Your tree will look like a blasted skeleton, but you may have saved it; if so, it will recover its vigor in due course.

THE FUNGUS IS IN THE SOIL, AND HAS BEEN FOR A LONG TIME

In Texas, they call this disease cotton root rot. It is found naturally where there are alkaline soils low in organic matter and a warm climate with mild winters. In other words, the Desert Southwest; more specifically, the lower elevations of Arizona, California, Nevada, New Mexico, and Texas. It also is found throughout northern Mexico.

You don't find cotton root rot across the eastern edge of this region because the strongly calcareous black soils of eastern Texas change to

This is what to look for: strands or ribbons of the Texas root rot fungus running along the roots. The ribbons are lightly attached, so lift the root to be inspected out of the soil after cutting both ends; don't strip off the ribbons by vigorously pulling the root out of the ground.

the acid, more organic soils of the Mississippi Delta.

To the north, *Phymatotrichum omnivorum* is limited by cold winter temperatures, owing in part to rising mountain elevations. It recently has been discovered that the organism exists at elevations previously thought to be free of the fungus, but at five thousand feet an infected plants stands a better chance of survival—or at least of a longer life while infected—than does a similar plant at a thousand feet or lower.

To the west, the sand hills and mountains of southeastern California once presented a natural barrier to the fungus. The efficiency of modern transportation has allowed the fungus over this barrier, however, and now the disease is in the Imperial and Coachella valleys.

If you've bought a house in a host area that was built on an old cotton field, more than likely there's cotton root rot in your yard. If so, your gardening and landscaping options are limited. Here is a list of plants that are susceptible to the fungus, resistant, or immune:

Susceptible trees — bottle tree, carob, chinaberry, cottonwood, elm, fig, ginkgo, pepper tree, poplar, and peach, plum, apricot, and almond trees.

Susceptible shrubs — buddleia, cassia, castor bean, silverleaf cotoneaster, lilac, Chinese photinia, flowering quince, roses, silverberry, and spirea.

Resistant trees — Aleppo pine, cedar elm, citrus on sour orange rootstock, Arizona, Italian, and Monterey cypresses, eucalyptus, evergreen tamarisk, Stribling or sycamore-leaved fruitless mulberry (but be warned: fruitless mulberry is a water-guzzler and a prolific pollina-

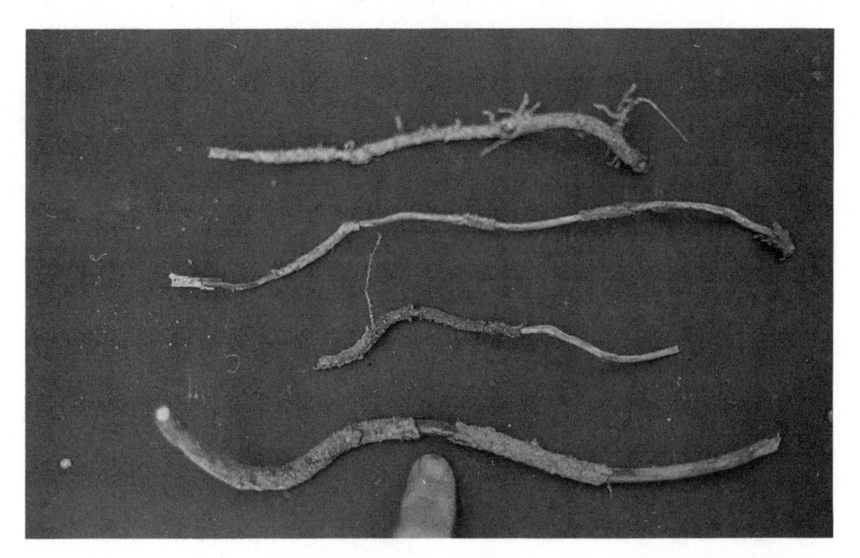

The soft flesh of these roots has disintegrated, but the bark and the woody central core have resisted the rot. This is *not* Texas root rot! It's overwatering, a common cause of decline and death that can easily be avoided by watering less often.

tor), mesquite, palo verde, American and Arizona sycamore, native black walnut, sweet acacia, lysiloma, salt cedar, desert willow, and canyon hackberry.

Resistant shrubs — cacti, crepe myrtle, Arizona elderberry, Japanese honeysuckle, jasmine, juniper, ocotillo, oleander, pomegranate, pyracantha, rosemary, Russian olive, Siberian pea shrub, hop bush, and creosote bush.

Immune trees — true bamboos, ornamental banana, and all species of palms.

Immune shrubs — agave, bird of paradise, dracaena, yucca, pampas grass, and giant reed.

DON'T BRING INFECTED SOIL OR PLANTS INTO YOUR LANDSCAPE

Usually, people move into an infected area as new housing developments invade old farming land, but eager landscapers can import the risk of disease by bringing in farm soil sold commercially under the name of topsoil.

If a homeowner needs a little dirt, he sometimes goes out and finds it under a mesquite tree, where years of leaf-fall have produced a rich brown soil, or he might go into a nearby drainage wash and dig out some soil or sand. This, too, is risky. Such materials can be loaded with the fungus, and your plants, especially if well-watered, provide good food for it. The fungus thrives and the plants die. More important, your soil is contaminated forever.

It's not likely you'll find infected plants growing in containers at your nursery, but it's possible that a friend, in offering you a plant he doesn't want ("Why doesn't he want it?" should be your question), can give you the fungus, too. And nursery trees grown in old cotton fields must be suspect.

GOOD PLANTING PROCEDURES MINIMIZE LATER RISKS

If you are planting susceptible trees in your landscape, you should do a thorough preventative job when you dig the hole. A good-sized hole is 5 feet square and 5 feet deep, and you must have good drainage. When you think you have done enough digging, fill the hole half-way with water and see how quickly it drains out. If it takes more than overnight, you need to start digging again—until you get through the caliche barrier and the water goes away.

The next stage is to mix amendments with the top 3 feet of soil you took out of the hole, as described in Chapters 6 and 7. Adjust the amounts of amendments according to whether your plants are susceptible to the disease or resistant. Desert trees and those that are immune to Texas root rot don't require such thorough soil preparation, but you mustn't forget about good drainage. Leave out the chemicals completely when you plant cacti and reduce the organic matter to a tenth of the volume of the hole, preferring compost over steer manure.

HOW TO REDUCE THE RISK TO EXISTING TREES

Don't force your trees by frequent applications of nitrogen and water. If summer rains are heavy, turn off the automatic irrigation system. Use your soil probe to determine when to water. Don't water on a rigid schedule, but as the trees need moisture. Every two years, in the spring, treat the area under your trees with the formula of organic matter, sulphur, and ammonium sulphate described earlier in this chapter.

Make sure there is good drainage. If there is not, it is sometimes possible to drill deep holes all around your tree at the drip line; fill them with pea gravel to keep them open. You have to go through the caliche layer to be effective. The holes should be 4 inches across. You can find drills at the rental places.

The ultimate solution is to replace susceptible plants with resistant ones. Your anxiety levels will drop and your maintenance obligations will be minimized.

13 WHEN YOU MOVE INTO AN EMPTY HOUSE

It's almost certain that the existing landscape played some part in your decision to buy your new home. A well-kept landscape often "sells" a house.

If the landscape is established and in good condition, there won't be much for you to think about once you move in, other than maintaining its pleasing appearance. If you have a different lifestyle than did the previous occupants, you may have plans for the landscape's future and you'll look forward to making changes. If you are a hobby plant person, you may want to restart a collection of specimen plants like the one you left behind.

In any case, you'll want to be in control again, to assert yourself, to make an impression, to be boss. It's only natural.

Unfortunately, the house was empty during the escrow period and no one looked after the landscape. If it didn't rain, everything is bone-dry. If it did rain, there's rank growth all over the place and much of it is weeds. In either case, you've got a lot of work to do.

FIRST, IRRIGATE EVERYTHING

Get things started again with a good irrigation. First, go for the flowers, if you think their shallow roots are still alive. If it's the growing season, water the brown lawn to bring it back to green. Next, irrigate the shrubs and small trees, especially those that appear to have been recently planted; you may be in time to save them. Last, give the trees a deep watering.

This initial irrigation prevents further deterioration of your landscpae. There won't be the same urgency if it has been raining for several days, but there's no telling how effective a rain was; a couple of rainy days aren't much help. You need to know how moist the soil is down around the roots. If you haven't got a soil probe, now's the time to get one. Read Chapter 4 for a complete discussion of how to irrigate in the desert.

By all means, get going on the cosmetic tasks, like pulling weeds, sweeping up fallen leaves, removing any messy dead flowers, and cutting out dead branches. Mow the lawn. You'll feel better for it. But now is not the time to remove plants that irritate you. And don't do any major pruning, even if a plant seems to be dead. Take your time. Do a little research and planning before you renovate.

TAKE AN INVENTORY OF WHAT YOU'VE GOT

If you have acquired an older landscape along with your house, it may resemble a jungle. The trees shade too much, the hedges are overgrown, the roses are too tall, and everything seems crowded. There's a strong temptation to get in there with a saw and do something about it. Instead, take a closer look. The large trees may give you shade on the patio, just where you need it. If you remove them now, it will be years before you get that shade back. The thick mass of Carolina jasmine may hide something unsightly in your neighbor's yard. The very closeness of the shrubbery may be a blessing, keeping dust and traffic noises out of your yard.

Learn to live with what you've got—for six months, if possible. Old plants are survivors that can take desert conditions, so you've got something of guaranteed value.

MAKE A MAP OF YOUR NEW LANDSCAPE

Take a clipboard with graph paper on it out into the yard and make a rough map of what you've got. What's each plant's condition? Do you like it? Why don't you like it? Is it too big? Is it in the way? And so on.

This exercise has two purposes. The first is to get you acquainted with your new plants before you start changing things; the second is to slow you down and prevent you from making changes hastily.

Once you've inventoried your landscape and lived with it a while, you'll know which plants really should be removed.

First on your hit list will be those plants that, when they were small, were planted too close together. Giving them the space they would need at maturity was unthinkable at the time, simply because they would have looked too lonely. As the plants grew and began to compete for light and space, it was hard to take them out. They had come so far that nobody wanted to spoil their progress. Instead, they were trimmed back and their shape spoiled, but they still were valuable in the eyes of the planter. Now something has to be done. Take out the most wretched specimens to make room for the better ones.

Another candidate for removal is the oft-clipped hedge with a tangle of short twigs on the top and sides. Their little leaves are so thick that they've shaded out the center and killed it. There's an old farm saying: "A tall hedge is a hollow hedge." In such a case, you have three options: (1) cut the hedge down to ground level and let it start again; (2) dig it up and replant; or (3) remove it entirely and thus get back the space it occupied.

Then there's water use to be considered. As water bills go higher and higher, some of the old favorite plants simply cost too much to irrigate. You may want to reduce the number of roses and fruit trees, shrink the lawn and flower beds, or say goodbye to the magnolia tree. Don't be hasty, but once you've made up your mind, do it before you get too used to them.

FINALLY, MAKE A LIST OF THE CHANGES YOU'D LIKE TO MAKE

Now that you've thought things through, develop a coordinated plan for change.

Will there be room for new plants without sacrificing older ones? If you decide to put in new plants, make sure they are arid-land plants that don't need a lot of irrigating to make them grow. Many different plants are available now, and the choice is expanding as nurseries become more involved in growing native and drought-tolerant plants.

Make a list of the family's activities. Athletic teenagers need room to blow off steam, and you'll want to remove vegetation that restricts their movement. A volley ball court, for example, doesn't need thorny plants or obtrusive branches nearby. Small children won't want to play on gravel or out in the hot sun, and the family dog needs grass and a running area where it won't send up clouds of dust.

As you plan, try to anticipate alterations to the landscape that changes in your family will dictate. Perhaps you'll want to spread the expense over a few years, so decide which things you'll do first.

Look at the irrigation system to make sure it's working and does what it's supposed to do. An old system that was adequate in earlier years may not properly serve larger plants. It may need a little fixing, it may need extending, or it may need renewal. Get it working efficiently; you'll spend a lot of unnecessary time hand-watering if you delay renovating broken-down systems.

Watch the first storm to see whether drainage from the roof takes excess water to a group of plants. If it simply carries it out of sight, you're losing an opportunity to harvest water from the roof and to save money. If runoff makes a mud puddle at the corner of your house, you've got a liability instead of an asset. Make changes.

14 WHAT TO DO ABOUT ROOTS IN DRAINS

It's not likely that you'll meet this desperate problem if you live in a new house, since modern plumbing materials usually prevent it from happening.

If you've bought an older home you'll have trouble with roots in the drains sooner or later. The reason is not simply that the older home is surrounded by old trees and hedges; it's that the old-fashioned clay tiles, which were butted against one another to make a drain, get dislodged and start to leak. By itself, the leak doesn't affect anything, except to make the earth soft and allow the piece of tile to settle a little more—and make a larger leak.

TREE ROOTS DON'T GO LOOKING FOR WATER

The leak won't attract tree roots. Although roots must have water in order to grow, they don't go searching through dry soil for it. If steady rains keep the soil wet for a long time, or if you give good deep watering, the roots will follow that water. If the water supplied from above meets the water leaking from the drain below, roots will grow into the drain through the crack. From then on, the plant will use the nutrient-rich drain water, even when the rains stop or you discontinue your deep waterings. The tree no longer needs attentive irrigating; it's getting enough water from the drains.

Roots won't force their way into a drain or a water pipe that is intact; they don't know that there's water beyond the obstruction. What's more, they are unable to distinguish a water pipe from a rock, or a brick from the gunnite wall of a swimming pool.

Nonetheless, roots growing strongly develop a great power. They can heave up sidewalks, push pipes around, and dent drains. A lot of people think they lift up the corners of houses by getting under the foundations, but it's more likely that the damage they blame on roots is caused by watering too near the foundation, which can cause soil to settle and walls to crack.

Roots really do come up through the toilet

I've heard some wild tales on the telephone. People tell me their shower floor is covered with roots or that roots are growing in the toilet. It's quite possible!

If the drains leading away from these plumbing fixtures spring a leak, no matter how small, the unchecked wetness eventually spreads until it reaches the roots of a shrub or a tree, which stimulates the roots to grow. The roots didn't go in search of the leaky toilet; the moisture from the leak reached the nearby roots.

Once a root, even a tiny root, gets into a broken tile, it thickens. A root has a terrific force as it grows. A misaligned tile will be further forced out of line. A tile with a small crack will be further broken. Your problems will increase.

SEARCH FOR THE CULPRIT

As soon as you realize that roots are in your drains, you'll demand to know which tree is doing it. Certain trees have a reputation for "getting into" drains, but any tree will do it.

Obviously, the faster-growing trees cause the greatest damage, so we hear that cottonwoods, mulberries, chinaberries, and oleanders are the worst culprits. Arid-land plants such as palo verde and mesquite also have invasive roots. So do palms, citrus trees, and roses. Any root that finds an abundant supply of water will take advantage of it. Wouldn't you?

In your search for the culprit, don't look for a particular kind of plant. The tree or shrub nearest the drain most likely is responsible.

Once you know you have a problem, don't wait for a disaster to happen. If you do, it will happen on a Saturday night when you have dinner guests. The time to take action is as soon as you sense that the water is not draining away from the bowl quickly enough.

You usually will find an inspection outlet for the sewer system near a kitchen or bathroom window. It may be overgrown with grass or weeds, but it will show itself by overflowing when the sewer backs up. If you live in an older house, keep the "clean-out," as it often is called, clear of weeds and ready for action.

Most people immediately call the plumber, and that's expensive, especially after hours and on weekends. If you catch the problem early enough you can avoid a plumber for a while, but chances are you'll eventually have to call one. Still, you can carry out the initial treatment yourself. Go to a hardware store and buy a "snake." The salespeople won't laugh at you; they know what you want. Don't buy a skimpy little thing. A snake three-eighths of an inch thick and 25 feet long will do for most situations.

Now find the inspection opening to the drain

Every house, no matter how old or whether it was built before zoning regulations required it, has an inspection opening to the drain. It may be overgrown and forgotten, but it's there. Usually, it tells you where it is because that's where the water first surfaces, before your toilet bowl overflows. If there's not an actual puddle of water, there'll be green grass or luxuriant shrubbery near it. Start by searching outside the kitchen or bathroom window.

Poke your snake into the inspection opening of the drain, making sure it doesn't kink on its way to the obstruction. Go both ways during this task—up toward the house and down toward the street. At this moment, you don't know just where the obstruction is. Stop when the snake meets resistance.

At this point, attach the loose end of the snake to a hand-held electric drill, tighten it, and gently squeeze the trigger. Try to get the "feel" of things down there. If you have a cutter end, you can try gradually to bore through the roots. If you have a spiral end like a corkscrew,

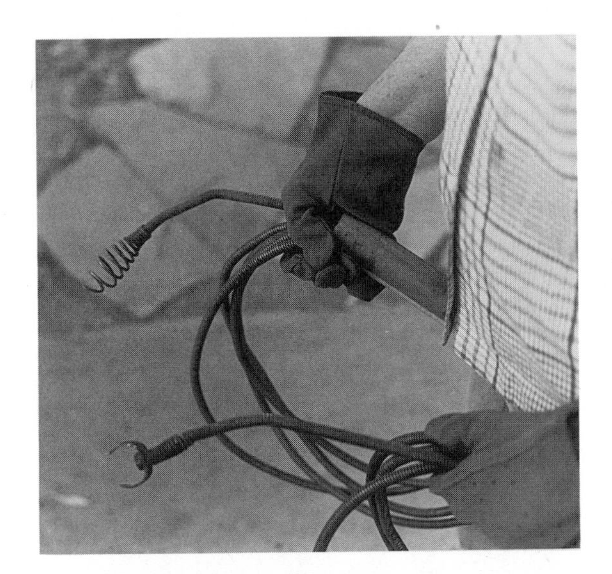

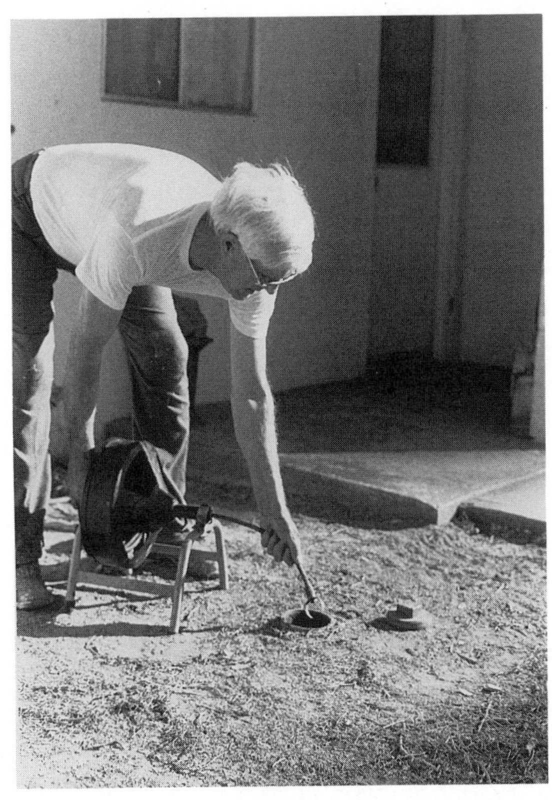

(Above left) There are different sizes of "snakes" for different magnitudes of obstructions.

(Left) If you catch the problem early enough you can take care of it yourself with a handheld electric drill.

(Above) Use a corkscrew end to pull out bits and pieces of debris, or a cutter end to chop through roots.

you can pull the obstruction out. Go gently. As soon as you have cleared the way there will be a satisfying rush of water down the drain. It's a nice sound.

REGULAR MAINTENANCE IS BEST

Snake out your drains regularly. Root growth occurs during, or just before, top growth, so spring and fall are the prime times to clear your drains. You might want to do it every month, just to be sure.

By snaking your drains regularly you are preventing roots from becoming too numerous. You can't stop them from coming into a broken line.

A word of caution

In the hands of an inexperienced operator, who is apt to use too much muscle, a snake might smash its way through the obstruction, taking broken pieces of tile with it. Now you really have a problem.

CHEMICAL TREATMENT IS UNRELIABLE

The standard recommendation to prevent this sort of thing is to put copper sulphate in the toilet tank. Every flush carries a dilute solution down the drain and bathes the invading roots. Copper sulphate is a plant poison, so the roots are supposed to die. They don't.

Other chemicals, quite corrosive in nature, sometimes are used, but they should not be. They affect all metal they come into contact with; if everyone did it, they would mess up the city sewage works, too. They certainly will mess up your septic tank, if you have one.

IT'S NOT ALWAYS NECESSARY TO REMOVE THE OFFENDING PLANT

The tree or shrub is not really the problem. The damaged sewer line is; it's leaking. It may seem odd to call a leaking line an "attractive nuisance," but that's the technical term for it—from the roots' point of view.

If you can put up with periodic do-it-yourself drain cleaning and with an occasional visit from a professional, you can let things alone. You'll actually save money.

If anything has to be done, it will be best to replace the broken drain. This will be expensive and inconvenient. Should you decide to remove the plant—and there's always the question, "Which plant?"—you'll still have a leaking drain. Eventually, roots from some other plant will get into it again.

Because no particular tree or shrub is good at "getting into the drains," don't remove any plant from your landscape just because it's on someone's list. Besides, if you have modern plastic drains with good joints, roots won't cause you a problem.

The soft white roots on the left grew rapidly in the nutrient solution of the sewer and could easily be corkscrewed out or smashed with a cutter powered by a handheld electric drill. The woody roots on the right had been in the pipe a long time and had to be ground out by a professional with power equipment.

15 HOW TO DIG UP PLANTS AND MOVE THEM

We decide to move plants for various reasons. We might just have moved into a house and disagree with the previous owner's idea of landscaping; several plants may be crowded now, when before they had plenty of room; we may be building onto a house and a plant is in the way; perhaps someone has given us a plant, provided we dig it up from their yard and move it to our own.

Whatever the reason, dig the new planting hole first. Chapters 6 and 7 will tell you just how big a hole to dig and how to enrich the soil.

BIG TREES CAN BE MOVED, BUT LEAVE THEM TO THE PROFESSIONALS

It used to be thought that only small trees and shrubs could be moved safely. It is true that the smaller the plant the easier it is to move, and not just because of the mechanics of the operation; a smaller plant seems to stand the shock better than a large one.

It's best to let a reputable landscape management company move a large tree. The cost is high, but they have the big diggers and the cranes and the trucks, as well as the experience.

CONSIDER THE HUGE SAGUARO: IT'S GOT TO BE OLD

A large tree has a future ahead of it. Large saguaros, on the other hand, took many years to reach that prize-winning size that will be the envy of your neighbors. Think before moving one. It could be past its prime and not worth moving—unless you are bent on salvaging a saguaro from destruction by "developers."

A saguaro's arms are delicately balanced and are in harmony with the rest of the plant. They can be ruptured—even broken off completely—during a digging operation, no matter how carefully it is done. An opening in the skin of a saguaro invites bacterial invasion, which often kills the plant.

And remember that removing a saguaro, regardless of its size, from land other than your own is called saguaro rustling; it's illegal. It also is illegal to transport saguaros and other native cacti over public roads unless you have a permit and the plants are properly tagged.

MOVING A SMALL SAGUARO

Small, in this case, means something smaller than you, a plant you and a friend can move without too much struggle. It won't have any arms to complicate things.

The first thing to do is to mark one side of the trunk; it doesn't matter which side, as long as you remember. Don't mark it with a knife or by punching a nail into the flesh. Use the knot in a piece of string—the spines won't let it move around the trunk—or masking tape. It's important to set the plant in the ground with the same orientation it enjoyed before. You don't want its north side, which has been shielded from the sun all its life and is, therefore, more susceptible to sunburn, pointing south. It will blister.

Use a sharp spade to cut the roots about 2 feet out from the trunk. A vertical angle and a strong push with the foot into wet soil will do it.

Wrap the trunk with a couple of blankets and set two 2×4s upright on either side. They should project above the trunk. Tie these to one another firmly to give you handles like those on a stretcher. The blanket saves the skin of the saguaro from damage by the 2×4s when you manhandle the plant.

Carefully loosen the soil around the plant. Saguaros have a shallow little tap root, like a big carrot, and this must not be damaged. One person carefully removes soil; the other prevents the plant from falling. When the roots are free, lay the plant down and take a rest.

It's a good idea to dust the cut ends of the roots with sulphur. This protects the succulent flesh from being invaded by bacteria and fungi, so that you can plant it the same day. Some landscapers prefer to leave the plant in a shady place for a couple of weeks and let the roots scab over by themselves. Either method is good.

Take the plant to the new hole, which has been filled in and is slightly mounded. Set it in the soil at the same depth as it was growing before. Remove the 2×4s and the blanket. Orient it according to the knot on the string and gently tamp the dirt around the plant to give it firmness. You don't want the plant to lean over. After a couple of weeks you can give the dirt a good soaking to drive out any air pockets, but constantly wet soil invites rotting of the succulent roots. Be careful of wetness.

Stake the plant if a lot of wind is expected. Drive in a long steel fencepost close to the stem, through the backfill and into firm, undisturbed soil. Place a wad of cloth between the post and the stem and tie the two together with soft cotton rope. Keep the saguaro staked until its roots grow out enough to support it. Provided the saguaro was set upright and it doesn't tilt, a year should be long enough. You won't see the post if you use a green one.

Provided you started with a plant full of water—it would have been round, instead of fluted—there's no need to water it for a year. Moisture reserves in the plant will be adequate, and too wet a soil leads to rot. That's why we like to have the new hole a little higher than the surrounding soil. Never make a deep well around a saguaro.

Follow the same steps for smaller desert succulents

It's the same story for prickly pear, barrel cacti, hedgehogs, cereus, and other succulents. Make a mark for properly oriented planting, cut the roots with a sharp spade, carefully lift the plant out, watch out for spines, dust the cut ends with sulphur (or rest the plant in the shade for a couple of weeks), and replant on the high side. Water once to settle the soil, and leave the rest to Mother Nature.

HOW TO MOVE AGAVES, OCOTILLOS, AND YUCCAS

These drought-tolerant plants are less succulent than the cacti. Treat them in much the same way, but give them more frequent irrigations after they have been set out. Water sparingly to keep the soil moist—not wet—in order to let the plant grow new roots.

Ocotillos are toughest and agaves the more succulent. The roots of all will rot in wet soil.

Summer, when the soil is warm enough to

Wet the ground around a plant to be moved. Then, without disturbing the soil close to the trunk, dig a trench around the plant. Chop the roots carefully, so that the soil stays firmly attached to the root ball.

Wrap burlap around the moist root ball and tie it securely with string. Now, undercut the ball to separate it from the deeper roots under the plant.

stimulate new root growth, is the best time to move these plants. Landscapers say the month doesn't matter, but it's best to stay with June, July, and August. These plants like the heat and summer rains are helpful, provided the soil doesn't stay wet all the time.

It will help to shade newly planted agaves if the summer is unusually hot.

HOW TO MOVE DESERT TREES AND SHRUBS

The end of natural dormancy, when temperatures are warming but before new growth flushes have started, is the best time to move desert trees and shrubs. April would be a good month in most places. Summer sometimes is suitable, but usually there is new shoot growth during summer rains. It's best to avoid moving any plant while it is in full growth.

You can prepare a plant for moving by letting it dry out a little. This slows down its growth—hardens it off—and when it reaches its new place the extra water you give it stimulates new shoot activity, or establishment.

It also helps to remove about half the foliage in an attempt to compensate for the loss of roots that is inevitable in digging up a plant. Either cut everything back to the halfway point or se-

Wrap burlap under the ball, too, and secure it with more string. The plant is ready to be moved. Plant it in its new home without removing the burlap, which will decay in moist soil.

lectively thin out half of the branches. The first method will give you a more robust, bushy plant; the second will preserve the natural form of the plant.

Have the new hole ready before you take the next step. It should have been dug deeply, so that irrigations will draw the roots down deeply.

Now, dig a narrow trench around the plant about 18 inches from the trunk. Cut the roots in two places, on either side of the trench. You want to be able to lift the roots out of the ground with as much soil on them as possible. This requires a damp soil, so an irrigation of the dry soil immediately before digging is called for. This will not, at this point, stimulate new growth.

Wrap the exposed soil and the roots of the plant with a large piece of sacking or cloth. Tie it tightly with strong string to make a solid bundle that will not crumble when you struggle to get the tree out of the ground. Lift the plant out, and then set it in the new hole at almost the same depth as before, only a little higher to allow for future settling. Keep the sacking around the plant. It will allow water in, allow roots to grow through it, and hold everything together until it rots.

Keep the soil moist with daily irrigations for a week. Then, provided the new shoots are not wilting and no leaves are falling off, stretch the irrigations to every two or three days. Watch the new growth at the ends of the branches; if it wilts and the plant looks sorry, go back to daily watering.

If the weather becomes unusually hot and dry, shade the plant and protect it from hot winds with a screen.

HOW TO MOVE A NON-DESERT PLANT

The best time to move an exotic plant is while it is dormant. That usually means December or January, sometimes February, but *not* if new shoots have started.

The new planting hole, which you will have dug well ahead of time, should be deep and wide. Backfill with a lot of organic matter, some sulphur, and ammonium phosphate, as outlined in Chapter 12, as a precaution against Texas root rot.

During the cooler times of the year you can dig up dormant plants without soil on their roots, provided you get them into the ground straightaway. That means immediately, not after you've had lunch and a nap. Help the plant to get established by including a little vitamin B in the water each time you irrigate for the first week.

It is not advisable to set the plant in a deep well. If you want to stop water running away from the plant, make a little berm around it—about as far out as the outermost branches—by scraping soil toward the plant from the outside.

Keep checking the moisture in the soil with your soil probe. Although the weather is cool and it might even be raining, keep the soil on the wet side for the first week. Gradually lengthen the irrigation interval as the plant puts out new shoots in the warming weather.

STAKE NEWLY MOVED PLANTS SO THEY DON'T BLOW OVER

Desert winds are gusty and your newly moved tree has lost its roots. If winds are always shaking the tree, its tender new roots are disturbed and can be broken off before they spread out enough to hold the tree up again. A newly planted tree can be blown over.

Stop this from happening by loosely tying the trunk in three or four places to a couple of stout stakes, one on either side of the tree. Drive the stakes into firm, undisturbed soil, not into the loose soil in the hole you just filled. If you drive the stakes into loose soil, everything will blow over.

16 HOW TO HAVE FLOWER BED COLOR ALL YEAR

Many people rightly assert that any effort in landscaping must include flowers. It's the first thing that comes to mind when we move into a house: "What flowers will look nice?" We usually think in terms of formal beds and containers rather than of wildflowers and blooming trees, but don't overlook the latter.

Flowers give us a rich return for our money. Even a small planting brightens and enlivens a landscape. If you have a good color sense, you can do a great outdoor decorating job with a few plants in a small space.

Desert conditions limit our choices because flowering seasons are short. We have to think of flowers in terms of summer and winter, which means two kinds of annual plants.

Perennials usually are slow growers. They require a full season, or longer, to deliver the goods. A desert twelvemonth has such extremes of temperature, moisture, brightness, and wind that perennial flowering plants often fail to give a good performance.

With perennials, you have to care for and water the plants all year in return for a week or two of color. Good examples of this situation are Shasta daisies and irises. Both have nice flowers, but they bloom for only a short time and often meet with some kind of disaster that

Always work in moist soil when you plant a flower bed. This patch is being pre-soaked by a drip system in preparation for planting in an hour or two.

detracts from the show. Shasta daisies easily sunburn, and irises freeze or get wind-blasted during their short flowering season. Still, irises are low-water-use plants, and many desert gardeners swear by them.

Geraniums can be a disappointment, too. They are wonderful in the cool months, then suffer through a hot summer and look awful at the end of it. To get the most from geraniums, it's best to treat them as annuals. Dig them up after they bloom and before summer stresses them. Buy new ones that are on the point of flowering in the fall. Enjoy them in the cooling weather, hope they won't freeze during winter, and continue to admire them during spring, until summer returns and kills them.

If you are intent on raising perennials, look to the natives and other desert-adapted plants for the best bets. Various salvias, verbenas, penstemons, and the desert marigold are reliable, tough, and water-thrifty.

FLOWERING ANNUALS NEED GOOD SOIL

Prepare the soil as you would for vegetables; flowers are something you harvest and you want a high yield. Before each planting—in fall and in summer—dig in an inch or two of steer manure, two pounds of ammonium phosphate, and three pounds of sulphur to each hundred square feet of flower bed.

Raise flower beds a little to get good drainage

It's better to plant on a gentle mound than in a shallow depression, because flower plants should not be kept too wet for long periods. This is especially important if flower beds are on the edges of lawns that get frequent irrigations. A number of soil diseases are favored by wet soil.

Don't repeat plantings in the same bed

If you keep planting petunias, for example, in the same bed year after year, you'll discover that soil organisms build up to the point at which they destroy your plants. You can treat the soil with fungicides and get some degree of control, but it's better to avoid the problem in the first place. Keep your flower bed full at all times, but use different plants each year.

Put your flower beds in the sunshine and where you'll see them

Most flower plants neither grow well nor bloom in heavy shade; some, such as the primroses, will take a little shade and still flower, but they and a few others are the exceptions. Most flowers take a lot of sunshine, even during summer.

Flowers are for looking at, so plant them where you can't help but see them. The traditional places are along the front walk, around the mailbox, under the windows, against a patio wall, along a fence, and so on.

Those are places for people on the street looking in; don't forget yourself looking out. The mailbox is still fine and so is the walkway. There's nothing wrong with the center of your desert landscape where the lawn used to be; if you still have a lawn, don't intrude on it with a shape that makes mowing more difficult. Long, thin beds running with the length of the lawn are better than diamonds and circles that require a lot of edging and lawn-mower maneuvering.

Set out plants, don't sow seeds

You don't want to wait ten weeks or so for seeds to grow into flowering plants; the seasons are too short. Seeds require constant attention from the moment you put them in the ground. Proper watering demands a lot of your time, and seeds are stolen by harvester ants and birds.

Go to a nursery and buy plants that are on the point of flowering. You'll know what colors you're getting, and you'll quickly get the results you're looking for.

Buy 10 percent more than you need, so that you can replace unsatisfactory plants with the identical kind. If you go back to the supplier after a week, she may not have the kind you bought and you'll have to fill in with a different kind.

If you want an instant neat appearance, plant in rows to a pattern; say, on the square or in a triangular spacing. This gives a deliberate design of green against the brown soil that is enhanced later by flower color. In any event, plant as close as possible to get a filled bed. A flower bed should be a mass of color from the beginning.

How to set out young plants

Tread the prepared soil (see Chapters 6 and 7) to firm it; you don't want air pockets around the roots. Use a trowel to dig out six or seven holes at the proper intervals. Fill these holes with a starter solution. You can buy starter solution or vitamin B solution at most nurseries. One is as good as the other, but you can avoid the expense by making your own: mix a tablespoon of ammonium phosphate, which you already have on hand, in a gallon of water.

Set out your plants quickly. Plant them at the same depth as they were growing in the container. Don't pull out a lot of plants and lay them

A small bed of closely planted annuals gives a colorful display and requires little maintenance. If one plant in such a dense planting dies, the survivors will spread to fill the gap.

(Above) Set out your potted bedding plants where you intend to plant them to see what sort of display they will make. If you are working with flowers of several colors and sizes, you can check out the massed effect before it's too late. Once you begin planting, work quickly. Plants in small containers dry out fast on a warm day.

(Below) You'll see light-colored flowers better if they are planted against a dark background, instead of, as here, against a white wall.

Remember that rabbits love flowers as much as you do. A low wall like this, with the extra height given it by its iron top, will keep them out of your beds. Chicken wire covers the spaces between the bars of the gate. Don't leave it open!

on the ground; their roots will dry out. Pull out and plant one at a time.

Come back the next day and check the moisture in the soil. More often than not, you'll need to water again. Be especially attentive to watering for the next eight or nine days—not too much, not too little. Check the soil with your probe.

SELECT YOUR PLANTS TO MATCH THE SEASONS

Winter bedding plants go into the ground in September and will last until May. Summer bedding plants go into the ground in March and will last until November's first frost. Lists of some reliable winter and summer annuals follow. Neither list is exhaustive.

Winter annuals

Full sun — pansies, violas, sweet alyssum, petunias, calendula, gypsophila, African daisy, candy tuft, sweet peas, mignonette, cornflower, Iceland poppy, nasturtiums, snapdragons, dianthus, stock, and gaillardia.

Shade — perrenial primrose (*Primula polyanthus*), freesia, sweet-scented stock (*Mathiola incana*), geraniums, fibrous-rooted begonia, baby's breath, Iceland poppy, and ranunculus. Hanging pots in trees or shaded patio: petunias, sweet alyssum, and lobelia.

Summer annuals

Full sun — French and African marigolds, zinnias, cosmos, tithonia, globe amaranth, hardy verbena, scabiosa, portulaca, periwinkle (*Vinca minor*), and salvias.

Shade — rain or fairy lily (a bulb), four o'-clocks, geraniums (they're risky in the summer), fibrous-rooted begonia, and periwinkle (*Vinca rosea*).

You don't see many beds like this one because it requires a great deal of maintenance. There are too many edges to trim, the effect is spoiled if even one plant dies and leaves a gap, and lawn mowing becomes a tedious chore.

Early season, shade — baby's breath, Iceland poppy, ranunculus, and annual primrose (*Primula malacoides*).

IN THE DESERT, BEDDING PLANTS ARE A COMMITMENT

Flowers look after themselves in milder climates. Here, they are unable to live without care and attention. You'll have to irrigate them, probably on a weekly schedule. Make sure the soil is moistened down to 12 inches, in order to develop deep roots. If you water shallow, the roots will be shallow and unable to withstand high soil temperatures.

Additional fertilizing usually is not necessary, provided you dug enough into the soil when you prepared the bed. If the plants pale out and slow down in their growth, you may apply half a pound of ammonium sulphate to a hundred square feet every two weeks until the color greens up again.

A lot of nitrogen in the soil makes for large plants with low flowering capability, so go easy on the nitrogen. In any case, stop fertilizing when your plants begin to produce flowers. Plants that are a little short of nitrogen produce more flowers than do those that are liberally supplied.

"DEAD-HEAD THE PANSIES!"

Years ago, this was the order given by head gardeners to apprentices learning the trade. It's a tiresome chore, but one that gives good returns. It means removing the spent flowers on young plants—and not just the pansies.

Since plants produce flowers for the purpose of obtaining seed, and thus perpetuating the species, flowering stops as soon as enough seed has been produced. You can prolong flower production far beyond its natural time by periodically going over your flower beds to pinch off the faded flowers. The more you dead-head, the longer your plants will give you color.

To pinch or not to pinch at setting out time

Flowers are produced, for the most part, at the ends of new growth; naturally it's a one-time deal. The first display is the brightest and the best, and it's often all the plant seems capable of. If you want more blooms over a longer period from the same plant, simply pinch off that single flower stalk when you set it out.

A good example is provided by stock, which flowers at the end of its central shoot. That flower soon goes to seed and the plant seems disinclined to flower again, although it doesn't die. You don't get much bang for your buck. If you pinch out that single flower stalk, side shoots develop very quickly. Each side shoot develops its own set of flowers over the next few weeks.

You'd hardly notice the death of a single plant in a planting as dense as this one.

Keep the edges of a curved bed tidy by sinking bender board into the soil to prevent grass roots from invading.

By pinching out at planting time, you exchange an early, large, single bloom for a series of smaller blooms over a period of time. Most gardeners are happy with this trade-off. The main disadvantage is that the first pinch delays the plant's delivery of color.

HOW TO BUY BEDDING PLANTS

Nursery plants in a six-pack give you more plants for your money, but they are smaller than single plants in 4-inch pots, which are sturdier. It's sometimes hard to decide which is the better buy; if you need a lot of plants, you'll probably choose the six-packs. Whichever you choose, always buy plants that are starting to flower; that way, you'll see what color you're getting. You can't trust the labels.

Leaves should be dark green and free of insect damage. You don't see a caterpillar that has been feeding on green leaves, because it is exactly the same color as its dinner. Pale leaves mean that the plant has run out of nitrogen; it might even be starving.

Take the plants out of their containers and look at the roots. Young roots—these are the ones you want—are white and fibrous. Old roots are brown and woody. Roots that are going round and round at the bottom of the container are too old.

Make a judgment about the size of the container, which holds the roots, in comparison with the foliage. If they are out of balance in either direction—roots too small and foliage too large, or lots of roots and small leaves—you're looking at a poor plant.

Few nurseries these days grow their own plants; they order them from far away. Find out which day of the week is delivery day and shop that day or the next. If you buy old plants, the price usually is the same but the quality is down.

Some nurseries are better than others in looking after their plants. The proper way is to keep them well-watered and, if they don't sell quickly, to keep them green with a little fertilizer in the water. Don't buy plants that have periodically dried out, that have become long and spindly, or that have paled or have dead flowers—even at a reduced price.

SOME SIMPLE RULES FOR BEST RESULTS

First, the obvious: put short plants in front and tall ones in back. Light-colored flowers look bet-

Let your plants bloom as they will if you want to avoid work. This stalk will have four or five small flowers. If you want bigger flowers you'll have to pinch out the smaller side buds.

ter in front of a dark wooden fence than do purple ones. The purple ones look better in front of a gray block wall than do the yellow ones.

If you spend a lot of evening time on your patio, you'll easily see light-colored flowers; you won't notice the reds and purples nearly as much.

Single colors are more dramatic than mixtures. If you must mix, try to stay with two colors, not three or four, and use complementary colors, such as yellow with blue. You can use several shades of the same color—white, pink, red—but use just a few of the more intense colors and plenty of the paler shades.

Avoid making color patterns—alternating blue flowers with white along a walkway, for instance—for fear that a dead plant will leave a disproportionate gap in the pattern. Creating your family coat-of-arms in flowering plants is an unnecessary accomplishment.

Maintenance will be easier if you use just one kind of plant instead of a variety. Watering will be the same, fertilizing will be the same, and the life of the bed will be the same.

Don't make flower beds under native trees

Native trees cast a most appropriately filtered shade for many flowers, as well as for people. Unfortunately, changing the soil to accomodate flower plants, together with the frequent watering they need, leads to a bad situation for native trees. Manure attracts grubs that eat the tree's roots, and the extra fertility and watering makes the tree grow too quickly. The quick growth is soft, inviting borer damage and rot in the roots.

Too many palo verde trees, which grew very well on their own until the houses came, have been killed by flower beds. If you want to use that excellent shade, grow your flowers in containers.

17 LANDSCAPE GARDENING WITH CONTAINERS

There's nothing new about growing plants in containers—it's been done for years, all over the world—but in the desert we seem to have overlooked the possibilities. Containers come in all shapes, sizes, and materials. You can successfully grow trees, shrubs, flowers, vegetables, and herbs in them.

Prices range from economical to ridiculous. The best value for a number of years has been the half whiskey barrel. The wood disintegrates in about seven years, but during that time you can plant a tree, a rose bush, a shrub, or seven years of annual flowers.

It's with annual flowers that containers prove their worth. They can be moved onto a patio to display their contents when flower production is at its peak and retired when the display is over. You can rearrange a number of pots or replace them, just as you treat the furniture inside your home. They give you variety and versatility. They don't take up a lot of space. By planting very closely, you can make a small number of plants produce an intense display.

A half whiskey barrel planted with herbs and placed by the kitchen door is as useful as it is attractive.

Containers give you an opportunity to have color all the time. All you do is replace poor performers with fresh new ones. An efficient way to do this is to grow the plants in a one-, five-, seven-, or ten-gallon plastic container, and then slip this plain container into a fancy display container when the plant comes into bloom. The outer container isn't spoiled by salt deposits, and you don't have to bang it around when you fill it and empty it. Remember that even your display container must have a drainage hole.

THE FIRST RULE: PLANT CONTAINERS MUST HAVE A DRAINAGE HOLE

No matter what kind of container you use, it *must* have a drainage hole to let the water out. If your container has no hole, make one. Plant roots left to sit in water at the bottom of the container will rot. It's surprising how often this mistake is made.

Even if you make a proper drainage hole, don't set the container on a concrete floor, where the hole will be obstructed by the floor. Instead, raise the container on bricks.

GOOD WATERING MEANS GIVING MORE WATER THAN THE PLANT NEEDS

When you pot a plant, don't fill your container to the rim with soil. Leave a couple of inches between the soil and the lip of the pot or barrel; this will allow you to put a lot of water on the soil quickly.

Each time you water that plant, overwater by about 10 percent. The extra water comes out the drainage hole, carrying unwanted salts with it. Salts are found in the water itself, as a residue in fertilizers, and in some soils. If you frequently apply small amounts of water, the soil holds it for a time and then it evaporates, leaving the salts behind. In a year or two those salts become uncomfortably corrosive to the roots.

Don't let the soil get too dry

If the soil in a container gets too dry, it shrinks away from the sides of the pot. When you irrigate, the water runs around the root ball and out the drainage hole without moistening the roots. The staves of whiskey barrels also shrink when dry, and water is lost between the staves. It's easy to see the problem with a barrel, but you don't see a shrunken soil ball in a pot unless you look carefully.

To correct the error, pack dry sand or a sandy soil mix in between the container and the shrunken soil ball when it is dry. The sand flows down to the bottom of the container and fills the space, stopping irrigation water from escaping too quickly.

Salt stains are unsightly

Salty drainage water leaves marks on concrete. You can reduce staining somewhat by wetting down the patio when you water, but the best thing to do is to give each container an adequate collection saucer. Use a large syringe to suck the water out, but don't put it back in the soil.

Even small containers, when artfully arranged, provide welcome color. They'll need diligent watering during warm weather, but they can easily be moved from sun to shade as the seasons change.

MAKE UP A SOIL MIX FOR USE EXCLUSIVELY IN CONTAINERS

A satisfactory mix can be made of equal parts coarse sand, perlite, peat moss, and ordinary garden soil. This mix will have both body and sufficient openness to allow good drainage.

The garden soil acts as a glue to hold the other ingredients together, but there's a danger in using it: it might contain weedkiller residues, salts, harmful bacteria, nematodes, or grubs. Be careful where you get it.

If you like, add a small amount of animal manure. It provides beneficial organisms, to be sure, but anything more than a handful to a cubic foot of mix is too much.

Mix everything together; don't make layers. If you find that you're a bit short, empty the container and mix the extra in with the original. In that way you avoid having two kinds of soil mix in the same container.

Don't use gravel in the bottom of the container

To some extent, a plant that grows in a container is handicapped because its roots are limited. For this reason, use as big a container as you can. You've already given up some soil space by not filling the container to the brim; don't give up more root space by placing a layer of gravel in the bottom of a container in the interest of improving drainage. You will improve drainage, but it's not worth depriving the roots of growing space.

Slow-release fertilizer can be added to the mix

There are several pelleted, or coated, fertilizers on the market (see Chapter 7), and they are very suitable for container-grown plants. They usually offer a balanced blend of the main nitrogen, phosphorus, and potash nutrients, and they sometimes have minor nutrients, too.

Make sure such a fertilizer is spread throughout the soil mix for efficient slow release of nutrients. The small-pelleted kinds are better than the big bullets or bricks. All of them release nu-

Containers easily build up salt deposits—from irrigation water, fertilizer residues, and the soil itself—and excess salts mean poor plant growth, even death. Reduce salt build-up by applying more water than the plant can absorb at one watering; be sure you have provided adequate drainage, so that salts are washed through the soil and out of the pot.

The shrunken staves of a whiskey barrel planter tell you that the soil is dry and the plant is ready for its next watering. Irrigate slowly, so that water does not simply run out between the staves.

A barrel and a tall circular frame are fine for sweet peas or other vining annuals. Start with a low circle of chicken wire at the base of the cage to give young plants something to hang onto.

trients slowly over about six months, but you want all of the soil mix to receive the benefit, not just certain parts of it.

You can plant as soon as you like. The slow-release fertilizer won't hurt the roots of young plants, provided you do not exceed the stated dose.

"Feed" as you water, too

Your plant's roots are growing in a confined space and are unable to find nutrients in an artificial soil mix. The slow-release fertilizer will change that, but quick-growing flowers also will benefit from applications of quick-release fertilizers.

In a week or two, after new roots have gotten going, you can add a balanced houseplant fertilizer to the irrigation water. Use the color of your plants' leaves as an indicator of well-being: a dark green color says that no additional fertilizer is needed, while a pale color suggests the need to fertilize. The preferred way is to add a teaspoon of fertilizer to each gallon of water every time you water, until the color improves. Alternatively, use a tablespoon at every other watering, or every third watering.

Use a stick to tell you when to water

Push a stick of soft pine to the bottom of the container and leave it there. When you get an urge to water your plants, pull the stick out and consult it, just as you would the dipstick in your car's engine. You'll see a water mark and you'll feel the moisture on the stick, but don't rely on this method alone. If the leaves begin to droop, it's time to water.

WHAT SIZE CONTAINER DO I USE?

Anything smaller than five gallons will need daily attention during the summer. Its soil will dry out too quickly and it will get hot enough to kill roots.

This rules out little window boxes and the touristy ornamental frogs, goats, and chickens with hollow backs that are supposed to sprout flowers. They're too small for the summer and barely big enough for winter, unless you like daily watering.

At the other extreme are gorgeous concrete bowls and huge urns of thick clay. They're fine for plants, but hard on humans; you can't move them.

In between is a wide range of sizes. Since portability is a major consideration, get the biggest container you can move without strain. Put it on wheels, if need be.

DRIP SYSTEMS ARE APPROPRIATE FOR CONTAINERS

You can lead irrigation tubing to an arrangement of containers and drop a "spaghetti line" into each one (see Chapter 5 for more on drip irrigation systems). One kind has a lead weight at the end to hold the line in place, in case fighting cats throw things around. There's another kind with a ring that encircles the stem of a tree or shrub and delivers water all around.

You can put a drip system on an automatic timer to cover for you when you are on vacation, of course, but because plants in a container have restricted roots and grow in a limited space it's easy to overwater and overfertilize them. They respond more quickly to outside influences and dry out more quickly when the weather turns hot or windy. All this means that you have to be more attentive to plants in containers than to plants in the ground.

TREES AND SHRUBS IN CONTAINERS NEED ROOT-PRUNING

The roots of annual flowers soon fill the space in a container, but because you take them out at the end of their season and replace them with smaller plants it's not a problem. With trees and

What could be easier to move than a flower bed on wheels? This mass of winter annuals is growing in an unopened but punctured bag of soil mix covered with black plastic. The "garden" rests on a sheet of plywood so that it can be moved off the wagon. Such an arrangement will not survive warm summer weather; it's strictly a cool-season tactic.

Even large containers need to be moved into a sunny spot in the winter and back into filtered shade for the summer. It can be quite a chore. Get a friend to help.

shrubs that stay for six or seven years in the same container, however, there's the problem of roots using up all the space and becoming crowded. What do you do? It's not easy, but you must take the soil ball out and cut the roots.

Lay the container on its side and roll it back and forth. If the soil is somewhat dry, it will separate from the walls of the container and you can grasp the stem of the plant—gloves, please, if it's a rose—and pull everything out. Because the roots are old, they hold the soil ball intact.

Press a sharp knife about three inches into the soil ball; cut from top to bottom at several places all around the soil ball. Remove bits of root as you go. Don't worry that some soil falls off.

When you've finished, wet the soil ball to hold things together and roll it back into its container. If a lot of soil falls off in the pruning process, place new soil in the bottom of the container and put the pruned plant on top of it. If you put the soil on top, you'll have buried the plant; it won't like it.

All this sound easier than it really is. You'll need a friend to help.

REPLACE THE SOIL MIX WHEN YOU SEE A HEAVY SALT CRUST

A good soil mix won't last forever. It eventually becomes salt-laden, which means your plants won't grow vigorously.

The sign to watch for is a crust of salt at soil level inside the container. Each time you water your plants this salt is washed into the soil. As the soil dries, the salt evaporates and collects on the insides of the container, where it waits for the next watering. It's time to change the soil mix.

It's easy with annual flowers: at the end of their season, tip out all the old soil and put in new.

With trees and shrubs it's both more difficult and more dangerous to your plant. Take the plant out, remove most of the soil from around its roots, and replant it. Do it in mild weather and enlist the aid of a friend.

Wide dishes are easy to manage, but rounded containers are not. To get the old soil out you'll have to disturb, perhaps even break, the roots.

Small containers need frequent watering; in the summer, that means every day.

18 STARTING WILDFLOWERS

The colorful show of wildflowers in the spring is one of the more memorable sights of the desert. It brings visitors with their cameras to the region, and if they decide to become residents they often try to duplicate that dramatic display in their own yards. In the wild, it's so natural and it looks easy.

One aspect of Mother Nature's performance is often overlooked: it doesn't happen by itself, nor is it a reliable performance. The gorgeous mass of wildflowers results from a combination of suitable soil temperatures and rainfall, which initiates germination and returns regularly to nurture strong plants. If the rain is inadequate or comes at the wrong time, the display is disappointing.

Another impression needs further analysis. When you look sideways from a car window across to the far horizon, the countryside seems to be filled with wildflowers. If you get out of your car and walk through the desert, you'll see that individual plants are widely scattered. In your smaller yard you should try to imitate this scattered population and not try to fill every square foot with wildflowers; if you do, the appearance will be unnatural, even displeasing.

A third consideration to bear in mind is that the flowers you see in the spring began with germination of the seed six months earlier, in the fall. Many homeowners start their program too late and are disappointed at the small size of their plants and their poor flowering.

FIRST, SOW THE RIGHT SEED

Sow the seed that is appropriate to your region. At present, seed in most commercial packets is collected in the higher mountain areas. Wildflowers from upland Colorado don't grow well in the intermediate deserts. Read the label to be sure you're getting local seed. Native plant societies, botanical gardens, and natural history museums are good sources for wildflower seeds and advice.

You may have to collect your own seed. Take a walk through the desert, remembering not to trespass on private property or wildlife preserves, and harvest the ripe seedheads before they explode and scatter their seed. There are strict laws governing the removal of wild plants from the desert, but it's legal to gather wildflower seeds, except in national monuments and other protected areas. When your plants go abundantly to seed in a good year, repay your debt by scattering seed in wild places or share the bounty with a friend.

Put the seed stalks in paper bags and let the bagged capsules explode in the dry air of your carport. Label the bags with the name of the plant, the date you gathered it, and the location where it grew.

To protect your seed store from mice, insects, birds, and damp, store the bagged seeds in airtight cans or jars; don't lose the labels. Seed that is kept dry will be good for four or five years.

There are two harvesting times

Cool-season wildflower seed is harvested in late spring; you will sow it next fall in cooling soil. The plants will flower in March or April.

Summer wildflowers, of which there are

fewer, are harvested in late summer; their seed will be sown early next summer as the soil heats up. The plants will flower in July and August.

A question for the purists: Is African daisy a wildflower?

In southern Africa's Namaqualand it is a wildflower, a native called the Namaqualand daisy. In the Desert Southwest it grows so well that it has "escaped" from deliberate plantings and "gone native." Many people are quite happy about this, because African daisy has an attractive flower and is easy to grow. Others are not so pleased with its vigorous reseeding.

In some national monument areas there are so many African daisies growing on the sides of roads, where the wind has blown their seed, that the rangers spend their time pulling them up for fear visitors will think they are a native plant. The pretty wildflower has become a weed.

Don't worry; in your yard it will not be a weed. Seed packets of African daisy and Arizona or California poppies are becoming more common in the nurseries, as are potted penstemons and desert marigolds. Other wildflower seeds, depending on where you live, may be harder to find.

IF YOU WANT GOOD RESULTS, PREPARE THE SOIL FOR WILDFLOWERS

This seems strange when you think that the plants grow so well by themselves in poor soil, but desert wildflowers are short-lived precisely *because* they grow in infertile soil that does little to support and sustain them. If you want strong plants with lots of flowers, you'll either have to improve a desert soil or take advantage of an old flower bed's fertility.

In the latter case, no special preparation is necessary. The residual fertility will be enough, and the soil will have been tilled sufficiently deep to encourage strong roots.

If you are starting fresh, you must prepare the soil. It's simply not good enough to scratch the soil, throw the seed over your shoulder, and expect it to grow on its own.

First, wet the soil 7 or 8 inches deep, then pull the weeds. Cover the ground with an inch of steer manure and scatter ammonium phosphate at the rate of two pounds to every hundred square feet. Dig the soil a foot deep, mixing everything thoroughly. Tread over it to firm it down.

Chop the big lumps with a hoe until you can make rake marks. Scatter the seed into these little furrows, and then rake across lightly to bury the seed. Don't sow too thickly; shoot for something resembling pepper on a baked potato. If you buy seed, you'll need about an ounce for each hundred square feet.

Wildflowers call for a random style

Don't sow the seed in a regular, geometric bed or in straight rows. This destroys the charm of wildflowers. Instead, sow scattered patches or strips through your desert landscape. A good way is to dig a narrow band, say two feet wide, snaking it randomly through the landscape. That way, the plants will look natural and the seeds will scatter at random to colonize the area in years to come.

Pre-emergent weedkillers won't allow wildflower seeds to grow

Don't underestimate the power of pre-emergent weedkillers. When you treat an area that you think is too weedy, you prejudice any deliberate sowing of seed in that place for several weeks. The chemicals don't know the "good" seeds from the "bad." This is something a lot of homeowners overlook.

Remember that desert wildflowers are sun-lovers

Wildflowers like the sun so much that on cloudy days they don't open up. Stay away from the shade of walls and other plants to get the best results. The light shade of a desert tree won't bother annual wildflowers, but the heavier shade of imported landscape trees will not allow them to do their best. Fortunately, desert trees are leafless during most of the wildflower season.

One reason that wildflowers of the mountains don't do well in the desert is that they prefer shade, even up there. The other reason is that the desert is too hot and dry.

THERE ARE TWO SOWING TIMES FOR DESERT WILDFLOWERS

For spring flowers—those that flower in March or April—September is a bit too early to sow seed, October is good, and November usually is too late. It's soil temperature that decides the best time; it's about right when the soil is 65 degrees in the top inch at midday.

For those plants that flower during July and August, the best time to sow seed is March, as the soil is warming up.

In both cases, true wildflowers need a regular inch of rain a month during their six months of growth.

The soil must be kept moist

From now on, you've got to care for your plants. They may be wildflowers, but if you want them to perform you've got to care for them.

If rain doesn't fall, you must water the soil to get the seeds to germinate. Treat the area as if it were a row of vegetable seeds. Keep the harvester ants off by finding the nearby nest and pouring *Diazinon* down it, provided your gardening philosophy allows for the use of chemical poisons. You can cover the seedlings with a length of bent chicken wire to keep the birds and rabbits from eating them.

As the seedlings grow, reduce the frequency of irrigations. You need to keep the roots growing downward with deep soakings, but you can let the surface dry out between waterings.

If the seedlings seem to be pale and short of nitrogen, don't be afraid to give them a light scattering of ammonium sulphate—something like a half-pound to every hundred square feet once a month. Apply the fertilizer during an irrigation.

Thin out the crowded seedlings

In your walk across the desert wildflower carpet at the beginning of this chapter, you didn't see many plants nudging one another. They were spaced far apart, even lonely. Try to imitate this naturalness.

Remove the crowded weaker plants and throw them away. If all your plants are strong and vigorous—and you are careful—you can transplant them into empty spaces. To successfully transplant wildflowers the soil should be wet—a rainy winter's day is your opportunity—and for a few days after you should water the transplants. Shade them if the days are hot, sunny, and windy.

To get lots of flowers, reduce water when first blooms appear

Annual plants naturally flower at the ends of their life cycles. If conditions remain favorable for growth, they continue to grow and don't flower as much as when conditions—usually hotter and drier—change for the worse. You can "terminate" the life cycle by interrupting the irrigations. Don't stop completely; resume watering a little after the initial stop that stimulates first flowering.

PERENNIAL NATIVES ARE STARTED THE SAME WAY

Those plants that live for several years, even though they seem to give up during the hottest months, can be introduced into your landscape by seeding. Collect the seed when it is ripe and before it is lost to the wind and animals. Store it, then sow it in the spring, in February or March.

You also can start perennials by making cuttings

The perennial penstemons, chicory, Mexican primroses, mallows, and verbena are woody, which gives you an opportunity to make cuttings. The best time is at the beginning of the normal growth cycle, usually in the spring.

Cut the stems into lengths of 4 or 5 inches, apply *Rootone* to the lower end, and put the cutting in a small container of equal parts perlite and vermiculite.

After a couple of weeks of gentle watering—overwatering is the danger here—each little stick will have grown delicate roots. Keep the new plant in its container until its roots fill the space, and then transplant it into a gallon can filled with desert soil. Keep the plant in this pot until it again fills the container with its roots, which might take six months.

Set out plants in the fall, with a rain

If you grow your own plants from cuttings or buy them from a nursery—the good news is that more nurseries are carrying these desert plants—you'll find that fall is the best planting time. Air temperatures are milder than in the spring and the soil is warmer. This is a better combination than hot air and cold soil in February or March. In summer, you have the worst of both worlds: hot air, hot soil, and too bright a sun.

19 STARTING A LAWN

There are obvious changes coming about in everyone's landscaping practices, owing to the scarcity of water in the desert and its high cost. The major water-guzzling component of a landscape in the desert is the lawn. It's a real expense. Besides, the purists among us will say, "Lawns aren't proper in the desert; they don't look right."

Be that as it may, most of us like a patch of grass. We value it for a number of reasons: it cools the air by its evaporation, it keeps the dust down, it works on our psyche (green is cool), it's kind to our children's bare feet, and the dog likes it, too.

It's hard to give up the thought of a lawn, despite the care a good lawn demands, so the trend is to have a smaller patch of good quality grass in a strategic spot. No longer do we carpet a vast unused frontage just for the neighbors to see. Instead, we put a lawn where we can see it through a sliding glass door, close to the house where it readily becomes a part of our outdoor living space.

In effect, we value lawns more highly under these conditions. The areas may be smaller, but they are of better quality and we use them more. This means we must take better care of them.

GOOD LAWN CARE STARTS WITH SOIL PREPARATION

No matter what size lawn you want or the kind of grass you'll grow, it's absolutely necessary first to dig the soil and improve it; see Chapters 6 and 7 for methods and materials. Don't think of a lawn in the same terms as you think of covering an old floor with shiny new linoleum. A lawn is a living crop, not a cover-up. Deep digging is the key to success.

If you move into a house with a lawn that's suffered this sort of careless treatment, you'll have to start all over again. Soil compaction caused by the cars' weight and contamination by dripping oil and antifreeze make it necessary to thoroughly rehabilitate the soil before you plant anything.

Mowing is neither easy nor efficient when a sidewalk is higher than the surrounding grass. Plant your lawn at the same level as walkways, which may mean filling to raise the grade level.

Install the sprinkler system at this point

Lawns must be irrigated by a buried sprinkler system. You can't use a drip irrigation system and the old-fashioned method of flooding a lawn is simply too extravagant these days.

Quarter-circle sprinkler heads go in the corners, half-circle sprinkler heads are set at the edges, and full-circle heads in the middle of the lawn. You need some engineering facts—such as minimum water pressure in the city supply, pipe sizes, number of heads, kinds of heads, and so on—to determine exactly where they should be set. You can do it yourself, but it might be better to call in a sprinkler installer and have him do it.

Once you know where the heads will be, you know where to dig trenches. Obviously, it makes more sense to dig them before you put the grass in. Test the installation before you bury the pipes. Each sprinkler head should overlap the next one by 15 percent at the lowest operating water pressure. You don't want dry spots caused by wind or by inadequate water pressure.

It's important to have the top of the sprinkler heads flush with the finished grade of your lawn. They should not stick up to be caught by the mower or be sunken to cause pockets of wetness.

The next step is to roll, rake, and level the area

If your lawn-to-be is surrounded by walkways, finish the lawn at the same level as the walkways. This lets you mow evenly up to the edge, with one set of wheels on the grass and the other on the concrete or bricks. Both sets will be level. If your lawn is lower than the walk, you'll have a tufted strip of tall grass along its edges because one set of wheels will be up on the walkway and the other will be lower down on the grass. The result will be messy, and that messiness requires extra time-consuming trimming.

Soil that has been dug deeply invariably settles, so you need to hasten that process by rolling the soil. Go slowly back and forth, and then crossways. Sprinkle the soil, but don't get it wet and plastic. Put water in the roller to give it

(Above) Here's a nightmare of a lawn. The shapes are awkward, the mounds make mowing difficult and they dry out on top, there are trees and boulders to drive around, and there are what seem like miles of edging to keep tidy.

(Below) This is another awkward lawn to maintain. Sunken tree "wells," boulders, and wavy margins all add up to a maintenance headache.

weight. You'll now see how uneven the lay of the land is. Rake soil off the tops of the "hills" and put it in the "valleys." Roll again. Rake again. Roll again. When you think you've done enough, turn on the sprinkler system and thoroughly wet the area. This helps to settle the soil, and puddles show you where the low spots are. A puddle should be filled in with a little soil from those high spots that dry out more quickly.

If you want a nice-looking lawn, the soil

This lawn can be maintained quickly and easily. There's a long straight run for the mower, the margin at right is a gentle curve, and trees have been planted at grade level.

should be perfectly flat. Grass grows evenly if the soil is uniform (from your digging) and if there are no dry and wet spots that invite weed growth later on. Besides, you can't properly mow an uneven lawn.

You may need to bring in additional soil; if you do, make sure it is the same as the soil you've got. To eliminate any irregularities, mix in the topsoil; don't lay it on top.

Think of future maintenance when you install a lawn area

When it comes to mowing, the most efficient shape is long and narrow; you mow all the way on the long axis with few turns to make. A square shape is bad enough, but odd shapes with extra bulges and sharp corners make mowing a horrible, time-consuming chore. It's even worse when you have rocks and trees in the way. Try to make simple, long shapes for lawns.

A flat lawn is easiest to maintain. Those that have undulating surfaces and steep slopes are difficult to irrigate evenly and are dangerous to mow if you use a power mower. They are awkward and tiring if you mow them by hand.

THE BASIC CHOICE: A WINTER OR A SUMMER LAWN?

In the low deserts, there isn't a grass that stays green all through the year. The extremes of winter and summer are too severe. A year-round lawn requires two grasses, one for winter and one for summer.

A lot of water is needed for a lawn during summer, when you may prefer to stay indoors where it's cool, anyway. No doubt you'll look at it a lot, but you won't use it much. Mowing grass when the temperature gets into the hundreds is no fun, either.

A winter lawn is never stressed as much as a summer lawn, and winter rains are more efficiently absorbed into the soil. Irrigation is less vital. Because you spend more time outdoors during the cooler months, you're more likely to use and enjoy a winter lawn.

TO START A LAWN QUICKLY, SOW SEED

For a winter lawn, use ryegrass or fescue, either a single kind or a blend that has been formulated especially for lawns. Sow seed in early October when the soil temperature has fallen to 75 degrees 2 inches deep. These grasses will give you eight or nine months service, until the weather gets hot in May or June; then they will die of the heat. The seeding rate for a thousand square feet of lawn is as follows: annual ryegrass, 15 pounds; ryegrass blends, 10 to 12 pounds; tall fescue, 10 pounds.

For a summer lawn, you could sow seed of common Bermudagrass, but it's not a good idea. Common Bermuda is a coarse, invasive grass; it grows into flower beds and cactus patches with abandon. It's not easy to control or to get rid of when, invariably, it misbehaves. When it flowers, its prolific pollen maddens allergy sufferers. The hybrid Bermudagrasses, which are sodded rather than seeded, are much to be preferred.

Separate lawns from flower beds by edging with bender board. Be sure the edging extends high enough above ground level to keep hybrid Bermudagrass from crawling over the top. Common Bermudagrass is even more invasive; don't plant it.

Try these seed-sowing techniques for an even coverage

Calculate how much seed you need and make two parcels of it. The first you apply up and down the area; the second you apply across the area. This gives you a better coverage than does sowing in just one direction, which might leave strips unsown and thus invite weeds.

If you have flower beds next to the lawn, you need a helper to hold a large sheet of plywood on its edge to bounce back any wayward seed you throw too far.

Prepare the soil for seeding by making sure it is firm. Use a rake to make small furrows for the seed. Furrows should be three or four times as deep as the size of the seed; be sure the furrows are of even depth. After sowing the seed, cross-rake to bury it at about twice the depth of the seed size. Be careful when covering the seed. If you sow too deeply, or use a lot of covering material, you'll make the seeds work too hard to push their way through to the light. The seed will break through thin and weak and ready to die.

On a small area, you can bury the seed by gently washing down the ridges into the furrows with a light sprinkling, but this requires considerable care. Using the existing soil to cover the seed is better than smothering it with steer manure, or peat moss, or "mulch."

You musn't let the seed dry out, not for a moment!

It is most important to keep the soil around the seed moist all the time. If you sprinkle faithfully for a couple of days over the weekend—the usual and best time to get things started—but then fail to come home at the first coffee break of the week to water and the soil surface dries, even for a half-hour, the seed is at risk. It might even be dead, and you won't realize it until another week passes.

Back off the watering as the grass grows

Watering three or four times a day, then twice a day, then once a day, then every other day is the progression to aim for. The weather, the condition of the soil, and so on determine how quickly you can do this.

Follow the old advice on how to water: "Keep the soil around the roots moist." In this case, the roots begin at soil surface, so you start with light and frequent sprinklings. As the roots grow downward, you water a little longer each time. the heavier waterings last longer, provided dry winds don't blow or a heat wave develops. Use your soil probe; in this case, a screwdriver can be considered a soil probe.

Don't sprinkle the young grass when the sun is shining on it. This is not easy at the beginning, but you want to avoid overheating the young blades. Water droplets magnify the sun's brightness.

Don't buy sod that has a layer of clay in it, especially if your soil is sandy. A layer of clay keeps water from soaking down to roots, so that the sod dries out and shrinks. That's what happened on this west-facing slope, where the chances for this lawn's becoming established are poor.

There's extra mowing and trimming when sprinkler heads are set lower than the surrounding lawn. The remedy is easy: Lengthen the risers until the heads are level with the surface of the ground.

KEEP OFF THE GRASS!

As much as you can, keep off the young grass. Roots are taking hold and the plants are fragile for a couple of months after sowing. After that time, go ahead and enjoy the lawn.

Be careful with the first mowing

The new grass gathers strength as it grows. There should be enough nutrients in the soil—the ammonium phosphate and manure you put there—to keep it dark green until it is 2 inches tall. That's the time for the first mowing. This actually is a pruning that stimulates side shoots in each seedling and makes the lawn thicker.

The grass should be dry and the mower blades sharp. A reel mower is better than a rotary, simply because the blades can be made as sharp as scissors, sharp enough to cut paper in a test. The blades on a rotary mower work, even if sharp, by tearing off the ends of the grass. Besides smashing plant tissue and allowing diseases to enter, the result is untidy to look at.

A good lawn is the result of constant attention

From now on, you're committed to maintaining your lawn. It's not a thing you can neglect. In a way, you're caught in a trap: the more frequently you mow, the more you need to fertilize; this makes the grass grow stronger, and the stronger it grows the more it will need mowing. The more you water, the more the grass grows and the faster it uses up the fertilizer. It will then need fertilizing to keep it growing, and the more it grows the more it needs mowing!

MOWING TECHNIQUES

Dry grass and sharp blades are the key. Don't let the grass get away from you; you don't want to be mowing a hayfield. When the height is 2 or 2½ inches, get out the machine and take off about a third of the length. If the grass grows quickly, this will need to be done more often than once a week.

If the grass is long and growing strongly and the cut material is wet and heavy, it's best to

You'll have to dethatch a Bermudagrass lawn at summer's end if you plan to grow a winter lawn. This great harvest of thatch in September tells us that economies can be made next summer in fertilizer and water.

catch the clippings and take them to the compost pile. If everything is dry and the cut is light, there's no harm in letting the clippings find their way to the soil surface to decay. This is especially true for a winter lawn.

Most of the time, mow in the most efficient direction; once in a while, however, mow crossways to avoid pushing the grass the same way every time. You'll be surprised at how much difference it makes.

If you want a first-class appearance, mow one way and then mow crossways over it before you put the machine back in its shed. This extra work removes those strips of tufted grass you left when the mower veered to one side as your mind wandered.

SUMMER LAWN ESTABLISHMENT

Grasses that do well in the summer months are the several hybrid Bermudas and St. Augustine. All of them go dormant and brown when the weather turns cool. They look dead, but they'll come back, like the swallows, when the weather warms up again.

Dichondra and Lippia are not grasses, but they make a good substitute if you are generous with the irrigations. They stay green all year, but will be damaged by a sharp frost.

The best Bermudagrass is a variety of hybrid that turns green early in the summer and stays green late into the fall. Santa Ana might be that kind for you; it is good for most parts of the lower deserts.

Laying sod is the way to start a summer lawn

Once you've prepared the soil (as for seeding), laying sod is as simple as laying tile in the kitchen. In season, which is during the warm weather between spring and fall when the soil temperature is more than 70 degrees 2 inches deep, you go to a nursery and buy a number of pieces of your favorite grass. Every piece measures 16 inches by 44 inches, or about 5 square feet; each is about an inch thick.

Buy sod fresh. Find out which day the delivery is usually made and be there on that day. Some of the poorer nurseries stack these pieces about 5 feet high; at best the grass becomes pale; at worst, the pieces heat up and the grass is ruined. You don't find out, however, until after you've laid them out at home.

Each piece of sod has a thin layer of soil, and you should look to see that strong roots are coming through this layer. You want pale vigorous roots, not brown woody ones. The sod should have been in its prime when it was cut. You don't want baby stuff with no strength to it, nor should you buy sod with a layer of dead grass (thatch) between the soil and the green blades.

The soil layer should not be so sandy that it falls off as the pieces are loaded into your car, but neither should it be a clay soil. A layer of clay, no matter how thin, won't let water through easily; this means your sod will be very wet on top and dry underneath every time you irrigate. New roots won't grow into your prepared soil. Your management problems have begun on the first day, and they won't go away.

First, stagger and roll

Lay the sod, end to end, on the long axis of your lawn. It should be level with the sidewalk; you don't want a sunken lawn. Start the second row with a half piece, so that you stagger installation just like the bricks of a patio floor. Work your way across the area, row by row, making sure that the ends and the sides are butted close together. Don't leave "mortar joints;" they look untidy and the pieces dry out at the edges, giving a checkerboard appearance.

Shade is wonderful for people, but not for Bermudagrass lawns. The dark area here is more a bald patch than a shadow. If you're really attached to your grass, thin the dense branches of the tree and let more light in.

The roots need to lay directly on the soil, so firm everything down and sprinkle lightly as you go along. Don't wait to sprinkle until you've laid the last piece. Then, when you've covered the area, gently roll your new lawn this way and that, and then diagonally. You don't want a heavy roller, and you don't want the ground too wet. You just want to make a good contact.

Now you've got an instant lawn.

Plugs make the money go further, but give you more work

One piece of sod can be cut into 176 pieces, each measuring 2 inches by 2 inches. Each piece is planted level with the prepared soil at a distance you can afford. If you set them 8 inches apart, you'll need thirteen pieces of sod for 1,000 square feet of lawn. This will give you a quicker lawn than spacing them at 12 inches, for which you'll need only six pieces of sod, a 50-percent savings in material. If you economize further by spacing plugs 18 inches apart, there's a danger of weeds growing up between them. You'll also have a much longer wait for your lawn.

When you've finished, roll the moist soil to make sure the plugs are all at the same height. Water diligently.

Stolons are a third way to get a lawn started

Stolons are little bits of grass shredded from pieces of sod. They look like wet hay when they arrive at the nursery in a plastic-lined box. Order ahead of time and collect your stolons from the nursery the minute they arrive. One bushel of stolons covers a little less than 100 square feet. They have no soil attached to them and they are vulnerable. They must not dry out, not for a moment. Prepare the soil (as for seeding) ahead of time, so there is no delay in getting them planted.

The soil should be wet when you scatter the stolons over it. You can lightly cover them with soil—not peat moss or steer manure—and gently roll them to make sure of a good contact with the soil. The little pieces are green and leafy, but they don't have much of a root system. Because they lie on top of the soil, they don't take long to dry out. If you are working a large area, don't wait until you finish the whole job before you sprinkle the stolons. Ten minutes is all that's needed—even less on a dry, windy day—for stolons to dry out. Stop every five minutes to sprinkle what you've scattered.

Begin your operation on a Friday evening; that way, you've got the whole weekend to devote to the matter of keeping your stolons alive.

Gradually lengthen the period between waterings as the sprigs grow deeper roots. You'll have to inspect them carefully and frequently to see how they are getting on. Your new lawn will turn a richer green as the days go by until, after three or four weeks, you can do the first mowing. Make sure the blades of your mower, preferably a reel mower, are sharp. You don't want to uproot the young plants by a rough mowing.

20 MAKING AND KEEPING A GOOD HEDGE

Hedges do more for a landscape than mark its boundaries and provide privacy. They create a microclimate by keeping out strong desert winds, which blow hot in summer and cold in winter. Hedges collect the dust carried by winds, too, keeping our living areas cleaner and healthier.

Admittedly, a wall or a fence does the same thing, but homeowners usually soften those structures with a planting of some kind, anyway. A hedge is less formidable, and it looks better.

There are, of course, limits to the usefulness of a living hedge. A lot of us expect hedges to quiet traffic noises or to muffle loud neighbors, but studies have shown that they don't help a great deal, even if a double row of plants is used. Hedges take up space and cast shadows. This means you are losing some landscaping potential, because their roots also take up space and steal water from nearby plants.

HEDGES FOR KEEPING PEOPLE—AND DOGS—OUT

Hedges will keep animals out, but they are not so good at keeping a determined dog inside your compound. For that, you need a fence or a wall.

A lot of desert plants, because they have thorns, are good for hedges. One of these is the century plant, the agave. There are several kinds, ranging from small and compact to large and spreading. Agaves last eight or nine years before they become untidy by sending out basal

This straight-trimmed hedge looks neat and will stay that way if trimmed very frequently. The danger in this sort of hedge is of the bottom leaves dying for lack of light; the dense top shades them too heavily.

suckers, or "pups." These are the plant's natural replacement system; they appear when the mother plant is about to flower. The tall flower stalk cannot be stopped and it precedes the death of the plant. To keep an agave hedge complete and in a straight line, remove old plants and replace them with pups. It may not be the tidiest of hedges, but it will be effective in keeping animals out.

Other desert plants with thorns include the cat-claw acacia and the white-thorn acacia. Both are trees, but they can be trimmed to keep them small; they can even be pruned annually to hold a defined shape. They are tough plants; they take heat and drought and have few pests.

Sour orange is another tree that can be made into a thick hedge. It has wicked thorns and it stays green all year. It is moderately drought tolerant, so that if you forget to water it you won't immediately lose a plant. A hedge looks awful if one or two plants die and are not replaced.

Prickly pear makes a good hedge, too, but it needs to be planted in a double row to provide the thickness that keeps animals out. There are several kinds to choose from; even the "smooth" ones have irritating fuzzy hairs.

A hedge of ocotillo will define an area, keep people out, and even keep dogs in, but it won't give you much privacy. On the other hand, ocotillo requires almost no maintenance. Its stems are leafless most of the year; the whole planting looks dead until a rain stimulates leaves to shoot out. The leaves die and drop just as quickly when the soil moisture dries out. Nevertheless, a hedge of ocotillo adds an artistic touch to your property if you have the right kind of house and desert vegetation. It looks silly with a lawn and flower beds in front of an "eastern" brick house.

HEDGES FOR A SOLID SCREEN

Pyracantha, privet, xylosma, sour orange, oleander, Arizona rosewood, Russian olive, and saltbush all grow thickly if they are watered adequately (they are listed here in descending order

Prickly pear can make an effective hedge, owing to its density and its thorns. The mature hedge requires almost no water and little maintenance, other than a light pruning (of whole pads) every other year.

Pictured here is a combination fence and hedge composed primarily of ocotillo. The plant is leafless most of the year, reducing its value as a privacy screen, but its thorns make an effective physical barrier all year round.

of thirstiness). All grow to eight feet and all can be trimmed.

Plants that screen, but need a support

If you want to cover a chainlink or open board fence, you can use honeysuckle, Carolina jasmine, or the Tombstone (Lady Banks) rose. All have flowers. Jasmine's yellow flowers are the first to appear each spring.

There's something to remember when you train a vining plant on a chainlink or open fence: don't weave the new shoots in and out of the links or spaces. It seems a neat thing to do at the time—to spread the new growth and hold it in place through a hole—but in a year's time you'll find the plant so firmly attached to the fence that you won't be able to take it down without breaking it, and you may want to move the fence or repair it in the years to come. Keep your plants all on one side of the fence and tie up the new shoots with string.

Don't use deciduous plants if you want a screen

A number of plants produce abundant foliage during the spring and summer—mulberry and grapes are two examples—but, because they drop their leaves in winter, they don't make a good hedge if your prime purpose is to screen out the public or to hide something ugly across the way.

TO TRIM OR NOT TO TRIM?

Trimming gives a neat appearance, but it's work that has to be done frequently, as often as once a week in spring and fall. If you forget, or fall behind, you lose the neatness straightaway.

A trimmed hedge complements the straight lines of a house and walkways. (To line a walkway with a little hedge to keep people on the concrete, try boxwood or myrtle. This kind of

(Above) When a hedge gets old, the upper branches shade the lower branches, which lose their leaves. That means you lose the privacy you wanted when you planted the hedge.

(Below) An old hedge often will send out basal shoots when sunlight manages to penetrate to ground level. This is your chance to cut back the top growth and rejuvenate your hedge, before the new shoots are shaded out.

hedge is formal and will need to be trimmed frequently.) A trimmed hedge suggests formality, order, and discipline. It is out of place if you have a natural desert landscape.

Any hedge will need to be trimmed occasionally if you want to make it thick and impenetrable. Otherwise, the natural growth tends to range upward and outward in thin stalks. Cutting these back stimulates side shoots, which makes the hedge more solid.

You can keep a hedge looking natural if you simply remove the very adventurous shoots.

(Above) Cut an old hedge back just before a growth spurt in the spring—not in the summer, when heat and strong sunlight will burn the newly exposed bark and new leaves, nor late in the fall, when tender growth encouraged by pruning will be vulnerable to frost.

(Below) Ragged growth like this on a formal hedge indicates that it's time for a trim. To delay longer will be to waste the plants' energy in upward growth, when what you want is for the hedge to thicken up by in-filling. Regular pruning promotes in-filling.

To trim a tall hedge properly—which means leaving the base broad and the top narrower—requires the use of a template. The base of the template rests against a string strung in a straight line along the base of the hedge, and the upright leg leans slightly inward. This yields both a straight line along the length of the hedge and a slight inward slope from bottom to top, which helps keep lower growth from being killed by lack of sunlight.

Don't snip away to make a straight side and top; instead, cut back the longest top and side branches close to where they start. This will reduce the hedge's size without affecting its natural outline.

HOW TO PLANT A HEALTHY HEDGE

If you want good growth, first prepare the soil for a hedge as you would for a rose bush (see Chapters 6 and 7 for methods and materials). There's often a compelling reason to have a hedge—to hide something unsightly, to keep your sunbathing to yourself, and so on—so don't take short cuts, even if you are in a hurry to have it complete. Carry out all the steps; don't skimp.

Some planting times are better than others

The cooler weather of spring and fall puts less stress on plants, unless they are desert plants, in which case the warmer soil of May, June, and September are better for root establishment. Try to avoid the very hot weather of midsummer and the cold soil of midwinter.

Spacing determines how quickly a hedge will be functional

Because most of us want a quick result, close planting usually is preferred. Close is a relative term. It might mean 4 feet for oleanders, 3 feet

To give yourself a lot of work, decide on a trimmed hedge like the one above. To save yourself a lot of work, let your hedge grow as naturally as possible.

for privet and jojoba, or as close as 18 inches for myrtle. As a rule, however, close planting means 3 feet apart—it's seldom worth planting vigorous growers any closer—and economical spacing means 6 feet apart.

If you want to make a really thick hedge, you can plant two rows 3 feet apart, staggering the plants every 4 feet. The thought behind this measure is that the individual plants crowd one another into tall growth. Unfortunately, this sometimes leads to overshading of the lower parts of the hedge, which results in gaps.

After-care means watering

Keep the soil around the roots moist at all times. Irrigate by any method you like (Chapter 4 gives you the options), but remember that the purpose is to get the roots growing deeply and widely. Get water down at least 2 feet each time you irrigate. Use your soil probe to be sure. Try to make each irrigation last as long as you can. It doesn't matter if the surface of the soil dries out; the roots aren't on the surface.

THE FIRST YEAR SHOULD BE FERTILIZER-FREE

Because you put a lot of fertilizer and organic matter into the planting hole when backfilling, there should be no need to apply fertilizer during the first year. The main objective during this time is to get good roots growing; they will, if you dig a decent hole and keep the soil moist.

The second year calls for a little pruning and fertilizing

Just before growth starts in the spring, as shown by swelling buds, make sure the plants get plenty of water. The first heavy irrigation of the year should be interrupted halfway through by an application of ammonium nitrate. Scatter the pellets on wet ground on both sides of the hedge and wash them into the soil with the second half

This well-leafed hedge shows the beginnings of a wide top and a narrow base because it has been trimmed "by eye." It needs to be heavily trimmed on the sides to make the base broad and the top narrow.

of the irrigation. Use a pound, or a half-pound if the plants are small, to every hundred square feet along the hedge. (Find the area by multiplying the length of the hedge by 5 feet, which is the distance across the spread of the mature branches and the same as the spread of the roots under the soil.)

At the same time, cut off the top 5 or 6 inches of each plant to stimulate side shoots.

As the hedge grows, pinch it or prune it

Even if you want a tall hedge, keep checking the growth with a light pruning. Each cut will produce side shoots, resulting in a thicker hedge and a stronger one. A light pruning can be made after every 10 or 12 inches of growth to stop your hedge from turning into a few tall shoots, each with a bunch of leaves at its top.

If you leave a hedge entirely to itself, it will become straggly and open at the bottom. Somewhere between untended and closely cropped lies the optimum spread, shape, and appearance for your hedge. The choice is yours.

21 PRUNING TREES AND SHRUBS

Unfortunately, many people lose sight of the reasons for pruning. Too much often is done when little or no pruning should even be considered. As a result, many trees lose their natural appearance. In fact, they often are harmed by enthusiastic chopping.

New tree trimmers sometimes try to impress their customers with overkill. If more wood is taken off, they reason, then the price should go higher. Any tree that obviously has been pruned has not been pruned well. A good pruning job doesn't show; the tree looks natural both before the job and after.

Young shade trees should be allowed to grow to their natural shapes. Removal of the top bud is an interference with that natural growth. Many shade trees are topped in the nursery in the belief that they should have a strong frame-

Chop off large limbs or top a tree and you'll shorten its life, especially if you don't seal the cuts with pruning paint.

A tree's beauty can be destroyed by pruning back to the same point every year. This leads to dense shoot growth and to such fierce competition for light that the shoots grow long and weak and vulnerable to wind damage.

Leave trees alone, except for repairing storm damage and thinning (if necessary), and they'll live long and prosper.

work of branches that will turn into main limbs. That's good thinking for fruit trees, but the removal of a terminal bud on a young shade tree simply starts a series of problems. If you are lucky enough to own a young tree—perhaps a volunteer brought in by the wind or by a bird—treasure it, don't top it. It will provide you with a balanced series of branches and a beautiful winter silhouette of graceful limbs.

Topping a tree causes a spurt of growth in new side branches, to which the natural human response is to cut back the vigorous growth. This results in more growth, which calls for more cutting back. The nursery has started you on a routine that appears to invigorate the tree. In fact, a tree treated this way becomes too shaded by its own foliage, which makes it weak.

To restore natural shape to a tree that has had too much annual cutting back, stop cutting back and start thinning out. Where there are three or

This sort of thoughtless tree trimming amounts to vandalism. There's *no* good reason for treating a tree this way.

If the previous example amounts to vandalism (and it does), then this one amounts to murder. This tree's useful life is over.

four parallel limbs, reduce them to one or two. This will let light in, and the limbs will develop side shoots from their dormant buds. If there are knobs at the ends of limbs caused by pruning back to the same place year after year, cut below the knobs. You'll get a lot of side shoots as a result; be quick to thin these out before they get too crowded.

THE BENEFITS OF JUDICIOUS PRUNING

Pruning makes a tree look better if the tree is one-sided, has unwanted twin trunks, or suffers from congested growth.

Pruning makes a tree safer. Thinning out dense foliage that obstructs the wind lets the storm blow through the tree.

Pruning maintains the size of a plant. Junipers under windows, trees under power lines, and roses close to a walkway often get too big. It's really a planting mistake, but pruning helps to correct it.

Pruning maintains the shape of a plant. Neat hedges require constant pruning. Sculptured hedges must be trimmed each and every week. A lopsided tree needs to have the "extra" limb removed to recover a balanced shape.

Pruning repairs damaged limbs. By correctly removing broken pieces, you ensure that insects and diseases don't invade the damaged parts; a clean cut and a spray of pruning paint protect the exposed wood.

Pruning removes diseased and infested limbs, such as gall on oleander and stem borers in shade trees.

Pruning removes worthless dead wood, and a cut into live wood stimulates new growth from dormant buds.

No one can truthfully say that this is a beautiful tree, but many people follow this bad example in the belief that because others do it, it must be the right thing to do. It isn't.

Why was this tree beheaded? Whatever the reason, it was a poor one. The tree's natural growth and development have been stunted.

Pruning, as of roses, crepe myrtle, wisteria, and bird of paradise, creates new productive shoots that give larger blooms. Hedge shearing is a kind of pruning, too.

Pruning is not, or should not be, a contest to see who can cut the most off a tree in the shortest possible time over the largest number of years, but that's what it looks like in some neighborhoods.

There are two kinds of pruning

Major pruning—the removal of limbs and large branches—should be done during the dormant months. In the case of storm damage, however, prune as soon as possible after the damage is done.

Minor pruning—hedge trimming, cuts designed to yield maximum flower production, and removal of light new growth—is best done just before, or at the beginning of, a growth spurt.

Use sharp tools

Hand pruners are of two types: anvil and scissors. Scissor pruners are preferred, since they don't crush the bark and you can get closer to the work if you have crowded branches.

Long-handled loppers give additional leverage on twigs up to an inch thick, but they won't do a good job unless they are sharp. The cutting action should be smooth: if you have to strain and bend the handles, you're trying to cut something too large or too hard.

For larger jobs, use a handsaw. An ordinary bow saw is good for many situations, but use a pruning saw in a restricted space. A pruning saw has a tapered blade that lets you get close to the job. Because the teeth are set backwards when compared with a carpenter's saw, it gets a bite on the pull stroke instead of the push stroke. This is easier on you and on the tree. Saws need to be sharp if they are to do a good job.

In all cases, avoid tearing the bark off the tree.

Prune when the tree is dormant

Try not to cut limbs when leaves are on the tree and the sap is moving. That sap is sticky and sugary, just like maple syrup, and it is food for fungi and bacteria that are blowing around in the air. Pruning paint from a spray can seals the vulnerable ends of the branches and keeps parasites out.

Use a spray of pruning paint on every cut

The controversy over pruning paint, which originated in the eastern states, recently has reached the desert. Some tree trimmers, having been given an excuse to avoid this fiddly part of the operation, have enthusiastically adopted the idea that wounds should not be protected. They are not considering local conditions. In the desert, the sun is fierce, the air is dry, and the very trees are different.

It is true that old-fashioned materials, such as *Stockholm Tar*, don't work well in the desert. They dry out and shrink to form a loose-fitting cap over a wound, which offers no protection at all. Besides, they are not easy to apply properly.

Here's a case in which corrective pruning should have been done long ago. A low limb like this is a hazard to passersby and the tree is out of balance.

On the other hand, pruning paint from a spray can satisfactorily soaks into the newly cut wood, providing in-depth protection without hurting the cambium layer, the tissue that naturally seals a wound.

Unsprayed plants offer ample evidence of the drying that causes bark to peel back, of invasion by bacteria that cause slime flux, and of branch die-back owing to sooty canker. These afflictions hurt plants and can even kill them. Unprotected pruning cuts invariably are the starting point for these problems.

CUTTING BACK VS. THINNING OUT

We've already mentioned that it's best not to remove a tree's terminal bud. In tall trees, this op-

Aleppo pines are notorious for sending out low side branches. Don't let them get this big before pruning.

eration is called heading back or topping. Tall trees bend and sway during stormy weather, sometimes alarmingly so. It's then that a nervous homeowner is most vulnerable to unscrupulous tree trimmers. They ask, "What would you do if that tree fell on your neighbor's house, car, child?" They recommend immediate topping to make the tree safe, and their arguments *sound* reasonable.

Topping certainly reduces the height of the tree, but it also stimulates rapid growth of side shoots at the top of the tree, which soon grow thicker than the original foliage. Now the wind can't blow through the tree; instead it pushes against it. Under such conditions storm damage is all but certain. Don't have your trees topped.

Close, clean cuts will soon heal over. In this example, bark already has begun to grow over the wound.

Even a tall tree produces new growth according to a pattern determined by its surroundings. It grows well under optimum conditions; all its parts are in balance and growth is moderate. Only when a tree is overirrigated and overfertilized will it break out of that harmony with its surroundings.

A good tree trimmer knows this and does his corrective work in moderation. If he wants to reduce the height of a tree, he looks at the topmost branches and follows them down to where they come out of the limb or trunk. Then he makes a clean cut close to the trunk. Tall branches are removed, the excessive height is gone, and the tree still looks natural.

He has reduced the height by a process known as thinning. This has the merit of maintaining air space around each branch. He leaves no stubs where dormant side buds might break out to give crowded foliage later.

Remember that a properly pruned tree looks untouched. There are no stubs to show you where limbs used to be, there is no white wood

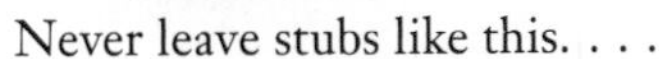

Never leave stubs like this. . . .

Or like this. They not only are unsightly, they also are potential entry points for disease.

on the cuts to show the inside of the trunk (tree paint covers them), and the beauty of the tree has been preserved.

Prune a young tree to raise its branches

If you eventually want to sit under a shade tree, you need to begin an early program of removing the lower branches.

There's no exact stage when you do this; you have to use good judgment. Do it too soon and you'll weaken the tree. Do it too late, so that you have to cut out strong limbs, and you've let the tree waste its energy; you're also throwing away good strong growth that you'd like to have higher up.

A good guide is to cut out low side branches when they are as thick as your thumb. Don't remove more than three such branches at any one time. In other words, remove them gradually to keep the tree growing at a regular pace. You want to avoid a young tree's responding to heavy cuts with great spurts of growth.

Cut close to the trunk. Leave no stubs. Use tree paint from a spray can.

Don't be hard on desert trees

You should go gently on all trees, treating them like a friend that needs a nudge instead of a push. This is especially true of desert trees, which are naturally somewhat untidy in their appearance. Don't try to prune them into formal shapes. They won't like it, your neighbors won't like it, and, sooner or later, you won't like it.

Don't fight the olive tree

Olives are notoriously vigorous. They send out a thicket of suckers at the base of the trunk; if you cut them off to keep things tidy, they send out even more. This is a habit of olive trees. Some are more persistent than others.

One way to get around the problem and still win the fight is to trim those basal suckers into a sort of bench or disk around the trunk. You have to keep trimming it if you want a tidy effect. Some gardeners disagree with this advice, arguing that the bench hides the tree's handsome gnarled trunk. You be the judge.

Storm-damaged limbs should be pruned out as soon as the damage is noticed. Make a clean cut close to the trunk and seal the wound with a spray of pruning paint.

You can't stop olive trees from growing a lot of basal suckers. One way to get around the problem is to trim the suckers into a deliberate shape. Whether this is any improvement over the natural growth is your call.

Repeated trimming reduces flower production

Earlier on, we mentioned that you need to prune roses in order to get blooms because flowers come at the ends of new growth. However, if you keep pruning roses as if they were a hedge, you'll always be cutting off flower buds. They never get a chance to develop. It's the same with citrus trees, bougainvillea, oleander, bird of paradise, and other plants with flowers at the ends of new growth.

Prune once, then let the growth develop its flowers and fruit. Prune again when flowering is finished.

If the repeated pruning happens to be done by a winter freeze, you're not likely to get flowers from your plants next spring when growth starts again. Depending on the kind of plant and the severity of the cold, you'll get new leaves, but that's all.

Frost is Mother Nature's way of pruning

Don't be upset if a frost lightly damages your old plants; it's just the outer growth that gets nipped. Once you're over the initial shock, it's obvious that you couldn't have done a better trimming job yourself.

In fact, a light freeze every winter is the best way to keep your plants to a reasonable size. It's an automatic adjustment. A tree that grows too big too quickly has more tender growth, which is more readily killed. Conversely, a tree that grows slowly has harder wood that is less affected by the cold. It doesn't need trimming so much, and it doesn't get it.

22 PALM TREE CARE

Palm trees are a potentially beautiful part of our desert landscapes. Unfortunately, many of them either are neglected by people who mistake them for desert plants, and so don't water them, or they are abused by overenthusiastic tree trimmers.

Palm trees should have a great green canopy, like a fluffy ball on top of a stick. The leaves should be bright and shiny, reflecting the sunlight. If they are gray-green and dull, with brown edges and dead ends, the tree is not getting enough water. Such palm trees don't die; they hang on, giving the false impression that they are arid-land plants. Like old soldiers, they just fade away. Their leaves get browner and browner and fewer new ones are produced.

DON'T PLANT PALM TREES IN COLD PLACES

All palms are frost-tender to one degree or another. Those planted in low-lying parts of the landscape can have their outer leaves killed by one night of frost during a cold winter (the leaves will be replaced by new growth in May and June). A young Queen palm, which is more tender than a Washingtonia, may be covered with a blanket during a cold night, but the larger palms are hard to cover.

Palms should be cared for as you would care for citrus, bougainvillea, and other frost-tender plants: by reducing irrigation frequency and by stopping fertilizing in September as the temperatures drop. We want palms to be ready for the first frost of November, and that means slowing their growth down to a stop.

PALM TREES ARE SUMMER GROWERS, SO INDULGE THEM IN THE HOT MONTHS

Palm trees grow vigorously from May to August, if you look after them. That means giving them good deep irrigations and monthly applications of ammonium sulphate (see Chapter 7 for more on fertilizer use).

Palm trees too often are watered incorrectly. They should get a three-foot deep soaking in a six-foot wide basin every ten or twelve days, rather than a shallow watering once a week. Use

Date palms are handsome landscape trees, but don't expect them to bear fruit unless you live in the hotter, lower deserts.

These gorgeous palms would look silly with fewer leaves.

your soil probe often. When the probe meets resistance because the soil is dry, it's time to water again.

Summer rains coincide with palm tree growth cycles

Summer rains should come at the same time that palm trees want to grow, and it helps to catch the rain in wide shallow basins around the trees. If insufficient rain falls—your soil probe will tell you—be generous with watering; otherwise, that growth urge will not be fulfilled.

Summer storms are not gentle

Palm trees blow around like crazy when a desert storm builds, even if no rain comes. But palm trees take it—it would take a hurricane to break them—so don't be frightened; all that can come down is some dead seed stalks. Palm trees never, or almost never, blow over.

Then there's lightning. To a lightning bolt looking for a contact with earth, a tall palm tree is the most prominent item in a landscape. You can't prevent lightning from hitting your tree, so keep your fingers crossed and hope for the best. Take comfort in the fact that if a palm is struck it doesn't fall down.

Once a palm tree is hit by lighting, it's the end. A palm tree has only one bud. Its leaves may stay green for a while, giving you false hope, but it should be taken down by an expert tree person as soon as possible.

A fungus can kill a palm's single bud in a wet summer

That soft-tissued single bud is vulnerable to a fungus disease during a wet summer. If the crown of the plant is always wet because of continuous rains and the fungus spores are blowing in the wind, you might lose the tree. There's little danger in a dry summer, because the fungus needs constant moisture to invade the soft tissues of the growing point. If, at the end of summer, you notice the crown of your palm is bending over, it's too late; there's no treatment. As with a lightning strike, it was bad luck.

There is no cure once the disease has struck, but you might slosh a solution of copper Bordeaux into the top of the palm before the weather turns humid. Use two tablespoons of the blue powder (available at nurseries) in a pint of water to get the right strength; slosh it in the center of the tuft of upright leaves at the very top of the tree. If the tree is tall, you'll need to

Palm trees have a tropically luxuriant look even in the desert, provided they are left unmolested.

This trio of palms has been left alone for years. Their skirts of dead fronds don't harm the trees, but they can be a fire hazard and they sometimes harbor yellowjackets. If you trim a palm's skirts, don't do it in the summer; the previously shaded trunk will be scorched by the fierce summer sun.

(Above) These palm trees have been well trimmed. They retain adequate foliage and leaf stalks have been cut close to the trunk.

(Middle) These trees exhibit the cone-shaped trunk that results from regular excessive frond removal.

(Bottom) Here's another example of what overenthusiastic skinning and frond removal can do. Instead of growing in a uniform column, this trunk has developed an hour-glass figure.

Here is a group of well-formed palms before an overzealous trimming.

And here is the same group after trimming. The green leaves in the foreground should have been left on the tree.

have this done by a professional with special equipment. If it keeps raining, you'll have to apply the treatment repeatedly. There's no guarantee, but you might consider it worth a try.

While you're at it, have the professional do a little more

While the pro is up there, have him remove any developing seed branches. These are going to fall out when they mature and make a mess on the patio and in the pool. By getting rid of them now, you'll avoid a plague of seedlings next year. There's really no need for the pro to do anything else, although he may want to, in order to earn more money.

DON'T MUTILATE YOUR PALM TREES!

Palm trees receive too much attention from hard-working, unskilled workers who want to cut out a lot of leaves and to remove last year's leaf bases. The palm tree doesn't benefit from either of these practices.

Dead brown leaves hanging from a palm tree may be unsightly—although many of us believe they add to the beauty of a palm—but they don't hurt the tree in any way. In fact, they help shade the trunk from strong sunshine. In the same way, the old leaf bases clasp the trunk and give it protection. For the tree's sake, it's better to leave them.

Palm trees need to have a lot of green leaves on top. If you don't like the idea of a palm tree in a skirt, it's easy to cut the dead leaves off. But never cut leaves that are showing any sign of green. Green leaves are working for the tree, manufacturing sugars from the energy of the sun. The tree needs lots of green leaves.

Besides, a palm tree that has had its leaves removed looks like a newly-shorn sheep, embarrassingly naked and uncomfortable. It doesn't look like a palm tree, but like a caricature of a shaving brush.

Unfortunately, we have too many displays in public places of overdone trimming jobs that lead us astray. We tell ourselves that professional workers must know what they are doing. It's understandable, but unfortunate.

This palm has been repeatedly punctured by the spiked boots of irresponsible tree trimmers. As a result, the protective bark is beginning to fall off.

It's the same with "skinning" a palm tree: it's often overdone in an effort to impress the customer. If you feel you *must* remove old leaf stalks, use a linoleum knife to make horizontal cuts into the trunk at the base of the twin stalks. Cut about a quarter-inch deep, no deeper. The broad paperlike base comes off with a slight tug. Keep cutting around the trunk, a little higher each time. As you go, you'll notice that the underlying color of the trunk becomes paler; stop when it is a light tan. You've gone too far when it turns a creamy color.

As you go higher, you're removing protection from the hot sun along with the old leaf stalks, so it's not really a job for the summer months. You can too easily expose bark to burns and blisters. This accounts for those palm trees you see in public places that have trunks of uneven thickness. The thin part is where someone a few years ago got carried away with skinning.

Look at your palm tree climber's boots

Going up a palm tree is a risky thing if you do it yourself, and it costs money if you hire a professional. If you hire someone, he should go up in a hydraulic lift.

Some energetic young men climb the trunk, using spiked boots to maintain a grip. Don't let them! Those spikes jab into the trunk and open it up to infection. If a trimmer must wear climbing boots, let him use those that have serrated bars instead of spikes. The bars are bad enough, but they are far less damaging to the trunk than spikes.

And make sure your tree trimmer is licensed, insured, and bonded. If he falls out of the tree, you shouldn't be held responsible.

23 CARING FOR SAGUAROS, OCOTILLOS, AGAVES, AND PRICKLY PEARS

Although these plants are different from one another, they share a common feature: they are landscape plants that call for very little attention. Together with the chollas, creosote bush, barrel cacti, yuccas, and aloes, they are the arid-land plants *par excellence.*

In undisturbed desert, these plants live in a harmonious mixture of species. They often grow in groups, so that the larger, older ones shelter the smaller, younger ones; a saguaro, for example, eventually will grow through a mesquite tree that nursed it as a baby. When you use

Bats are among the saguaro's best friends. The flying mammals are the principal pollinators of the giant cactus's waxy white flowers, which, if pollinated, give way to fruits that burst to display a scarlet interior studded with tiny black seeds.

Crested saguaros are unusual, and so command higher prices among plant collectors. This leads to their being "rustled" and illegally uprooted. Don't buy any landscape cactus unless it bears a tag testifying that it has been legitimately dug up.

The base of this saguaro rotted because annual flowers were planted—and watered—at its feet. This cactus will die.

This old saguaro is strong and healthy, despite the numerous "apartments" carved in its trunk by woodpeckers. Don't try to patch or plug holes like these. The dry desert air will allow them to scab over naturally, and the snug cavity that results will shelter a nesting bird.

arid-land plants in your landscaping, try to imitate this association of plant species. Look at the natural desert and you'll find it rich in variety.

These plants are quiet and retiring most of the year, but each is full of surprises. The saguaro presents a mass of white flowers at its top, followed by scarlet starburst fruits in early summer. Ocotillos spend most of their time as bare whiplike sticks, but they display red flowers at their tips in the spring and are quickly covered with ephemeral leaves after a rain. Agaves seem motionless for years until, one spring, they send out high-speed flower stalks that reach 15 feet in a month. Prickly pear, cholla, and barrel cacti produce a most amazing display of bright flowers in a rainbow of vivid colors.

What's more, they do it all themselves, without irrigation, or pruning, or fertilizing, or spraying, or any of the perpetual fussing we call landscape maintenance. Good management of these plants is based on a number of "don'ts."

DON'T DIG UP DESERT PLANTS WITHOUT A PERMIT

All the plants you see in the desert belong to someone; they are not there for you to help yourself. Those on the roadside belong to the state department of transportation. Those beyond the fence belong to the owner of the land, who may be a private person, an Indian nation, or the state or federal government.

State laws protect many species, requiring anyone who moves a protected plant to carry a statement from the landowner that he permits their removal. Each plant must carry an official tag while being transported, and the tag must stay on the plant after it has been planted. If you buy a native plant from a nursery you will see this special tag. It shows that the plant has been acquired legally. Don't remove it.

The laws vary from state to state, so get the appropriate information from your state's agricultural commissioner.

DON'T BUY A NATIVE PLANT THAT IS NOT TAGGED

Don't buy a protected plant from roadside or flea market vendors unless official tags are attached to the plants. There's a lot of plant rustling going on because of the value of these plants; don't encourage it by joining the black market. Besides, plants at these places are not always bargains. They might have been carelessly

The thick, asparaguslike shoot sent skyward by the agave signals the end of the plant's life. There's not a thing you can do about it. If you chop it down, the plant still will die, to be replaced by the "pups" that have sprung up around it or by plantlets borne on the stalk itself, depending on the species.

This little blemish on the trunk of a saguaro is the beginning of the end. Bacteria have gained entry through an open wound. Quick action is required. Scoop out the black, rotted flesh and sanitize the cavity with a rinse of 10 percent bleach and a smear of Bordeaux paste.

This rocky slope shows the kind of soil and situation that saguaros prefer. When you dig a planting hole for cacti you want to open up the soil for root development, not to "improve" the soil with manure and fertilizers.

dug up in a hurry and damaged. The damage doesn't show until several months after planting, and guarantees are seldom provided by the sellers.

DON'T KILL THESE PLANTS WITH KINDNESS

Don't dig a deep planting hole. These plants have shallow roots—perhaps extending only a foot below the surface—but they spread out over a wide area. This suggests that you dig a couple of feet deep and 6 feet wide, but only in the interests of loosening the soil so that roots will grow easily.

Don't mix in steer manure, ammonium phosphate, or sulphur. These plants are attuned to poor fertility and prefer an alkaline soil. Adding sulphur is the worst thing you can do. A handful or two of organic matter, in the form of leaf mold, compost, or peat moss, won't do any harm.

Don't plant in a saucerlike depression where water will collect, and don't plant where there is caliche. These plants will take a lot of water from an occasional heavy rainstorm, but they must have good drainage; otherwise, their roots will rot.

Don't place these plants where they will receive a lot of water from sprinklers serving a lawn or flower beds. Watch out for runoff from house roofs.

Don't use a drip irrigation system on these plants. They need infrequent, wide-area waterings, instead of regular waterings just against the trunk.

Don't grow annual flowers around these plants. Their water needs are not alike.

Don't fertilize these plants. They don't need extra nutrients, and it's a mistake to turn them dark green by using nitrogen.

Don't dig the ground near these plants. They have shallow roots and you can easily chop them if you do more than a light hoeing to remove weeds.

Don't apply weedkilling sterilant chemicals near these plants. Their extensive roots will pick them up and the plants will die.

Don't spray these plants; they are practically unaffected by insects and diseases. Even the nesting holes made by woodpeckers in saguaros should be left to scab over on their own. It's a mistake to plug a hole in the trunk of a damaged saguaro with concrete; let it heal by itself.

Don't prune these plants. Prickly pear pads and stalks break off naturally when they reach a mature size or after frost: the fallen pads grow roots into the soil where they fall. The natural form of prickly pear is a thicket of vigorous young plants on the edges, with a dead center of old stems.

Agaves naturally send out basal shoots to form a dense mass of spiky young plants. These can be removed and planted elsewhere, but it is normal for agaves to grow in clumps; the older central plants die and nourish the youngsters as they disintegrate. Agaves send up a stout central flowerstalk just before they die. There's no point in trying to prolong the life of a prize specimen by cutting this stalk. The plant will die anyway.

Chollas grow in an untidy manner. An out-of-balance plant eventually will drop the heavy side to the ground to begin new roots where it falls. Don't go near a cholla. There's no need for any maintenance.

Don't do *anything* to a saguaro. There's no need.

Don't cut back an ocotillo. They are meant to have long thin branches. An alternative name for them is coachman's whip, or buggywhip cactus, and that's what they are supposed to look like. It's a mistake to cut them back; you won't get more flowers, as you would from cutting back a rose bush.

(Above) Saguaros can heal themselves if given a chance. They need dryness in order to keep bacteria and fungi from attacking their succulent interiors. The edges of this wound have healed but they will not grow together, as happens in plants with bark.

(Middle) When a saguaro runs short of water, it shrinks. This is a perfectly normal mechanism to temporarily overcome hard times. When the rains come again it will absorb moisture and fatten up.

(Bottom) This is what a saguaro looks like in a year of good rains. There is no need to irrigate such a healthy plant.

(Left) A dying saguaro seldom falls over, at least not at first. It just disintegrates. Eventually, the only thing left standing will be the bare ribs.

(Above right) Many homeowners prefer to leave the remains of a dead saguaro standing for as long as possible, delighting in the skeleton as natural sculpture. Saguaro ribs are much sought after, however, and sometimes are "collected" by unscrupulous people.

DO USE COMMON SENSE

Do start off by planting on a mound for good drainage, rather than in a depression.

Do plant in well-drained soils.

Do plant in the sunshine. These desert plants won't do well in the shade of a house or under a shade tree.

Do use a strong jet of water to squirt off cochineal scale from prickly pear pads. That white stuff that looks like wet tissue paper is a small insect that sucks the vitality from the plant; if left unattended, it will kill the plant.

Do treat soft rots in the succulent trunks of saguaros. (This is an exception to the rule above.) Bacteria thrive on the sugary juices of the plant. Entry is gained through a wound caused by a bird or vandals, and damage is quick. Scoop out the wet, black, rotted flesh and put it in a plastic bag so that you don't infect the neighborhood. Keep scooping—a spoon is bet-

If you're feeling neighborly, nip off the sharp points of an agave planted near a walkway.

ter than a pointed screwdriver—until you see firm green flesh. Then spray on a solution of 10 percent bleach with water once a day for three days. Let the wound heal over by itself, which it will do in the dry desert air if the cavity does not collect and hold rainfall.

Do irrigate these plants during long periods of dry summer heat if they show wilting, as in the case of yuccas and agaves, or shrivelling, as in the case of prickly pears. Don't pay the same attention to such signs during the winter. These plants lose water in a frost-resisting tactic. Diluting their body fluids with an irrigation weakens their resistance to cold.

Do read Chapter 15 for the best way to transplant.

THE SECRET TO SUCCESS WITH SUCCULENT DESERT PLANTS: LEAVE THEM ALONE

Don't fuss over them. They do very well with a minimum of attention. The difficulty is in disciplining yourself not to feel sorry for them. Don't go out to help; sympathetic irrigations will kill them.

AGAVE WEEVILS AND ALOE MITES: TWO MORE EXCEPTIONS TO THE RULE

There's not much you can do when the agave snout-nosed weevil strikes. The larvae enter the plant at ground level and destroy the juicy base, preventing the roots from supplying the plant with moisture. Most people miss the very first signs of distress, and when they see the obvious wilt—the lower leaves making a flat rosette on the ground—it's too late to do anything. The damage has been done.

The plant should be dug up, together with any grubs and adults, and removed so that nearby plants are not infested.

Even after the parent plant has died, the persistent agave stalk can be quite dramatic. The dead stalk makes a good hanger for bird feeders or holiday lights.

There's some satisfaction, at least, in treating nearby plants in an attempt to protect them. Start with the older plants, which have gathered sugars during their lifetimes in readiness for the growth of their flower stalks; it's the plants with sugars that interest the adult flying beetle. The beetle lays her eggs at ground level, where they hatch and burrow into the flesh of the plant.

Dilute liquid *Diazinon* with water according to the directions for white grubs; you won't find agave snout-nosed weevil in the list of pests printed on the label. Slowly pour the diluted mixture over the top of the plant so that it trickles down, leaf by leaf, until it soaks the ground at the base of the plant. The liquid will find its way into any beetle holes on the sides of the plant, and with luck will kill any grubs inside. The water reaching the ground will irrigate the plant and enable it to grow away from a slight damage.

The best times for this treatment are April or May and September, when conditions are favorable for insect activity. There's little point in applying it during the dormancy of hot summer and freezing winter. There's no point in applying it after the agave is flat on the ground; you're too late.

The Achilles heel of aloes is a tiny mite that chews on new growth, creating grotesque bumpy leaves and flower stalks. Because aloes grow in clumps, the mite finds it easy to move from one plant to another and to do a lot of damage, or at least to create an unsightly mess.

Spraying with chemicals has little or no effect. The best thing to do is to pull out the infested plants and haul them away before other plants are contaminated.

One last exception to the rule

Aloes are more sensitive to sunlight than agaves are, and so grow better in filtered shade than in bright sunshine. They also are more frost-tender and will be severely damaged by a few hours of temperatures at 28 degrees. A mature plant will recover and grow again when spring returns.

24 Hard Work and Some Disappointments
ROSES IN THE DESERT

Roses are beautiful. They are the most popular flower of gardeners and non-gardeners alike, so it's no surprise that roses are bestsellers, too. Everyone wants to grow them.

Growing roses in the desert is a challenge. You may be inspired to try it by nostalgic childhood memories of grandma's rose garden, or by a desire to flex your gardening muscles, or to join the fray on the battlefield of the flower shows. But even after a lot of effort, the roses you grow in the desert are not really like the ones you knew before. The buds don't stay tight, but quickly "blow" out into open cabbagelike balls because of the heat. The edges of the petals blacken with frost, and scorch with the hot dry air. There's little fragrance and the colors fade. The reds wash out and the whites have a tinge of green to them in summer. Yet we keep trying, year after year.

Growing roses in the desert is a task that involves all those things we must do when we try to grow imported plants. We have to completely alter the environment to suit a particular plant's needs, and then we are not entirely successful. Here is another reminder that we really ought to select plants that are suited to the desert environment, rather than attempting to alter the environment to suit the plant. If you are determined to have roses, despite the odds, read on.

SELECT AN APPROPRIATE SITE

Summer heat and bright sunshine tell us to plant roses on the east or north sides of a building, where they will enjoy morning sun and be sheltered from afternoon extremes. Don't plant roses directly under the shade of trees or roof overhangs; these places are too dark and cause the plants to stretch toward the light, wasting their energy. They will be weakened in the effort and become susceptible to mildew.

Mild winters allow roses to grow vigorously in the cooler months, but a sudden cold spell can nip the tender growth of new leaves and damage the petals of the flowers. If you live in a cold part of town, provide roses a sheltered place where a cold wind won't get at them.

Roses grow during the short seasons of fall and spring. In September, after a blasting twelve weeks of summer, they revive and bloom nicely until mid-December, when a few days of frost may check their exuberance. After such a setback, the severity of which depends on the number of freezing nights, they resume growth in mid-January and produce flowers until May or June, when they again go dormant in the heat. Half the year they are growing, half the year they are not.

Better blooms are produced in the fall, when the soil is warm and the air is cooling, than during the spring, when the soil is cold and air temperatures are rising.

ROSES ARE NOT ALIKE!

Most of our modern rose varieties come from Europe and were developed for planting in the cooler parts of this country. There are hundreds of them, but only a few have characteristics appropriate to the desert; even these owe their suitability to pure happenstance, not to design.

One of the characteristics we value in roses is

The six photos grouped here depict three days in the life of a rose in bloom in the desert. A: Monday morning brings three buds. B: Tuesday morning yields one perfect flower. C: Tuesday afternoon: the desert heat has accelerated the flower's opening. D: Tuesday evening: the flower is all but spent. E: Wednesday morning: there's not much left. The faded blossom should be cut to make way for the side buds. F: The side buds will yield a nice progression of flowers, but they won't last long.

resistance to mildew. Never plant a rose that is prone to mildew. Overall, the pink-flowered kinds seem to do best. The deep reds fade and the whites turn greenish during the hottest months. The yellows fade, too. In the desert, the All-American annual selections usually disappoint, and their reputation doesn't outlive the initial fanfare.

For simple landscape purposes, the "wild" single-flowered types that are used as rootstocks grow most easily, but they are low in rosarians' estimation. If the top of a rosebush dies, for one reason or another, the rootstock often survives and grows vigorously with plenty of blooms, especially if it is adapted to alkaline soils, as is the single-petalled red rose Dr. Huey.

ROSES NEED A LOT OF WATER

Keep the soil moist all the time, because roses have shallow roots. Deep watering encourages deep rooting, and basin flooding is the best way to achieve this. Roses will do very well on a drip system, provided you keep the water dripping for a long time to get a deep soak. An organic mulch helps to keep moisture near the surface and keeps the soil cool during the summer months. Don't use a mulch in winter; it's better to have bare soil that allows the sun to warm the root zone.

During the summer, rose leaves take on a pale, chlorotic appearance because people water them too much in an attempt to keep them cool and comfortable. It's hard to hold back on the watering when temperatures reach 120 degrees in the sun. The best routine to follow during summer is to water deeply and let the surface dry out a little before the next irrigation.

ROSES NEED GOOD SOIL PREPARATION AND A LOT OF FERTILIZERS

First, dig your planting hole and enrich the backfill as detailed in Chapters 6 and 7.

Twice a year, with September's and February's spurts of growth, scatter ammonium sulphate around the bush at the rate of 2 pounds to every hundred square feet; water it in with a 2-foot-deep irrigation. This will support a rose's vigorous growth.

If there are signs of iron chlorosis, check the soil's moisture before you rush to the nursery and buy iron sulphate. Too wet a soil encourages the pale leaves with dark veins that is the iron deficiency symptom.

The desert summer sun is hard on roses. Give them filtered shade like this, or plant them on the east side of your house for afternoon shade.

The first step in pruning a rosebush is to remove old, thick canes to make way for new growth. Stand back, walk around the plant, and see what needs to be done. In this case, the heavy cane on the left must go.

This is the same bush after pruning. The woody canes to the right and left will be removed next year. Removing them at this pruning would have punished the plant and been counterproductive.

PRUNE ROSES PRIOR TO SPURTS OF GROWTH

Flowers are produced on new growth, and you get new growth when you cut back the old stalks in late August and late January. Don't cut back so heavily as do rose growers in the eastern states. Removing a third or a half of the growth is enough.

Open up the bush's center by cutting out old, woody canes at ground level. Cut close to the ground to remove some outer canes, leaving no more than five as a main framework. Then cut back each outer cane to a bud that points outward. New shoots follow the direction of the buds, so it would be quite a mistake to cut the canes so that all new growth goes back toward the center.

Remember, too, that if you cut high up on the branch, into thin material, the small bud there will produce a small bloom. It's better to cut into a branch that is thicker than a pencil, where a fatter bud can be found: this will give you larger flowers. You'll never get a big flower to grow from a small bud on a thin stalk.

In the desert, there are two spurts of growth, in September and February. Prune just before these bursts of activity. In October, when temperatures are falling, the growth rate of the shoots is slower and the buds are tighter and remain closed longer than do buds in the spring. In other words, the flowers are better. Admittedly, there's a danger of frost spoiling the appearance of winter flowers, but most of us, including visiting family and friends, enjoy our winter gardens more than the summer ones. Roses that develop from a February pruning grow rapidly in the warming weather of May and June, so rapidly that they burst into wide-open flowers without pausing in the bud stage.

Prune hardest in the season whose blooms you prefer. Some rose growers who prune in the spring like to remove all the green leaves from the plant. They say new branch growth begins quicker that way, but it seems a strange thing to do; each and every leaf is needed to capture the sun's energy to make a strong plant.

Fall-pruned roses that grow into a cold winter need protection

Rosebushes grow vigorously after the September pruning in a warm fall. If a sudden frost is brought in by a cold front in November, it means danger. New shoots and flowers are tender and will be blackened by a frost. Protect roses in the same way that you protect citrus trees: cover them on a cold night.

ROSES SUFFER FROM TEXAS ROOT ROT AND CROWN GALL

Both diseases originate in the soil and enter the plant through a wound. Both are killers. Texas root rot usually invades an established bush—the fungus is already in the soil—but crown gall more often comes in the soil of the nursery container or has already invaded the stem at ground

This rosebush is a prime candidate for pruning on several counts, not just because it is leaning rather outlandishly to the right. Before you undertake any delicate surgery on such a plant, level off the overgrown top. This lets you see where to begin.

level before you buy the plant. Inspect your purchases for good root development and possible root congestion, and always carefully inspect the stem at ground level for a crusty black growth about the size of a walnut. Don't contaminate your soil with crown gall bacteria from a nursery purchase. It will remain in the soil for several years and attack later plantings.

PACKAGED OR POTTED: WHICH IS THE BETTER BUY?

Packaged roses are tightly wrapped in plastic. Their roots are squashed together and you can't see them. Break open the plastic to see if any have been broken by the wrapping machine. Their branches are visible through the clear plastic, however, and if the plants lie out in the sun for a few days the greenhouse effect of the wrapping forces the buds to break out into long weak shoots. This is not surprising when you realize that the plants were dug out of cold soil a week or two ago. Sunny desert temperatures, even in January, reach 80 degrees.

There's just a short time in the spring to take advantage of packaged roses, and even then you need to buy the best grade of plants. Packaged roses at bargain prices seldom are good buys.

On the other hand, the more expensive container roses are those that the nursery selected from among its packaged stock and planted in containers. If this was done a day or two ago, there's no advantage in paying more money for a container plant; its roots have not grown at all. Check by lifting the whole thing up by a branch; if the soil mix falls apart and the can drops to the ground, don't pay the higher price for a container plant.

There aren't any packaged roses in the fall; they've all become container plants. Although you'll pay more for them, they are better buys because they've survived the summer, have an extensive root system, and are ready to put out new growth with the return of nice weather. Because fall is the better time to plant, these plants are the better buys. Plant them, prune them, and away they go.

It really isn't advisable to order rose plants through the mail after reading the Sunday newspaper supplements. For one thing, the plants aren't available at the best planting times. For another, those roses usually are someone's mistake; too many were propagated and they have to be got rid of. More important, they are plants intended for the eastern states, where the soils are acid. Their rootstocks are not suitable for our desert alkaline soils. Your local nurseries know best, and they will have specified an appropriate rootstock when they made their order.

Fall is the best time to dig up and move a rosebush

If you can get a "freebie" from a neighbor, or you discover that a bush isn't doing well in too sunny a situation, prune it back, dig it up, and replant it. September is the month to do this. There's more about transplanting in Chapter 15.

SPRING BRINGS APHIDS

As plant growth starts up after the spring pruning, we find another kind of growth keeping pace with it. The temperature encourages aphids and the young growth is soft and tender enough to allow them to feed on the plant juices. You find clusters of them around the buds. Because they give birth to live young, their numbers increase rapidly.

Aphids can be kept in check if you attack them while their numbers are small. Start by squirting water at them; if that doesn't work, try soapy water. If that doesn't work, you have to use chemicals like *Diazinon*, *Malathion*, or *Orthene*.

Some fertilizers incorporate insecticides. The idea is that you "feed" the plants and give them a shot of medicine at the same time. The idea is a good one, but a lot of insecticide is needed for the measure to be effective. Further, since aphids are present for several weeks, a lot of fertilizer—too much—has to be applied to take care of the problem. There's a further danger in that some rose varieties are "allergic" to the systemic chemical; they show side effects of the treatment. (A systemic chemical is one that is transported throughout the plant's system of tubes that carry water and nutrients up and down the stem and branches.)

HOW TO COPE WITH SUMMER STRESS

You can't do much about the high temperatures—often forty consecutive days of temperatures above 100—but you must fight the tendency to overwater in response. This leads to leaf chlorosis and rotting roots, which often kills plants.

By all means make sure that the soil remains moist. It is true that roses will need a lot of watering, but the best measure you can take during summer is to cover the soil with a shading mulch. Soil temperatures can be greatly reduced by a 2-inch-thick layer of organic material. Leaves and straw blow away in the desert, but other materials are suitable: carpet underlay, even a piece of carpet, *new* cooler pads, layers of newspaper, or cardboard. Don't use old cooler pads; they are full of salt and will harm the roots.

A mulch keeps the soil cool and it keeps the soil surface moist. This helps the rosebush, but

(Left) The desert spring is unreliable. A warming trend in February can be followed by a freeze in March, just as flowers start to open. Tender petals are easily damaged by cold nights.

(Center) The warming weather that makes roses grow also encourages insect activity. They like the petals of new flowers, and their chewing can spoil a blossom.

(Right) A few days of strong sun as the petals open will burn them. Some varieties are more susceptible to sunburn than others. Consult your nurseryman.

the improved microclimate also encourages pillbugs, crickets, and earwigs; these are not the rose plant's friends.

Stem borers show up during summer stress periods

If, when you pruned in the spring, you left the ends of the canes open, you offered entry to a flying insect that may have laid an egg on the soft central pith of the stalk. If so, the egg hatched into a grubworm that ate its way down inside the stalk. Its progress becomes very evident during summer. Stalks die back and leaves turn brown, sometimes right down to the ground.

You should immediately cut out the damaged stalk, including the grub itself. Next time you prune, make sure you protect the exposed ends with a dab of Elmer's Glue, nail varnish, or a spray of pruning paint.

The final step in rose pruning is to seal cut branch ends with a spray of pruning paint, nail varnish, white glue, even chewing gum or lipstick. That way you'll keep boring insects from doing the damage seen here.

LEAF-CUTTER BEES CAN BE TROUBLESOME, BUT THEY'RE NO THREAT

These are small, gray, fly-sized bees that build their nests in keyholes, straw ends, and any small opening they can find. A few eggs are laid at the end of the tunnel, which is packed with fresh green leaves. These leaves may come from rosebushes or from other plants.

The damage shows up as neat holes on the edges of leaves, giving them the appearance of Swiss cheese. At first it's a puzzle; there's no perpetrator in sight and spraying has no effect. If you are patient and watch quietly, you'll see the little bee fly in, quickly chomp out a circle, and fly off with a piece of leaf as big as itself in five seconds flat.

The leaf's appearance is spoiled, but the damage is minimal—just cosmetic—and there's no reason to get angry about it. Once the nest has been built, the stealing will stop.

DIAGNOSING FLOWER BUD DAMAGE

Young buds are delicate. They are easily damaged by cold, heat, and dryness, as well as by insects.

If the point of the bud seems to have been eaten off to give an even, level, blunt end, the damage has been done by grasshoppers, thrips, or nitidulids. They simply chew off the edges. Frost and heat, on the other hand, scorch the tender paperlike petals, leaving a blackened stub.

Sprays of *Diazinon* or *Malathion* give a small degree of protection from insects. The problem is that you need to get poison on the insect itself; there's not much point in spraying the flower bud in anticipation of the insect coming along later. Besides, the poison discolors the delicate petals. There's no easy solution.

ROSES ARE A LOT OF WORK, AND THE REWARDS ARE ELUSIVE

If you like roses and don't mind a lot of work seasoned with a dash of anxiety, you'll want to persevere in your efforts to grow them. You'll hear of experts who are successful and who are happy with their fifty different rosebushes.

But if you want to conserve your energy and keep your frustration level low, here's an easy way out. In the fall, as soon as the weather cools, buy rosebushes in five-gallon cans. Plant them in the best possible place (maybe it's in a portable half whiskey barrel) and grow them during the best time of the year. Protect them during frosty weather (you can move the barrel to a warm spot on the patio) and they will give you blooms until the hot weather arrives in June. Then you throw them away. Start again in the fall with a fresh planting. This program will save you, and the plants, from the rigors of summer, which is an unproductive time for roses anyway. It won't work with the large varieties or the climbing roses, because they need plenty of time to get established and to produce flowers. It will work very well with the quicker-growing miniatures.

This idea will horrify rosarians. Don't tell them where you read it! If they challenge you about it, tell them it's for the common man, not for experts who grow roses for years and years.

25 LANDSCAPING WITH CITRUS

Even if you don't like to eat oranges, grapefruits, or lemons, the varied foliage of citrus trees is attractive. Citrus trees look solid and, because they are evergreen, they provide a cozy privacy to a patio, effectively screening out unsightly things beyond your fence.

It's a pity that citrus trees don't make good shade trees; they are too small for that. Even when you make space by removing the lower branches, you don't get enough room for a patio table. Citrus trees are naturally low-branched and they don't look right when you prune them to look like lollipops on a stick.

What's the best kind of citrus to plant? The kind you like to eat is the simplest answer, but there's a bit more to it.

CITRUS TREES WON'T THRIVE IN COLD PLACES

Winter temperatures determine what kind of citrus to plant, too. If you live in a cold part of town that consistently has freezing nights during the winter, you should forget about citrus. Remember that they are subtropical plants and are sure to be damaged, and perhaps killed, by the dozen or so freezing nights we can expect each winter.

Find out what your winter temperatures have been in the past. Don't go by the official records; they tell you what happened at the airport weather station. If there aren't any records on paper, you can find records in the neighborhood. Nearby houses with lemon trees, bougainvillea, jojoba, sweet acacia, and ironwood in

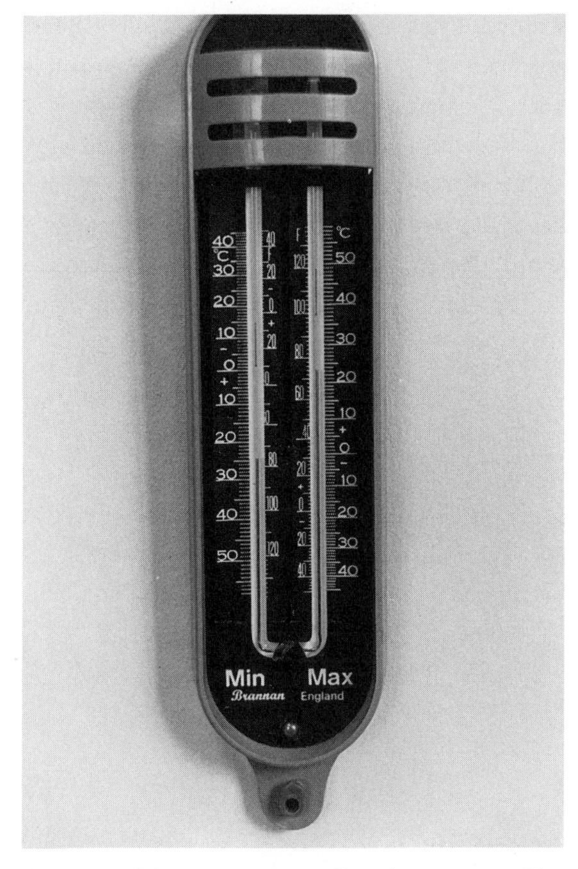

A minimum/maximum-recording thermometer like this one will tell you what happens in your yard, not out at the airport weather station. Install one or more near frost-tender citrus and other plants and keep a record of overnight lows at your place, as well as the official low temperature at the recording station. Then you'll know how seriously to take freeze warnings and when to cover your plants.

It's important for citrus trees to be budded to frost-resistant roots. All three plants here were subjected to the same frost. The citrus macrophylla in the center was hardest hit, the rough lemon at left suffered minor damage, and the sour orange at right escaped unscathed.

their landscapes tell you that it wasn't cold enough to kill them and that it's quite safe to plant citrus. You might want to install a minimum-maximum recording thermometer and keep your own records.

Citrus varieties vary in their tolerance of freezes

The most tender are limes, followed by lemons, oranges, tangerines, tangelos, grapefruits, kumquats, and calamondin, in that order.

The rootstock also influences tenderness. Citrus trees at the nursery have two parts: the roots, which are quite different from the branches where the fruit is formed, and the upper, fruit-bearing part, which was grafted onto the roots by the nurseryman who grew the trees. The roots are important for several reasons, but at present we are interested in them because of their tolerance to cold.

Among rootstocks, trifoliate orange has the greatest tolerance to cold, followed by citrange, sour orange, sweet orange, grapefruit, rough lemon, and, most tender, macrophylla. By selecting the appropriate rootstock, you can overcome, to some extent, winter's cold temperatures. You'll also reduce the amount of maintenance your trees will need.

ROOTSTOCK INFLUENCES FRUIT QUALITY AND TREE SIZE

If fruit production is your prime reason for growing citrus, make sure you get quality fruit by choosing the best rootstock. Your choice also will have an enormous influence on the way your tree grows and performs. Most of us prefer small trees because our yards are small. Besides, how many lemons do you eat each year? One lemon tree is more than enough.

Here's a rundown on the common rootstocks, starting with the one that's most suitable for desert planting.

Sour orange — makes a small tree. It gives a good flavor to all kinds of fruit, does well in heavier soils, helps a tree to resist frost, and is resistant to Texas root rot and phytophthora root rot.

Rough lemon — makes a large tree that grows quickly. It does very well in sandy soils. The fruit quality is poor, but the yield may be heavy. It has poor resistance to frost. Texas root rot and phytophthora root rot attack this rootstock.

Macrophylla — is like rough lemon, only more so. It is not a suitable rootsock for home planting. The tree is huge and the fruit is insipid, but the yield is heavy.

Troyer citrange — is a slow-growing rootstock, which keeps the tree small. It does well in heavier soils and gives good protection against frost. Fruit quality is good, but the yield is light.

Trifoliate orange — is like Troyer citrange, but more so. It does not do well in sandy or alkaline soils, so it is not a good choice for the desert. It gives good resistance to frost because it goes dormant in cold weather.

Sour orange is a good tree to have in the landscape. It stays a beautiful green all year and in the spring its handsome flowers are fragrant. As shown here, fruit and flowers can peacefully coexist.

ROOTSTOCK TAKEOVER CHANGES THE NATURE OF A CITRUS TREE

There are times when a citrus tree starts to produce two kinds of fruit. This doesn't affect the landscape qualities of the tree, but the tree begins to produce a lot of poor fruit. As the years go by there is more poor fruit and less good fruit, but the tree stays vigorous and healthy.

When you find rough lemons appearing on your tree instead of sweet oranges, or sour oranges instead of grapefruits, you wonder what is happening and why. It's not cross-pollination or peer pressure from adjacent trees that causes this to happen. It's the rootstock taking over. This often happens after freeze damage to the tree, or after a period of neglect when the tree was short of water. On recovery, the roots' energy is too much for the damaged branches; latent buds on the roots, below the graft, break out with great vigor and form branches that grow through the foliage to the sunshine above.

Unless this situation is corrected, the tree turns entirely into the rootstock kind of citrus. For landscaping purposes, this doesn't matter at all; in fact, you most likely will have a stronger tree than before. If you want to maintain the kind of fruit you started with, you have to remove all the "wild" growth that starts at the base of the tree. It usually is easy to see the two kinds of wood, because they are of different colors. If the "wild" shoots at the base of the tree are not obvious, you need to start in the top of the tree where the "wild" fruit is and follow its branches down to the bottom of the trunk.

SMALL SIZE IS IMPORTANT; PRODUCING CITRUS SHOULDN'T BE PRUNED

When you plant a tree, bear in mind the space it will occupy when it is mature. Plants that take

Here are two fruits from the same tree: at left is a sour lemon from the root, and at right is the Valencia orange the grafted tree was supposed to produce. After a hard frost, the root of a grafted citrus tree may send out a shoot that stretches through the damaged foliage. You notice the invasion when the shoot produces a different kind of fruit. Cut out the root sucker before it takes over.

A citrus tree pruned to a single trunk usually responds by growing a lot of vigorous suckers, perhaps from the root. It's better to let a citrus tree grow the way it wants to, as a great round thing with branches sweeping to the ground.

up too much space or that rub against walls and roofs become a nuisance and look unnaturally restricted. Citrus flowers are produced on two-year wood at the ends of branches, so any cutting back automatically reduces fruit production; you can't help snipping off flower potential as you trim.

Citrus should be allowed to grow naturally, even in the early stages. A three-year-old tree sends out vigorous vertical shoots that, because of their untidiness, invite cutting off. Don't do it. Let them grow longer and they eventually will fall over; along the bend of the arch, buds will break out and thicken up the tree's profile with new foliage. If you tie weights on the ends of these long shoots to keep them bent, you'll get a quicker development of new foliage.

Trimmed citrus hedges make effective boundaries

Almost any kind of citrus can be used to make a formal and impenetrable hedge, but remember that repeated trimming to keep the hedge's shape reduces flowers and fruit production. Citrus trees make good hedges because most have sharp thorns and all keep their leaves throughout the year, provided they are not damaged by frost. You may have a tall hedge 8 or 9 feet high to form a backdrop or screen, or you can keep it as short as 2 feet to act as a traffic director.

Dwarf citrus is a novelty in the desert

A young tree grafted onto certain rootstocks grows very slowly and gives the impression of being a dwarf variety, but over the years the tree eventually attains full size. It wasn't a dwarf at all. In such cases, grafting is used as a horticultural trick; it works for quite a while. True dwarfs are dwarfs because the plant's genes make them so. True dwarfs are rare. Unfortunately, they also are stingy in their flowering.

You don't get much yield from dwarf citrus, except in the case of the Meyer lemon. It's a very prolific little tree that you can grow in a half whiskey barrel for several years. The fruit is juicy and flavorful, pleasant in appearance, of good size, and plentiful. The plant is more frost-hardy than the other lemons, making the Meyer lemon a decidedly useful component in patio landscaping.

Lemons growing in a barrel usually are safe from frost. You can move the barrel to a warm spot in winter and you can easily cover such a small tree on a freezing night.

WHAT TO DO ABOUT FROST DAMAGE

A slight scorching of the foliage following a light freeze is nothing to worry about. Consider it natural pruning. Serious damage, in which more than half the foliage has been killed, calls for careful handling.

First, don't do anything until all danger of further frost has passed. You might have to wait a couple of months. If you are hasty and do some pruning the next morning, you could stimulate buds to break out and their tender new leaves could be killed by a later freeze.

When spring and bud growth return, you'll be able to see how much damage was done and how far to cut back. Don't just cut off the dead twigs. Go further back, so that your cut includes two buds that are breaking out. (See Chapter 9 for details on how to avoid and repair frost damage.)

If your tree is more severely damaged, you'll have more cutting to do and there may be little left of the tree. Don't worry; it will grow back. It may grow back *too* strongly if the roots were undamaged; in that case there will be a profusion of new shoots at the base of the tree. Start by thinning these shoots out so that only three or four are left. These will be the tree's framework in a year or two, from which smaller, fruit-bearing branches will develop. Tidy up your tree by cutting out all the dead branches as soon as you can see where the new framework is going. Take particular notice of whether new shoots are starting up from the root wood below the graft; remove these as soon as they start.

To protect citrus trees from frost, put a light bulb or two on the ground to produce a few degrees of heat that float upward through the foliage. A covering helps keep the warmth in and a framework like this makes covering and uncovering easier.

Don't fertilize a frost-damaged tree for at least a year. The new growth will come quickly, and there's no point in hurrying it along.

Recovering lemons are vigorous growers; they need pinching

Lemons recovering from frost damage send out long, vigorous shoots that have to be controlled if you want a regularly shaped tree. In fact, wild shoots will be found on all lemon trees in the spring; they need to be suppressed. Don't allow them to grow so long that you have to saw them off where they originate. Simply pinch out the tender tips with your fingernails before the shoots grow longer than 6 inches. Take a walk around your lemon tree during the spring growth flush and check this vigorous growth before it gets too big. The pinched shoots will quickly send out side shoots and your tree's foliage will thicken up.

Other kinds of citrus also have a spring flush of growth, although theirs is not so vigorous. Pinch if necessary.

Apply fertilizer if the soil is short of nutrients

If foliage is uniformly dark green, there is no need to apply fertilizer. The soil is rich enough and is providing the needed nutrients.

The common recommendation is to apply ammonium sulphate in February, May, and August. There is good reason for this only if the tree is short of nutrients. Don't do it just because the "proper" month has arrived. If you apply too much fertilizer, the tree grows too quickly and is weakened by its rapid growth. More fertilizer does not make sweeter fruit or more fruit; it just makes the skin thicker.

This is what happens if you force growth with fertilizer and liberal waterings just before frosty weather.

The *good* reasons for applying fertilizer three times a year are these: In February, the tree begins its spring growth and that growth needs nutrients. In May, the flowering is over, the fruit has safely set, and the tree is settling into production. In August, the soil has lost nutrients because of summer rains or heavy irrigations during the dry weather, and a fertilizer application restores fertility in time for the fall growth spurt.

Fertilizing after August encourages late growth that will be damaged by an early frost. Frost-tender trees should be in a state of dormancy before frost arrives in December, or maybe even November.

How to tell when fertilizer is needed

If the leaves on your citrus trees are small and pale and the tree has not grown much, it could be short of nitrogen. Remember that light irrigations could also be responsible, so be careful. A lot of small fruit is another indicator of nitrogen deficiency. Perhaps the most telling indicator, however, is a number of older leaves in the center of the tree that are uniformly golden yellow, while new leaves at the ends of the branches are green; in effect, the nitrogen has gone from the older leaves to the new growth.

A shortage of iron is shown by new leaves that are yellow between green veins, but don't confuse this symptom with damage done by weedkillers or other excess chemicals in the soil. (See Chapter 8 for a complete guide to troubleshooting.)

Fall weather and spring growth flushes also give yellow leaves. These are natural occurrences. In the fall, it's simply a case of older, dying leaves giving up their nitrogen to younger leaves, even if they are not actively growing. During a spring growth flush, it's the young leaves actively taking nitrogen from the older leaves, but the result is the same: lots of yellow leaves.

Spring and fall are not good times to assess the nutrient condition of your citrus trees, unless you make allowances for nitrogen mobility. In any case, get an overall view when you look at a tree; don't study the extremes.

How to fertilize citrus trees

If your tree hasn't grown much during the past year or two, it could be time to apply nitrogen. A citrus tree in good health has large, dark green leaves from top to bottom. Lots of small, pale leaves all the time indicate starvation.

As detailed in Chapter 7, scatter two pounds of ammonium sulphate for every hundred square feet under the spread of the branches. Don't follow the recommendation that calls for a pound of nitrogen for each inch of trunk diameter. This recommendation is a case of spurious science making a simple operation unnecessarily complicated.

To correct an iron deficiency, spray iron sulphate on new leaves. Use a tablespoon of iron sulphate in a gallon of water every two weeks in the spring and fall, while new leaves are coming out.

How to irrigate a citrus tree

Citrus trees are irrigated in the same ways that other trees are irrigated. See Chapters 4 and 5 for detailed recommendations and methods.

CITRUS SUFFERS FROM SUMMER STRESS

Because citrus trees are semi-tropical plants, they don't like the hot dry months when the sun is intensely bright. They go dormant during such uncomfortable weather. If the tree be-

Grapefruit is a cold-hardy tree. Much of the fruit is sheltered by foliage from freezes and from the scorching summer sun.

comes short of moisture, both the fruit and the leaves are burned by the sun's radiation. Keep your trees well watered.

Whitewashing citrus tree trunks is mostly cosmetic

Whitewashing the trunk of a tree does reflect the intense heat of the sun, but a naturally grown citrus tree shades its trunk and limbs with plenty of foliage that sweeps to the ground. If you have to remove that protective foliage for any reason, it's advisable to paint the newly exposed bark to prevent it from being blistered and killed.

The trunk of an old tree that has been pruned hard develops a thick bark as it gradually adjusts to the sunlight. A low sun, even in summer, doesn't hurt it, and at high noon it is shaded by

Spring growth coincides with insect activity. Thrips will deform fresh young leaves like these by rasping on the tender skin and sucking the juices. The damage is not noticed until later in the year, when it's too late to do anything about it.

Exposed citrus fruit will be sun-scorched during the heat of summer. Severe scorching hardens the skin. Later, during a growth period in the fall, the enlarging fruit simply has to split.

its remaining foliage. Whitewash on such trees is largely cosmetic, and draws attention to a tree that has been unnaturally shaped.

WHAT TO BUY AND HOW TO PLANT IT

It's not likely that you'll find a bare-root citrus tree. Once in a while someone tries to sell bare-root trees at a discounted price, but it's not worth buying them. The roots dry out very quickly, and because such trees usually have come a long way they are half dead before you can plant them.

Buy a tree in a five-gallon container, ignoring the invitations in the advertisements to plant a larger one with fruit already on it. A larger tree usually has had its roots severely trimmed in order to get it into its box.

Nurseries sometimes sell citrus trees growing in cardboard containers and advise you to plant the whole thing, container and all. You're told that the cardboard will rot and that the roots will grow through it. This claim is not borne out by experience. What's more, the cardboard acts like blotting paper to soak up chemicals; new roots are damaged by the resulting concentration of salts. If the cardboard dries out, it becomes very hard and won't allow moisture through. The soil inside the container usually is different from yours, and the cardboard acts more like a barrier than a bridge between them.

When you plant, dig a big hole, get through caliche, and amend the soil as advised in Chapters 6 and 7.

Allow your tree enough room to grow. Lots of people don't realize that planting a citrus tree closer than 15 feet to anything else leads to its being frequently trimmed before it reaches maturity. A trimmed tree is a spoiled tree.

THINGS THAT GO WRONG WITH CITRUS

Citrus trees are good trees for a carefree landscape. Not much goes wrong with them. Apart from frost damage, yellow leaves are the commonest complaint and concern, and they are easily corrected if it's anything more than aging leaves.

If the soil at the base of the tree is kept continually wet, there is the danger of a soil fungus invading the tree and killing it. The treatment is to cut out the affected part and to apply a Bordeaux mixture. Phytophthora rot is easily prevented by keeping the soil surface dry; do this by irrigating properly.

Blossom drop and fruit drop will happen if the spring is cold and windy, or if the change from mild spring to severe summer is sudden. Fruit and leaves will sunscorch during summer if the tree is improperly irrigated.

Then there are nuisance things, such as orange dog caterpillars, the larval stage of the black-and-yellow swallowtail butterfly, which chew on the leaves. If you are interested in fruit as well as landscape value, you won't like birds that make holes in ripening fruit. There's not much you can do about birds except to keep them out with a fine-meshed net.

26 Plants, Play, and Water-Saving SWIMMING POOLS

There's a connection between landscapes and swimming pools: they both require our attention for their upkeep, they both give us pleasure and provide recreation, and they both require water. If you are careful in the management of both, you can make the most of their benefits and minimize the conflicts.

IF YOU BUILD A POOL, STAY AWAY FROM NEARBY TREES

Trees drop their leaves, dead flowers, and seeds. Caterpillars and bugs drop out of trees. Trees harbor birds that drop things. For these reasons, you don't want to have tree branches above a pool. Build your pool beyond the drip line of a tree, and add a bit for future growth. This simple precaution saves you from forever cutting back your trees and spoiling their appearance.

Although a poolside tree offers a picturesque landscape effect, if you put your pool too close to a tree you'll have to cut roots. New roots usually form at the cut, and they'll stop when they reach the wall of the pool. Such a tree will have a one-sided support system, which might fail during a windstorm.

ABOVE-GROUND POOLS CALL FOR SPECIAL SOIL TREATMENT

The plastic liner of an above-ground pool seals in moisture in the soil beneath; it can't get away and the ground remains damp. It gets quite wet if your pool is built below grade level or if a leak develops. Then, you'll discover, roots from nearby trees "come to the surface" in this wet soil under the plastic liner.

Avoid this danger, first, by applying a soil sterilant *only* on the area that you are going to cover with the pool. As long as the chemical rests under the pool, it will not be washed down by rainfall or irrigation. Provided you don't scatter the chemical outside the pool area, roots of nearby trees will not be damaged. Second, add a layer of sand a few inches above grade for the plastic to rest on and settle into smoothly. Third, dig a trench all around the pool about 3 feet deep, in order to cut any roots of nearby trees that might grow under the pool.

MAKE A SIMPLE LANDSCAPE AROUND A POOL

There's a lot of activity around a pool, so you don't want thorny plants that will scratch naked bodies. You don't want groundcover plants that sprawl into the area and trip people up or that have to be trimmed back frequently. You don't want plants that shed a lot of leaves, flowers, or seeds. You don't want flowering plants that attract bees; a pool, by itself, does that well enough.

If you want a bit of shade, don't plant eucalyptus trees. They are always shedding leaves or seedpods that stick into bare feet. Palms are perhaps the best trees to have near a pool, because their large leaves stay on the tree and their seed stalks are seasonal; if they fall, they are easy to collect. A group of palms casts as much shade as you want.

A grass area around a pool is nice to have. Hybrid Bermudagrasses stay short if there's a lot of traffic over them. If you mow any grass, make sure you collect the clippings. If you leave them on the lawn, the wind is sure to blow them into the water.

LANDSCAPE PLANTS RARELY ARE AFFECTED BY POOL CHEMICALS

The solid chemicals you throw into the pool are quickly swallowed up by the water. You may smell chlorine, but it's not enough to hurt nearby plants. On the other hand, chlorine gas that bubbles out of the water, especially on a still day, can cause leaf discoloration. Only rarely, through carelessness, will plants be killed by chlorine. If you do it right, backflushing can save you money on summer water bills.

Backflush water can be used to irrigate salt-tolerant landscape plants

The reason you have to keep adding chlorine in one form or another is that it quickly gets used up. Chlorine gas from cylinders leaves no residue in the water; for the sake of your landscape plants, it's the best kind to use.

Most pool chemicals are compounds of chlorine and either sodium or calcium. It's the residue, after the chlorine has been used, that we have to worry about, especially if it's sodium. Liquid formulations usually contain sodium, whereas the powders and solids contain calcium. Avoid using the liquid formulations; sodium is a plant poison.

After three or four years of chlorination and evaporation, the percentage of total solids, either sodium or calcium, in the water becomes excessive. Your pool chemical supplier can test the water and tell you when it holds more than 1500 parts per million of salts, or solids. At that point, you don't want to use it for irrigation.

Don't irrigate acid-loving plants—the "imported" trees, shrubs, and grasses—with alkaline water. Save it for Bermudagrass and for desert trees and shrubs that grow naturally on an alkaline soil. If you are blessed with a patch of undisturbed natural vegetation, that's the place for swimming pool water; it will keep those plants green and growing during the hottest of summers when rainfall is light.

But remember that desert plants like a period of dryness between waterings; they can't stand being wet all the time. Move the water from one clump of plants to another, and then to a third before you come back to the first.

You can dilute the effects of salty water by alternating it with faucet water on plants that are sensitive to salts. The signs that a plant is getting too much salt are brown dead tips on leaves, a bluish color instead of a shiny green, and leaf edges dying and turning brown.

27 LANDSCAPE MAINTENANCE WHILE YOU'RE AWAY

We all take time out and go away from home occasionally. If we're gone for a short period in winter, we don't have to worry about our landscape plants while we're gone. They can live without us. If we go away for a vacation during the summer months—or if we are snowbirds and leave our homes in the desert as soon as the weather gets hot—it's a different story. Something has to be done while we're away.

The first rule is this: Don't start anything new just before you leave. Any new project needs your attention for some time after you think you've finished it. Don't set out flowers, plant a rosebush, change the irrigation system, construct a pond, or start anything else the week before you leave. You won't be able to follow through.

FOR A SHORT ABSENCE IN SUMMER

For an absence of just a week, your indoor plants will survive with a good soaking at the last moment. Cluster houseplants together so that they share one another's humidity. If a particular plant seems to thrive in only one place in the house, leave it there and cover it with a clear plastic bag. Keep the bag off the foliage with two sticks. To avoid sweating, leave the bottom open.

For a two-week absence, houseplants will survive in the bath with an inch or two of water to provide moisture and humidity. Unfortunately, most bathrooms are too dark for plants, but this is an emergency measure and they'll come through.

If you don't like the bathroom idea, another way to get water to plants is to use lengths of cotton string to "wick up" moisture from a pan of water. Remove the plant from its container and bring four pieces of string up through the drainage hole and against the insides of the pot, one strand for each of the four points of the compass. Put the plant back, keeping the strings against the insides of the pot. Place the four strings coming through the drainage hole in water in a pan under the pot.

Outdoor plants in small containers should be grouped together in a shady place, sheltered from the wind, and given a good soaking. They will survive better if they are placed on a dirt floor that has been wetted thoroughly. Don't put them on concrete; it gets hot and quickly dries.

All the other plants in your landscape should be well watered. Don't assume it will rain while you're away.

FOR A LONGER ABSENCE

It's probably best to give or loan your houseplants to a friend. If you don't, use the wick method and make sure the pan of water is big enough for the length of your absence.

Outdoor container plants, especially the smaller ones that have to be hand-watered, are probably best given away. Everything else will have to be cared for somehow. One way is to install a drip irrigation system with an automatic timer. A better way is to have someone come in and look after things as if the landscape were his own.

Survival with a drip irrigation system

It's supposed to rain during the summer. Even if it does, there's no guarantee that it will rain on your property. Summer rains are fickle and you musn't assume you'll get enough. On the other hand, there's sure to be increased humidity, which appears to provoke plants into growth. That summer growth must be supported by water at the roots.

If you want a drip irrigation system to keep your plants alive while you're gone, get it finished and test it for a month before you leave. Make sure it's working properly. Use your soil probe to be sure water is going deep enough. Make adjustments until you are satisfied. (Read Chapter 5 for details on organization and assembly of your system.)

A week before you leave, adjust the controls to give more water in anticipation of the forthcoming increase in temperatures. Check everything to make sure it's working satisfactorily.

The problem with a drip system is that it can't think; it simply follows the clock. It's possible that a rainstorm will occur during one of the irrigation delivery times, but that won't matter very much. If it's a really wet summer, however, your plants will suffer—perhaps even be killed by Texas root rot—if the system continues to water a wet soil.

There's also the possibility that the electrical control mechanism of your system will be interrupted or damaged by summer storms. In that case, your plants won't get the water they need during dry spells.

For peace of mind, you need a summer caretaker

You need a back-up person who will check on things from time to time. There are three kinds of help: a friendly neighbor, a student on vacation from school, and a commercial landscape maintenance company.

A friendly neighbor probably knows your landscape and your landscaping practices. If things aren't quite to your liking when you return, however, that friendship can be strained. Leaving your property for a long time in the complete care of a friend is a good way to spoil a relationship. Landscape maintenance is a responsibility and a worry; things go wrong despite dedicated attention and good care.

Hiring a student on vacation appears to be a good thing to do. You could help develop his or her sense of responsibility and introduce a young person to a lifetime career. At least you will provide summer employment. But don't risk a friendship by giving the job to a neighbor or a friend's child; you could find yourself involved in emotions that obstruct efficiency. It may seem a bit chancy to hire a young stranger to care for your landscape, but you can ask for references.

An established commercial landscape maintenance company also should provide references. If you can, engage a caretaker on the strength of personal recommendation. Ask your friends whether they know a good person who can look after your property while you are away. Start interviews, check references, discuss what you need, make an agreement, perhaps even write out a contract.

Human activity deters thieves

A drip system on a time clock probably will keep plants alive, but it won't mow the lawn, or sweep up the leaves after a storm, or pick up papers blown in by the wind. It won't repair tree damage or call the police if something unusual happens. Your house will look empty.

If a thief is watching your house with evil intent, it's good to have a person arrive, stay awhile, and let everyone know that someone is around. It's better if your caretaker doesn't follow a regular schedule, like visiting your house every Tuesday morning at 10. If he can routinely call you to say that everything is okay, it will be good for your peace of mind.

You are entering into more than a service contract

It's important that your caretaker understands what you want. This applies especially to young people, who want to be helpful and sometimes overreach themselves in trying to please.

When you have picked your man or woman, tour your landscape together to show how you do things. Take pains that there's no misunderstanding caused by inadequate verbal instruction. People learn better by watching than by listening. Work from a list if you like, and be sure to have a complete list in your caretaker's hands before you meet again.

The second time around, it's your helper's turn to show you how to do what has to be done. Check, correct, and praise as you go around. If you start early enough, there's time to find another person if need be, or perhaps to train this one.

Keep in mind that it's maintenance you want

Keep it simple. It's not fair to throw in development tasks, such as building structures, laying pathways, or generally improving your property. That's for another contract with another person.

Be careful about the use of power equipment

Make sure all your equipment is in good, safe working order if you expect your caretaker to use it. This is especially important with young people. Demonstrate the safe use of mowers, hedge trimmers, string trimmers, and other power tools. Give your caretaker a performance test. Check with parents to be sure they approve their child's use of power tools.

If all equipment is clean, sharp, and properly adjusted, your worker will have no excuse for doing a poor job. Your equipment will last longer, and there won't be repair bills while you are away. Just in case, make arrangements with your repair shop and supply store before you go. If something needs to be repaired while you are away, it's better to have it done by a professional. A wrong spare part can ruin a piece of equipment. Besides, a young person may not have the money to make a necessary repair.

If you decide not to have your equipment used while you are away, lock it up. Lock up gasoline, fertilizers, and spray chemicals, too. There have been times when an inexperienced caretaker, trying to please, used the wrong thing the wrong way and did a lot of damage.

Talk with a young caretaker's parents

You shouldn't make the parents responsible for the work done at your house, but you should get approval for their child to work for you. Go and talk to them; you might make a friend. And be sure to give your young caretaker the name of a friend to go to in case everything falls apart the week after you leave.

Set some ground rules about work habits

You are liable for accidents that happen on your property, so you need to feel safe about having a young person working for you.

If he or she brings a companion, there's help on the spot if something goes wrong, or someone to dial 911. On the other hand, if he or she brings a gang of chums along there's a good chance of monkey business developing. If an admiring younger family member comes along to watch, he may be hit by something the lawnmower kicks out of the grass.

Try to think of the dire possibilities. Leave clear instructions; in these days of litigation, it might be a good idea to write them down and have your caretaker sign for them.

When you return and the job was well done, reward gladly

Praise your caretaker for a job well done. Give a written reference to build up a résumé. Pay gladly and gladly bestow a bonus if you promised one. Let your caretaker know you'll tell your friends he or she did a good job.

A STRATEGY FOR WINTER RESIDENTS

Some people own more than one house, and they enjoy the winter months in their desert location. They arrive after Thanksgiving when it's cool, and leave around Easter when it gets hot. Winter is a wonderful time of the year in the desert for plants, as well as for humans. Make the most of your winter landscape.

The first thing is to get started as soon as you arrive. Remove dead plants, dig the flower beds, empty old containers and refill them with fresh soil. Get rid of the weeds around your winter home. Dig the lawn area to get it ready for sowing ryegrass seed. If you intend to plant trees and shrubs, get the planting holes dug. Work hard for a couple of weeks to get things looking good as quickly as you can. You don't want to spend the next four or five months getting things ready for your departure; there's outdoor living to enjoy.

If you don't like this sort of activity, get a professional to do it for you. In any event, start early and get it over with so you can enjoy the flowers.

A number of winter visitors sensibly grow a ryegrass winter lawn and let it die in June when the weather gets too hot for it. There's no point in growing hybrid Bermudagrass, a summertime plant that is brown during winter, if you're not here to enjoy it.

28 CONDOMINIUMS: COMMON GROUNDS, COMMON PROBLEMS

You might think that people who live in condominiums have no landscaping worries. Trading off your expansive acreage for congested living was supposed to free you from daily landscaping chores and plant maintenance.

Condominiums usually come complete with landscaping, which initially is managed by the developer. This is fine, for a time. It's when the prescribed number of units has been sold and the residents take over the complex that trouble begins. *Their* management now becomes *yours*, but only through a committee, and that means it's not *completely* yours. It can be very frustrating for everyone.

WHAT ARE THE ANNUAL DUES?

After you have settled in, it's inevitable that the annual dues will increase. Before you buy, find out what they are. Have them itemized, so that you can tell whether you are paying for a swimming pool and recreation facilities as well as for upkeep of the landscaping. Are the dues meeting all the costs now? What about later?

A developer is tempted to "dress up" the property with plenty of green plants and lawns in order to make quick sales. Ask yourself what this costs today, and what it will cost if the price of water goes up by 7 percent. Will those quick-growing trees need a lot of expensive pruning? Will leaf-sweeping be costly? Are there a lot of little grassed areas that call for fiddly, expensive mowing? Do lawn sprinklers water the driveways?

Go ahead and appreciate the surroundings, but don't forget someone is going to pay for their maintenance. You may be excused from doing the work, but you'll be asked to pay. Try to discover the landscaping attitudes of those people already in the complex. A majority may be newly arrived and still thinking in terms of green lawns and flowers, trimmed hedges, and rose gardens, all of which are expensive.

ARE THERE PLANTING RESTRICTIONS?

It's not unusual to have restrictions on plant material for one reason or another. Will this bother you?

Some plants have a bad reputation, deserved or otherwise, for producing lots of pollen or for untidy habits. Some landscape committee members really throw their weight around and impose their own ideas, which are not always founded in fact, on the other owners.

Read the rules before you buy; don't rely on what the salesperson tells you. If you want to have your say in the management of things, you need to know what the administrative structure is. How easy is it to make your voice heard?

LANDSCAPE PROBLEMS ARE PEOPLE PROBLEMS

In theory, the front common areas usually are cared for by the landscape committee through a landscape maintenance company. In practice, many individual homeowners like to tell the workers what to do, how to do it, and when to do it. This leads to everyone's dissatisfaction.

In the interest of efficiency and happiness, it should be understood by everyone that those areas accepted by the group as common areas shall be the responsibility of the landscape committee. The committee should appoint one of its members to manage things by way of the foreman or owner of the contracted maintenance company.

Don't entice workers off the job

Then there's the possibility of a homeowner demanding an hour's work of a laborer in his own patio. "Just give me a hand with this," he says. A laborer should never be subjected to this sort of demand. He is supposed to be efficiently working on an assigned task. If the homeowner needs some help, it can be arranged for after hours and at an agreed-upon price.

Channel complaints through the committee

A concern about the way the common areas are maintained is best taken to the chairman of the committee. It's in everyone's interest to make the complaint in writing.

A laborer, the foreman of a crew, or the owner of the company should not be hassled by every homeowner with an opinion, by an over-eager committee member, or even by a well-intentioned first-rate gardener. It's too much.

Let the committee choose the maintenance company

A contract should be drawn up to make sure that everything is taken care of. To help the committee people—who more than likely are volunteering their time—it will help to put the job out to bid. The applicants can then list the operations they will carry out.

It's best to have the company itemize tasks; you can check on them better that way, and so can the foreman. A contract made up of general statements, such as "take care of trees" and "lawn maintenance," really doesn't tell you what the contractor will do and won't do. It's an invitation to an argument.

Keep contract periods short

You don't want to bind yourself for a long time to any contract. This may sound silly, but if you have disagreements it's better to finish them quickly than to drag them out. Start with a six-month contract and work up to a year if you are well pleased with the services; it might be better to renew the contract every six months. The reason for this is that most landscape companies are forever changing. Their work force is a very mobile one—here today and gone tomorrow—and, unfortunately, not always knowledgeable or well-trained.

Companies that develop a reputation for reliability are in great demand, and sometimes they expand too quickly. As they take on new accounts and increase their workload, management loses contact and control. Good workers are pulled off routine accounts to shore up those that are becoming problems. Things tend to slip a little.

WHAT TO DO IF YOUR COMMUNITY WATER BILLS ARE TOO HIGH

First, check consumption. Read the meter, check the water company statements, and make sure no accounting errors have occurred. Then read the meter on a daily basis—forever—and see if there is a pattern of heavy use on certain days. For example, does the swimming pool gulp a lot of water? Summertime evaporation is very high from an open pool, and children splash water out of it. Is water consumption on weekends higher than during the week, perhaps owing to people washing their cars?

Second, check the whole complex for water leaks. These will not appear in your records as sudden spurts of consumption, but a few leaking faucets (which you can easily see) and some broken lines (which will be indicated by wet soil patches and weed growth) will send your costs up surprisingly.

Third, peek at your neighbors to see whether any of them are wasteful water users. Be discreet.

Fourth, find out where water runs down the streets and correct the problem. It may be that the soil won't absorb the water quickly enough, or that the system is left running too long, or that the sprinklers shoot high in the air instead of delivering a low pattern, or that the pressure is too high, causing the water to mist and be blown away.

"It's-not-me" syndrome

Because many condominiums have but a single water meter and not one water waster can be singled out, it's always the other fellow who is at fault.

Use the monthly newsletter to bring everyone together. Copy the information from the water company bill, stating how many gallons were used last month and what it cost. Make a bar graph to show how the complex is doing relative to past months. Make everyone aware of what's going on.

Separate meters quickly deter the wasteful users, but it may not be feasible to install a meter at every home and have each individual pay his own water bill. Besides, the cost of irrigating the common area still needs to be shared.

Depending on how the water pipes were laid, it may be possible to install a meter for recording water flow—not to make out bills—to serve several homes and thus break down use by groups. If the homeowners' personalities allow friendly contests among groups, it may be possible to compare one group of residents and their water use with another. Praising conservative groups is a people-oriented method of getting cooperation in reducing water bills, but you need to have figures, not impressions, and that's where meters are useful.

Work with your landscape maintenance company

Ask whether the irrigation system is being used efficiently. Maybe the plants are being watered too much. Use a soil probe to find out whether water is getting down to the roots of plants; if there is a good reserve of moisture deep down in the soil, there's little point in watering every other day. A good soak once a week is better than a little sprinkling every evening.

Discuss whether lawn areas can be reduced. Ask whether the irrigation system can be improved by changing from sprinklers to bubblers, or from bubblers to a drip system. Perhaps the system was originally designed—if it was designed at all—for a greener landscape. The present plantings may not need so much water.

Ask whether it is safe to reduce water applications with a view to testing suitability of the plants. Gardenias and privets need a lot of water; hopseed bushes and rosewood don't. Try a reduced regime for a period during the hot summer, when water consumption is at its highest, and replace thirsty plants—those that suffered—with drought-tolerant ones.

Finally, make changes gradually. If you want

to keep a group of homeowners happy, don't make a lot of sudden changes.

WEIGH THE ALTERNATIVES TO A GREEN LANDSCAPE CAREFULLY

The extreme form of a "water-saving" landscape is one of stones, gravel, and concrete. Such a landscape will save water, but it also will heat up the community and you'll spend more money on cooling, thus nullifying the "savings."

Midway between a green jungle and a barren wasteland is a landscape that is shady and cool, and yet doesn't have a high water demand. You get this by the use of tall trees that shade the ground, buildings, and people. You won't get it by using cacti, agaves, and ocotillos alone. Instead, combine them with green plants that are water-thrifty and drought-tolerant.

PART II

A Month-by-Month Maintenance Guide

January

January is a quiet month, but one full of apprehension. Watch out for frosts and snow.

- Pay attention to the radio and television weather forecasts, especially if a frost or freeze warning is issued. If a warning is issued, cover your plants while they are still warm from the sun. In the morning, remove the covering to let the sun warm the plants again.
- If it is going to be really cold, or if there are several days when the winter sun doesn't shine long enough to warm up your frost-tender trees, you will have to put a source of heat under each tree and let the warmth float up through the branches. Keep your extension cords, a light bulb or two, a light blanket or heavy sheet, and cardboard boxes handy. A week or two of this messy procedure can save several years of growth on frost-tender plants. See Chapter 9 for more on protecting your plants from frost damage.
- Shake snow off junipers, roses, desert broom, and any other limber-limbed plants in your landscape. Snow's weight will break even stiffer-branched young trees, especially if they have poor branch structures.
- Repair torn limbs and cut off broken branches as soon as you see them. Young trees whose trunks divide equally are particularly prone to splitting at the fork under the weight of snow. If that happens, simply cut off one fork and paint the wound. Stake what's left.
- Leave snow to melt on bedding plants and lawn. It won't hurt anything. But don't walk on a frozen lawn; you'll leave lasting footprints.
- After a freeze, decide which citrus to pick and which to leave on the tree. There's little point in picking fruit as soon as the freeze warning is issued; cross your fingers and wait. The fruit on the inside of the tree usually is not affected at all, and it can stay there quite safely until you are ready to eat it. The outside fruit is more susceptible to damage. Cut one or two open; little white crystals or granules in the juice segments tell you to eat the fruit quickly and to give some to your friends and neighbors before it spoils any further. You also can turn the fruit into juice now. Dry, pithy fruit—the next stage—is useless. See Chapter 25 for more.
- Leave frost-damaged plants alone. Wait a few weeks for warm weather to stimulate buds to sprout; only then will you know where to prune.
- Keep your flower beds filled. Set out bedding plants now to fill any empty spaces. Nurseries sell large plants on the point of

flowering, often with enough flowers on them to make good color. The new plants won't grow until warm weather returns but you will have some sort of display, which is better than a bed with dead plants or gaps.

- Control weeds that emerge in response to winter rains. Winter rains also nourish wildflowers, however; learn to tell the good guys from the bad.
- No weeds means no rain, which means you must irrigate. Check ryegrass lawns and flower beds with your soil probe to see whether the soil is adequately moist at root level. If you sowed wildflower seeds in October, you'll have to water them, too, if it doesn't rain.
- Don't water the lawn at night. Annual ryegrass is a succulent, watery plant and easily succumbs to leaf fungi. Irrigate down to eighteen inches in the early morning and let the sun dry the leaves. Use your soil probe to tell you when the soil is drying out around the roots. Don't irrigate until it does.
- In the warmer parts of the desert, plant trees.
- Large numbers of yellow leaves on trees and shrubs in January are a warning that the buds soon to break into new spring growth will need extra nitrogen. Anticipate this growth by applying nitrogen fertilizer this month. See Chapter 7 for more on appropriate fertilizers and their use.
- Don't use fireplace ashes on desert soils. It seems a waste to throw wood ashes away, but it's the best thing to do in the desert. Ashes are very alkaline, and desert soils already are too alkaline for many plants.

February

February is much like January, but there's an occasional suggestion that spring is on its way. The days lengthen a little, and during warm spells daytime temperatures reach an enjoyable 70 degrees. These are false alarms if you are looking for the end of winter. Night temperatures regularly fall to 40 degrees, and there's still a chance of frost.

- If it doesn't rain, you'll have to irrigate. This becomes more important as the weather warms and plants start to grow again. Use your soil probe to tell you when to water. Don't forget the wildflowers: annual wildflower plants will die if the weather turns warm and the soil is dry. Give them a six-inch deep irrigation to encourage deep roots if you want a good display of color in March or April.

- Yellow aphids appear from nowhere on oleander and must be eliminated before they build up their populations, which they do quickly. Small infestations can be rubbed out of the tender growing tips of the shoots using finger and thumb, or you can use an insecticidal soap, which will dissolve an aphid's waxy coating and cause it to die by dessication. If aphid populations get out of hand, spray with *Malathion* or *Diazinon.*

- If you trim an oleander hedge in late February, you'll cut out the aphids before they build up a heavy infestation. If you leave hedge trimming until later in the spring, you'll cut off a lot of flower buds—after the aphids have weakened the plants.

- Look out for green aphids (some people call them greenfly) on roses. You'll find them on the ends of new growth, sucking the juices out of the soft shoots and buds. Eliminate them before their populations increase.

- Another pesky insect that comes to our attention in February is the white grub, the larva of the May beetle or June bug. It comes to the surface as the soil warms and begins to eat organic matter, usually leaf mold and manure, but also tender roots of your plants. Grubs are no good. As you dig your flower bed, pick these creatures out and squash them. Alternatively, you can spray the bed with *Malathion*, *Diazinon*, or *Sevin+*. Adding more organic matter now invariably means a new generation of grubs; its smell attracts flying adults, who lay their eggs on it.

- Get those weeds! If you missed them in January, they're a lot bigger now. Don't procrastinate. See Chapter 10 for more on weed control.

- February is planting time. Set out junipers and other trees and shrubs. See Chapters 6 and 7 for how to prepare the soil and how to plant in the desert.

- February is a month for pruning, and fertilizing with a deep watering should always accompany pruning. All three operations complement one another to support plant growth. Don't prune shade trees heavily and don't top your trees (any work that is done should be so subtle that the tree looks untouched). Shrubs, roses, and grapes on an arbor should be pruned now, as should hedges. See Chapter 21 for proper pruning methods.

- Give your dormant plants a good watering in early February. This is a critical month for all dormant plants, especially trees and shrubs; warming weather stimulates buds to swell and to break out into leaves or flowers. Now is the time to fertilize, too. Remember that ammonium nitrate works faster in cold soil than does ammonium sulphate, and that it's more concentrated.

- There's still a strong possibility of a late frost that can kill new growth; be ready to cover your flowering trees on a freezing night.

- In winter you see things that were hidden by summer foliage, such as infestations of parasitic mistletoe in desert trees. Mistletoe is a green plant, and as such uses the sun's energy for growth, but it also saps a tree's strength by taking nutrients from its branches. Mistletoe won't steal a lot of nutrients, but a heavy infestation will shade a tree's foliage. It's best to remove it. A long, hooked pole is the right tool for the job; just pull the parasite off. If you cut the branches to which it is attached, you often spoil the natural appearance of the tree. If mistletoe grows back, pull it off again. Don't use weedkilling chemicals on mistletoe. If you do, you'll poison your tree, too. The parasite and its host are closely connected and share a common source of moisture and nutrients.

- Don't be hasty with the spray gun and shoot down everything that flies out of your plants. Some of the insects hatching now are your allies. Lacewings, for example, are spring's first predators to come out and gobble up aphids and red spider mites. They are a delicate green and have appropriately lacy, transparent wings.

- Inspect last year's plant ties and loosen them. This year's buds grow out and last year's twigs grow thicker. If those twigs were tied with string, watch out. The string doesn't stretch as the twig gets fatter; instead, it cuts into the soft tissue and strangles the twig. It's worse if you use wire ties; the wire cuts into the flesh of the plant. Even soft cotton string can strangle a twig. Old-time gardeners used raffia, an organic fiber that disintegrated in a season; modern technology has given us soft plastic that doesn't degrade but that does stretch with the growth of twigs. Climbing vines—

grapevines on the arbor, honeysuckle and climbing roses against a wall—are notoriously prone to string strangulation. Make string inspection a routine task during growth spurts.

◆ Later February is the time to spray citrus trees for thrips, but there is considerable danger in doing so. Thrips chew on tender leaves just starting from the bud. You don't see the damage they are doing until June or July; then the leaves are twisted and cupped and generally misshapen. Distorted leaves function just as well as do normal leaves, but they spoil the appearance of a landscape tree.

To control thrips, you can spray them with *Diazinon* when the leaf buds are breaking out in February. The danger of spraying thrips is that you also will be spraying the pollinating insects that guarantee you a crop of fruit; you'll kill them all if you spray. Citrus flowers are one of the first and strongest sources of food for bees. If the winter has been a hard one, they need this nectar and pollen. Don't kill them by spraying!

March

Winter weather in the desert is fairly mild, but even here March is notorious for its strong winds. They shake the leaves and dead branches out of trees and cause a mess. Winds rushing past the new leaves of trees and shrubs dry them out and sandblast them. Newly planted trees can dry out before their roots are able to replace the lost moisture. March is a month for vigilance.

- Clean up, but don't overdo it. There's some controversy about leaf litter. One argument is that it acts as a surface mulch and keeps the soil cool and moist in hot weather. However, in this cool moisture there lurk pests and diseases. Privet weevil, a small beetle that spends summer's days hiding and comes out at night to nibble the privet leaves, and mildew of euonymus, roses, and grapes, a disease that hides in leaf litter, are two such hazards. Minimize the risk by raking up leaf litter around these plants. Save the leaves if you like mulches, but discard the leaves of eucalyptus, Mexican palo verde, and oleander. It's thought they contain poisons that harm plant growth.

- Protect new growth on grapes, roses, and euonymus from powdery mildew during March by spraying the young leaves with wettable sulphur once a week. Sulphur can burn tender new growth when it's hotter than 90 degrees, so now is the time to start your control program.

- Stay alert for aphids. Last month saw the start of these pests, and they'll continue into April. Look for green aphids on roses and yellow aphids on oleanders. Until the soft tissues of new shoots harden, these and other plants will be weakened by juice-sucking aphids just as they begin spring growth. Squirt aphids off with a strong jet of water or spray with *Safers Soap.* If that doesn't work fast enough, finish them with a spray of *Diazinon* or *Malathion.*

- Remove oleander gall now. Cut out oleander gall every time you see it. The gall is a black crusty growth seen where the old flowers were. The bacteria that cause it hide in leaf litter. Cut *all* the galls out. If you leave just a few, they will grow further into the plant and kill it. The bacteria that cause galls also can be spread on your pruning tools. The textbook recommendation is to dip tools in a can of 10 percent bleach before each cut. Send the diseased bits to the dump; don't leave them lying around to act as a reservoir of infestation.

- Protect newly planted shrubs and new leaf growth from wind with a temporary screen. If you have just moved into a brand new subdivision that has no shelter, it's worth setting up a length of four-foot-high snow fence. If you want greater protection, fasten sheets of plastic on the windward side.

- Warm weather makes hedges grow again, so be quick to trim them before the vigorous growth becomes untidy. You don't want the plant to waste energy by producing growth that you'll cut off. Start lightly trimming as soon as warm weather stimulates new shoots. Remember that every cut you make encourages more growth, so you thicken up a weak hedge by a series of light trimmings. A hedge that has become too wide and too untidy can be severely cut back now. If you wait too long, a summer sun will scorch the inside branches that are no longer protected by the outer foliage. By letting in the light now, the inside branches will send out new shoots and the smaller hedge will thicken up. An old hedge that has lost most of its lower leaves can be brought back by cutting everything off at a height of a foot or two. The stumps will quickly grow new leaves. If you wait until summer to do this, the strong sunshine will kill the newly exposed bark of the inner branches. The sun in March is right for stimulating dormant buds to break out on the old branches. For more on proper hedge maintenance, see Chapter 20.

- Now is the time to repair frost-damaged plants. Many frost-tender plants begin to put out new shoots this month. As soon as buds break out into new green shoots, you know the extent of last winter's damage. Cut out the unsightly dead wood and include two live buds in that cut; a cut into live wood encourages new growth.

- Use frost damage as a planting guide. If a lot of your plants were killed by last winter's frost, let it be a lesson to you. Replace them with hardier plants.

- A late, late frost is possible in March, so be ready to protect new growth on hedges and roses, flowers on citrus trees, and newly planted summer bedding annuals. All can be damaged by just one night of frost. The first warm days of March bring ants out from their rest beneath the soil, gophers and squirrels become active again, the birds sing, bees gather nectar, people are at work on their rooftop coolers, and construction workers take off their shirts, but these signs are not reliable. A more trustworthy (but not infallible) sign is the appearance of mesquite flowers, the long yellow blooms that hang from the twigs like catkins. After mesquite flowers appear, it's usually summer all the way.

- Water diligently. Windy days lead to dryness, so March is often a dry month, as well as the month when plants start growing strongly because of the warmth. Dull and bluish leaves indicate that a plant is short of water. Plants that have just been set out are particularly at risk. Use your soil probe a lot this month.

- Flowering fruit trees need water, not fertilizer. Flowers are delicate and are easily damaged if they become too dry; their stalks break and the wind blows them away. The stalks also break if the tree is fertilized during flowering; it's too much of a shock. Fertilizer at this time can cause young fruit to fall, too.

- Keep after the weeds, especially if it rains. Those that germinated before Christmas are probably flowering by March, and flowers turn into seeds. Your first objective is to prevent flowering and seeding. See Chapter 10 for more.
- March also is the time to use pre-emergent weedkillers. If it rains, or if you intend to regularly irrigate an area, get with it at once. These chemicals are not effective after seeds have germinated. Don't forget that pre-emergent weedkilling chemicals have no discrimination; they prevent *all* seeds—of wildflowers or lawngrasses, too—from becoming plants. Don't expect "good" seed to grow in an area that has been recently treated. Because pre-emergent weedkilling chemicals don't affect established plants, you can safely spray the lawn against summer weeds and you can keep the cactus patch clean for the summer without having to spend much time in it.
- Rains in March, coupled with warming temperatures, make ryegrass lawns grow vigorously. You'll have to mow more frequently, perhaps every five days. Don't let ryegrass get away from you; keep it at 2 inches. If there's a dry, hot spell in March, the ryegrass will suffer from the heat and the underlying Bermudagrass will come out of its dormancy. Now, there's great competition between the two grasses and you can work this to your advantage. If you want to encourage the Bermudagrass in anticipation of summer, mow the lawn as close to the ground as you can. This will weaken the struggling ryegrass. The operation also will expose Bermudagrass thatch, a layer of dead leaves and stalks, so that you can get rid of it. One advantage of taking out the thatch in March, while it's cool, is that the soil does not burn. If you de-thatch during summer, strong sunshine can kill the exposed Bermudagrass roots, especially on high spots in the lawn. After de-thatching, irrigate well and fertilize.
- First the mulberry and then the olive become nuisances in March. Both send out pollen into the air, and some people suffer from one or the other. The news media have made people think that these two trees are a nuisance all through the year, but a mulberry (only a male produces pollen) puts out pollen for just a couple of weeks; the olive flowers over a little longer period. In dry springs flower production is low; in wet springs the pollen is washed to the ground instead of blowing around to bother you. Don't chop down your established mul-

berry or olive trees for the sake of preventing two weeks' flowering.

- To reduce pollen production in olives and mulberries, spray the flowers with water. This washes the pollen to the ground. Nurseries will sell you a chemical called *Olive-Stop*. It's diluted with water to make a spray that kills the flower. *Olive-Stop* is designed primarily to prevent fruit from forming, but it also reduces pollen production. It also works on mulberries.

- To get your olive tree to produce bigger olives, let the first flowers develop into fruit, then spray the second and third waves of flowers with *Olive-Stop*. This eliminates competition and the first fruits grow bigger. Of course, your tree has to have the potential for producing big fruit. Some kinds are genetically small-fruited; they'll never give large fruit, no matter what you do. There's even a variety of olive whose flowers produce no fruit.

- There is often a lot of exciting growth on your grape arbor during late March that has to be taken care of. Thin out the crowded shoots by firmly snapping them at their base. Spread the remaining, more vigorous ones and pinch off their grasping tendrils to prevent them from hugging one another into a tight bundle. You want an even covering on your framework that is well ventilated. This will reduce mildew infestations.

- Finally, pay extra attention to your plants in containers. Their soil dries out quickly, and they must have adequate moisture if they are to grow and flower. For more, see Chapter 17.

April

Prickly pears put on a gorgeous display of bright flowers this month, wildflowers bloom, and perennials like desert marigold and mallow brighten the landscape.

- There are two kinds of buds on old prickly pear pads: flower buds and those that produce new pads. Now's your chance to keep a large prickly pear in check without hacking it about, which seems to be the fate of many large old plants. Let the flower buds grow into flowers, but cut out the young pads; they become *nopalitos*, which are eaten as a pickled delicacy or sauteeed. A cut now saves the plant's energy. It's silly to allow a plant to grow too big and then chop it back.

- Although succulents seem to manage without a lot of watering, it's a good idea to try to remember whether they have had adequate rains to support spring growth. Use the soil probe to see how dry the soil might be. In April, a supporting irrigation often is called for.

- Desert trees and shrubs call for your help, too, if it hasn't rained. The older, well-established mesquites, acacias, and palo verdes will start up and flower on their own, but trees and shrubs younger than two years should get a deep irrigation now.

- Anything just planted needs deep watering once a week; you want their roots to grow as deep as possible and as quickly as possible.

- Stake newly planted trees against the wind. This will keep them from being blown over, of course, but the wind also does more insidious damage to newly planted trees, especially if the soil is kept too wet by a continuous drip irrigation system. The soil in the planting hole becomes a well-lubricated mud; the tree's foliage acts as a sail and its trunk as a lever. As the tree sways in its muddy planting hole, any new roots growing out of the planting ball are sheared off and broken. This means your plant won't become established. To stake your plants, sink two stout poles into solid ground and pass soft cotton rope between them and the trunk at three places up and down the trunk.

- Take another look at last year's string and plastic support ties. Make sure they are loose enough to let branches grow without hindrance.

- Mesquite trees weep black sap in the spring. All plants that go through a dormant period start up their cycles with a flow of sap; it's what makes the leaves come out. Sometimes, the pressure inside the plant is so great that the sap bursts out at a weak spot and forms a gum as it dries. (When this happens to acacias in the deserts of Arabia, the result is called gum copal, gum arabic, or frankincense.) Admittedly, gumming can be a sign that something is wrong with the tree, but if it happens in the spring and lasts no more than a day or two, don't worry about it. On the other hand, if weeping occurs after you have cut a limb, the message is that you should not have. It's better to cut limbs while a tree is dormant. Don't forget to seal the cut with a spray of pruning paint.

- Some landscaping plants suffer from nutrient deficiencies that cannot easily be corrected by ground treatment. The answer is to "feed" young leaves as they come out of the bud; delicate, thin-skinned leaves absorb liquid fertilizers. Use any soluble houseplant fertilizer, but read the label to be sure it's appropriate as a foliar spray; when the heat of the day has gone, thoroughly wet the new leaves. Do this once a week as long as new leaves continue to appear.

- New leaves also invite mildew, so check again for powdery mildew on euonymus hedges, roses, and grapes. If you find it—it first shows itself as white blotches—spray with wettable sulphur.

- If you see a black fluid dripping from a damaged saguaro, do something about it quickly. If you leave a dripping saguaro to its own devices, you lose it. The bacterial rot that causes the dripping will rapidly invade the soft tissues and kill the plant. See Chapter 23 for the appropriate treatment.

- Don't plant Easter gift plants outdoors. It's nice to receive azaleas and Easter lilies in the spring, but there are at least two reasons for not putting these plants in the ground. First, they have been grown under controlled conditions using growth-regulating chemicals; they were grown in a hurry so that too much money would not be spent on their culture. Second, they are not garden varieties. Even if they were, they are not desert plants; they won't take the heat of July and August.

- You'll get more rose blooms if you harvest your flowers on a long stem; try to get 18 inches of stem. In this way you carry out a light pruning each time you harvest a bloom. A long stalk means cutting into fairly thick stem, and the bud below that cut has a chance to produce a big flower later on—provided the new flower doesn't grow into the hot weather of June and July.

- If you haven't already done it, repair your Bermudagrass lawn or start afresh. Use sod or plugs, depending on your budget. See Chapter 19 for how to do it.

May

In May, it's your elevation that tells you whether spring is over and summer is beginning in your part of the desert. At the cooler, higher elevations, there's still time to plant trees and shrubs. They will establish themselves a lot more easily now than if you try it next month, when hot weather arrives. In the higher places, flowering winter annuals are still good enough to keep a little longer. In the lower areas, time has run out and they need to be replaced with summer annuals. No amount of dead-heading will rejuvenate the pansies, stocks, poppies, snapdragons, and so on. The time has come to pull them up and start over.

- If you have a raw new yard, this is a good time to improve the soil, as detailed in Chapter 6. Your summer annuals will be glad you did.

- Buy summer annuals that are on the point of flowering to be sure of getting the color you want; you can't rely on plant labels. A plant on the point of flowering is the right size to set out. Remember that close planting gives you more color per square foot more quickly. See Chapter 16 for details.

- Don't make a flower bed around a desert tree. Flower plants grow well in the filtered shade of palo verdes, acacias, and mesquites, but if you plant flowers around their trunks, there's a good chance you'll kill them; the irrigations you need to keep the flowers performing nicely will be too much for the trees. To use the shade of these trees without killing them, put your summer annuals in containers. Remember that any container with a capacity of less than five gallons is going to be a nuisance when hot weather arrives and requires you to water every day just to keep the plants alive. Besides, daily watering keeps roots too wet and hot when temperatures hit the hundreds. See Chapter 17 for more on container gardening.

- Irrigating becomes critical in May, which usually is not a rainy month. Good watering reduces the stress of hundred-degree weather. Give first consideration to the newly planted things in your yard. Then irrigate the plants that are visibly growing, putting out new shoots. Next, irrigate everything else, even the cacti.

- May is a cactus month. You'll have noticed the prickly pear flowering; look in the flower centers and you'll see a lot of bees rolling in the scuppers like drunken sailors, overcome by the nectar. Now look up and see if there are any flowers on your saguaros; most likely there are. No doubt you'll want to take a picture. Do it now; they won't last long.

- Plant or transplant cacti now. These heat-loving desert plants are best moved during the month of May, before temperatures soar too high. See Chapters 15 and 23 for how to do it.

- Treat saguaro soft rot. See the April calendar and Chapter 23 for details.

- The new pads on prickly pear that appear at the same time as the flowers are edible. You can buy them at gourmet food stores, ready to eat, or you can make your own *nopalitos.* Cut off the soft new pad and singe the spines over a flame. The skin will become loose, so that you can remove it. Then fry the slices or pickle them in vinegar with herbs of your own choosing. They make interesting vegetables.

- Bee swarms are common in May. Don't be frightened when you see a swarm of bees clustered on a tree limb, on a roof overhang, or even at your front door. Don't get out the spray gun to blast the swarm with insecticides. Don't squirt them with water. In fact, don't go near them, for their sake as well as your own. You need to know that they won't "go for you." They are simply waiting for a new home, having been ejected from their old hive by overcrowding. Each bee is full of honey with which to start a new home, and so is unable to bend her body to place her stinger in the right position to do you harm—unless she has to, because you are a nuisance to her. In a day or two the swarm's scouts will have found a permanent home and the swarm will disappear. Sometimes the bees' future home is behind a small opening in the walls of your house; then you have to do something, and quickly. Look in the yellow pages under "B" to find the names of people who remove swarms from awkward places. They usually do it for free because the swarms are valuable. Very seldom do they have to break open the wall to get the colony, unless the bees have been in residence for a number of years.

- If you have a grape arbor, keep a sharp watch for the inch-long, blue-black moth that hatched out of its chrysalis during March. It's the adult of the grape leaf skeletonizer, a most appropriate name. It's a daytime flier and is easy to see in the early morning when temperatures are cool enough to slow down its flight. It sits out on the sunny leaves to warm up. It's then that you catch it between finger and thumb. If there are a lot of them, you can catch a dozen at a time with a butterfly net. If you see two of them tied together by their tails, you can expect the next stage of their life cycle very soon, the eggs. These are laid in clusters of twenty or more on the undersides of leaves. Before the end of the week they will hatch into tiny caterpillars. Tiny caterpillars quickly turn into larger ones, and by this time their damage is evident in a few tattered leaves. If you ignore them, there'll be much more damage; whole branches will be skeletonized. By now the caterpillars are an inch long and have black and yellow bands around their bodies, like rugby jerseys. Control of this pest in its early stages is easy. Simply pick off a sluggish moth, pick off a leaf holding an egg cluster, or pick off any leaf that has a swarm of caterpillars on it. After the caterpillars have munched their way over several leaves, you may have to spray with *Sevin*, *Malathion*, or *Diazinon*. Sometimes it's possible, in the cool of an early morning, to shake them off the arbor. They won't find their way off the ground back to the leaves.

- Dichondra lawns get flea beetles in May. These small insects show their presence first by jumping off the leaves in clouds as you walk over the lawn, and then by leaving a brown trail of damage to the leaves themselves. A lot of them will exhaust a lawn. To control them, spray with *Diazinon* or *Malathion* in the evening after the heat has gone out of the sun.

- Agave snout-nosed weevil gets active this month, too. You won't see the little black weevil until it's too late to do anything about it. It hides in the stems of agaves and yuccas, chewing away on the soft tissue until the plant can no longer absorb water from the soil, at which point it collapses. The infested plant is finished, but the nearby plants should be protected as quickly as possible. In fact, you might want to adopt a routine of treating all your agaves in May and again in September, when the beetles lay their eggs. See Chapter 23 for the appropriate treatment.

- The standard treatment for powdery mildew on euonymus is a spray of wettable sulphur, but don't do it after temperatures reach 100 degrees; the spray becomes corrosive in high heat. The fungus is supposed to die of the heat, but there's a "Catch-22" situation here: the plant prefers shade, but so does mildew; sunshine kills the mildew, but the plant can't take full sun either. This is a classical instance of a plant that should not be used in the desert.

- Cultural practices can reduce mildew attacks on euonymus. Observant gardeners say there's more mildew on hedges that have been systematically and frequently trimmed than on hedges that are left to grow more naturally. Trimmed hedges are tight and compact, and so are shaded by their own growth; further, their density doesn't allow air to circulate and ventilate the foliage. These factors favor the growth of mildew; they also weaken the hedge, making it more vulnerable to attack.

- Roses need help in May. Roses are at their peak at the beginning of this month, but they begin to feel the heat at its end. Mulching is one of the best ways to provide comfort to your roses during the summer months. It shades the soil and keeps it cool, prevents moisture from evaporating, and keeps weeds from growing. Although a mulch may provide a home for pill bugs, earwigs, and crickets, it's usually worth it. See Chapter 24 for more on how to care for roses in the desert.

- Work early in the day, but check plants in the afternoon. Temperatures reach into the hundreds during May, and outdoor work is best done in the early morning when it's cool; you feel comfortable and so do the plants. They don't show any stress at this time of day and it's easy to assume they are doing fine. But, beware! Take another look at them at midafternoon; if your plants show discomfort by wilting, an irrigation is needed.

- Vigorous new growth calls for gentle pruning. Hedges of oleander, privet, and boxwood may need to be tidied up by a light trimming. Don't trim oleanders if they are showing flower buds, however; you'll lose the hedge's spring color. Delay trimming until after flowering. Vigorous growth on citrus trees, especially lemons, also needs to be watched. If you let it grow too long, the trees lose their compact shape, look too open, and take up too much room. Go around the trees, pinching the soft new growth with your finger and thumb while the tips are tender. While you're at it, check the new growth spilling over hanging pots, especially those containing trailing African daisies, nasturtiums, hearts-and-flowers, periwinkle, and verbena. Trim out the long, straggly pieces—use them as cuttings for new plants, if you like—and you'll get new summer growth near the center of the plant. This fosters the appearance of "bushing up," which is what you want.

- Remove any remaining twigs that have been damaged by frost.

- If you go by the calendar, it's time to fertilize citrus. As a rule of thumb, you may fertilize citrus trees in January, May, and August, but there's nothing sacred about the operation or its timing. If the leaves are dark green, there's no need for fertilizer. See Chapter 25 for details.

- A lot of winter's weed plants turn dry and brown in May, but that's not the end of them. If left to themselves, they will scatter their seeds. Gather the dying plants into bags; don't let their seeds fall out on the ground. Summer weeds are starting now, too, so stop them from developing further. For more, see Chapter 10.

June

June is the month when we start getting larger water bills. If your landscape plants don't get the water they need, they tell you. A dry lawn looks silvery gray to start, and then turns straw-colored. Privet and roses wilt and develop brown sunburn patches on their leaves. Trees produce lots of yellow leaves on their "insides" and new growth looks dull instead of shiny. If the drought continues, they drop the yellow leaves; *Rhus lancea* is a notable example, but pine trees do it, too. Citrus trees might drop young fruit under the double stress of increasing temperatures and inadequate water. You usually can head off trouble by paying attention to your plants' water requirements. You'll have to water more often than you did last month, but don't make the mistake of watering too often—say every evening—with a light sprinkling that only wets the top three or four inches of soil. See Chapter 4 for the right ways to irrigate in the desert.

- It's not likely that your lawn is suffering from fungus in June. Garden store salespeople, with an eye on the cash register, are quick to tell you that a silvery appearance on the lawn means you have a dreadful fungus disease that can only be cured by fifteen dollars worth of *Brand X*. Don't believe them. Fungus lawn diseases are encouraged by constantly damp conditions, which we don't have in June. Check the "diseased" areas with your soil probe. If they are hard and dry, you're not watering enough. If you accept the disease theory and buy *Brand X*, it's almost sure to work for a time. The reason is that the chemical has to be applied with plenty of water; it's the irrigation that "cures" the problem.

- Help your lawn survive June by mowing a little on the high side, so that the grass shades the soil. An inch-and-a-half is a good height for hybrid Bermudagrass.

- Save water by using a mulch. A mulch is any material that covers the soil, keeping moisture in and the hot sun out. Desert plants don't need mulching, but you can help your roses and other thirsty plants through the stresses of summer by mulching them. Perhaps the best mulching material is new—not used—evaporative cooler pads. Gardening books from other parts of the country often recommend placing grass clippings, pulled weeds, crop residues, and old leaves on top of the soil around your plants. If you do this in the desert, you'll soon have an untidy mess. Everything will quickly dry out and desert winds will scatter it all over your landscape. If you keep it moist, it will provide a home for pill bugs, cockroaches, crickets, earwigs, and maybe snails. Both organic and black plastic mulches have a limited value in the desert.

- As trees grow, extend their watering basins in June. Remember that you want a wide, shallow basin around the tree, not a deep well. If your landscape includes sloping ground, you have an opportunity to collect rain that falls up slope. This time don't encircle the tree with your extended basin; leave it open on the high side to collect runoff.

- Watch out for hot hoses! A garden hose lying out in the June sun for a couple of hours holds water hot enough to scald your hands and hot enough to do a lot of damage to both plant foliage and shallow roots. Before you water your plants, turn this hot water onto a part of the landscape where it won't do any damage; use it to wash down the dust on a patio or add it to the swimming pool.

- Sunburn on leaves shows up in June. The heat itself is a stress, of course, but so is the sun's radiation. If plants with broad leaves develop a dead patch in the middle of a leaf before the whole leaf is affected, there are two messages. The first is that the plant is not suited to the desert and should be replaced if the trouble persists. The second is that the plant may be short on water; dry leaves burn more readily than do leaves plump with moisture.

- Geraniums fizzle out with the heat this month and begin to die in July. Away from the desert they are perennials, but they can't take the summer's heat here. Container geraniums can be moved into the shade, but those planted out in a sunny place will suffer at least some loss. Some gardeners let geraniums take their chances; if the plants survive a dreadful summer, they cut them back to get fresh new growth in the cooler weather of September. If you try this, be warned that if you water them too much during summer's heat their roots will rot and the soil will be contaminated for future plantings. Geraniums are, to some extent, drought tolerant; it's better to water them lightly.

- Summer stress brings out symptoms of weedkiller residues. The worst chemicals are soil sterilants; they should never be used in urban landscapes, but they are commonly found on the shelves of garden stores labeled "vegetation killer." Killers they are, and they last a long time in the soil. If a tree or bush stops growing, develops mottled leaves, shows twig die-back, and finally dies for no good reason, you can suspect the nearby use of sterilants. A tree that is nice and green on one side and dead on the other graphically tells you that soil sterilants have been used on the dead side; it is, unfortunately, a common sight, especially in boundary plantings. The deadly chemical sometimes is applied in your neighbor's yard, but tree roots don't recognize property lines. Try to wash the poison out of the soil and away from roots with deep irrigations. See Chapter 10 for better ways to control weeds.

- Palm tree skinning is a summer job, but it often is an unnecessary chore. See Chapter 22 for details of good palm care.

- Will we get any rain this summer? Toward the end of June, this question is uppermost in a desert dweller's mind. Magnificent clouds build up in the afternoons, there's a hint of humidity, cicadas start to sing, and you might hear thunder in the distance. We keep hoping, and our plants keep hoping, too. Take a close look at them; they sense the humidity and, in anticipation of a storm, start a little new growth at the ends of their branches. If rain doesn't fall, give them an irrigation to satisfy their hopes. And don't skimp on the watering in the hope that it will be your turn for a soaking rain tomorrow. Put your soil probe to good use.

July

July is a month of false alarms. There are thunder and lightning, but the promised rains don't always come. Plants and people are under stress. Even desert plants show it; prickly pear pads shrivel and palo verde trees drop their leaves—until the rains arrive.

- And then there's Texas root rot. It's a wet summer when this dreadful fungus kills our trees, and so some people assume that every tree that dies during July, August, and September must have been killed by Texas root rot. It's not necessarily so. See Chapter 12 for the facts on Texas root rot and what to do about it.

- It's easy to jump to a wrong conclusion when something goes wrong with your trees at this time of year. The symptom that first catches your eye—the sudden wilting of leaves that don't drop—could be caused by an excess of fertilizer, by weedkiller chemicals, by grubs chewing on the roots, by overwatering, by poor drainage, by borers in the branches, by extensive cicada damage, or by sheer exhaustion. Or the soil could be dry. That's the possibility you should check first; it's the easiest to diagnose and you can quickly do something about it. Get out your trusty soil probe.

- While waiting for rain, take care of the hoses. Keep hoses in the shade. Hang them up. Don't let them develop kinks. Don't control the flow by bending a hose end over on itself; it's a sure way to shorten your hose.

- Beware of overwatering in the heat. You can feel the heat in leaves when a plant is short of water. After an irrigation, the leaves transpire and the plant cools down, just as we perspire and cool down after a good long drink. But we don't continue to cool down the more we drink; it's the same with plants. What's more, roots drown if they are kept too wet. The first sign of drowning is that leaves turn dull and droop. This is so similar to the symptom of plant stress caused by too little water that many people, particularly in July, rush to the garden hose. This leads to the second stage of stress caused by wet soil: leaves lose their nitrogen and iron, and become chlorotic. Lawn grasses turn yellow. The cure is simple: cut back on the watering. Use your soil probe regularly.

- It's amazing how a tired lawn perks up after a good rainfall. When the summer rains finally start, turn off the sprinkler time clock to save water and to avoid fungus diseases. Get out the mower and make sure the blades are sharp. Mow the grass more often, say every four or five days. If you let grass grow tall and thick during the rains, it will stay wet and fungus diseases will be encouraged.

- A natural rain is worth ten irrigations. That may be a bit of an exaggeration, but a good rain does release a lot of growth energy. Don't push your luck by fertilizing a fast-growing lawn that already is dark green; its color tells you that it doesn't need nitrogen. If you give it more than it needs, it will grow faster and weaker; it will exhaust itself and will succumb to fungus attack.

- Irrigate your lawn, when necessary, early in the morning. Sprinkling at night when humidity is high keeps the leaf blades wet and allows fungus diseases to spread rapidly.

- Take it easy in July; you're under stress too. Don't undertake any great garden enterprises this month. It's not the best time of the year for success in planting or digging. It's a time for steady maintenance and watching for trouble. Trouble can include insect activity, germinating weeds, chlorosis, fungus diseases, and so on. By being observant and taking care of trouble in its early stages, you can save yourself work. If you have to do anything strenuous, such as repairing storm damage, do it early in the morning. Take it easy, and leave some of the job for tomorrow.

- If you use them, apply pre-emergence weedkillers before it rains. The success of pre-emergence treatment lies in getting the chemical against the dormant seed before it swells with moisture and begins to germinate. Pre-emergence is what it's called, but it would be a better reminder to landscapers if it were called "pre-rains." If you apply it a week before the rains start it will wait in the soil for the seeds to start. In fact, it will wait for four or five weeks. If you apply it a week after the seedlings begin to show, it won't work.

- During last month's dryness and increasing heat, fruit trees were under stress. In spite of irrigations, fruit hardened in the strong sunshine; it became corky and inelastic. Now comes the rain; all of a sudden the tree gathers up an enormous amount of moisture. A lot of this goes to the young oranges, pomegranates, and peaches. The hard skin can't expand, the inside swells fast, and something has to give; the fruit splits. There's not much you can do to prevent this, even with liberal pre-rain irrigations, and there's nothing you can do after it's happened, except to remove the damaged fruit. If you leave it, it will attract flies and leaf-footed plant bugs.

- Remove broken limbs quickly after a storm has damaged your tree. Limbs and large branches should be neatly cut off as close to the main body of the tree as possible. You don't want any tears or stubs to remain as a result of your cutting. Paint the exposed ends with a spray of pruning paint.

- Don't try to splice a split branch or trunk. The repair will leave a scar, but, more important, the mend will always be a weak spot. The branch split because it was weak in the first place, and it's best to prune it out. Make a clean cut so that no stub is left, then apply the pruning paint.

- If a July storm pushes a small tree over, however, there's often a good case for righting it. To right it, first soak the soil to the point of making it a plastic mud pie. Then gently and firmly, taking two or three days if necessary, pull the tree upright again. If you can't do it manually, rent a ratchet "come-along" device. Attach it to the tree with a protective cloth, so that you don't damage the bark. The other end, of course, should be attached to something *very* stable; you don't want your tree to topple a porch pillar as you tighten the cable.
- The Mexican palo verde borer beetle grub can cause trees to blow over in a storm. We seldom see the grub—it lives in the ground for a year or two, eating the roots of softwooded trees—but in July we are very much aware of the three-inch-long adult brown beetle. During its evening flight, it clumsily bangs against porch lights, crashes into the reflected light from swimming pools, and bumps into newly arrived palefaces sitting on the patio. The grub is bigger than your little finger, and it is very good at destroying roots. The first noticeable sign is a dieback of branches and limbs, which turn light, and then dark, brown. After the soil has been thoroughly soaked and a gusty storm has blown an infested tree over, you see the chewed-over roots. At this point, you're too late; there's no cure. Chop up your dead tree and haul it away. If you want to save nearby trees, there's a treatment you can follow. It won't guarantee their salvation, but it's the least you can do. See Chapter 11 for how to proceed.
- There's another July emergence to watch for, or rather to listen for. Many small holes in the ground mean that cicada grubs have matured and come out of the soil, where they spent their grubhood feeding on plant roots. You don't see the flying insects, just the grubs' empty body cases with a split down the back. These are all over the place: on walls, on tree trunks, even on the tires of cars that have been parked for awhile. You may not see the cicadas, but you hear their mating calls. The female eventually chooses a tender new twig and makes a dozen or more saw-toothed cuts on it; into each cut she lays an egg. These hatch, and new grubs fall to the ground to begin a year of chewing on roots. All this looks worse than it really is, because leaves at the ends of the twigs usually turn brown and die, giving the impression that Texas root rot has struck. Reassure yourself by inspecting the stalks of the dead leaves; if they are serrated, it's not Texas root rot.

August

August is a continuation of July, but the weather is more intense: it's hotter, it's more humid, the insects have multiplied, and the diseases have taken hold. Storms are violent and they continue to be unreliable in location and delivery. Everyone but you seems to get the much-needed rain. Because of the increased humidity, it's uncomfortable. If you can afford it, it's a good month to take your vacation.

- During a lull in the storms, you may get a knock on the door from a young man who tries to talk you into having your trees topped. Don't let him. If, on the other hand, he wants to thin out the limbs, it might be worth listening to him. Old trees blow over because their foliage is too thick. They gather the wind like a sail, especially if the foliage has thickened because of a previous topping. Thinning, not topping, is the proper preventative. For details, see Chapter 21.
- Palms stick up into the sky and act as lightning conductors. A tree that is struck by lighting usually is finished. A tree expert, with his expensive equipment, will have to be called in to remove a stricken palm little by little, starting at the top. Check your insurance policy to see whether your company will pay for the tree's removal. Use neighborhood safety as the reason for the request.
- The same young man who knocked on your door asking to top your trees might come back and want to clean up your palm trees. Don't let him do that, either. Too many workers remove too many leaves. Any tree-trimmer carrying fronds to the dump should be fined five dollars for each green leaf. Let your tree look natural.
- During a continuously wet summer, there's the danger of a fungus being blown into the top of a palm and infecting the bud. A palm tree has only one bud; if that is destroyed, the palm is finished. The proper preventative in this case is to treat the top of your palm tree with copper Bordeaux before the rains begin. For more on palm tree care, see Chapter 22.
- Apart from a general browning of the inside needles, which is normal and to be expected during the summer, Aleppo pines sometimes show hand-sized patches of dead needles on the outer branches. The experts haven't found a specific reason for this condition, so it's called summer stress or "blight." Let this "tell-tale" remind you to give your trees a good deep watering this month, even if it rains. Be extra vigilant with the soil probe.

- Another summer problem is eriophyid mites. You don't see them, but you see the damage they do to pine trees: new growth at the ends of branches becomes deformed into a compact bunch of twisted needles; you see the same thing on Mexican palo verde trees. The tree needs a miticide spray. At the nursery, the stuff you want is called "mite-killer" or some such name; whatever the product, it contains nicotine; be careful when using it as a spray. Mite-damaged foliage also can be clipped from trees. Put the pieces into a closed bag for disposal. It would be silly to snip them off and leave them lying on the ground, allowing the mites to get back on the tree.

- There is a branch nematode that infests pine trees, too. It's hard to say where it came from, but we know it is spread through an urban area by tree trimmers and their tools. The symptom is similar to that of summer "blight," but nematode infestations don't clear up; it takes but a couple of months for a perfectly healthy tree to turn completely brown and die. An infected tree should be removed and hauled away. (In fact, the whole tree should be burned to kill the infestation, but local laws usually prevent this kind of clean-up.) After cutting up the infected tree, make sure your tools are clean; soak them in disinfectant, such as a 10-percent bleach solution.

- Roses take a rest in August. There's not much to be done about it, either, except to be careful with your sympathy; don't give them "food" and don't keep them too wet. Just be content to get them safely through the rest of the summer. If you planted some on the west side of your house—the worst side for roses—it will help to cover them with a white sheet to throw off some of the sun's radiation.

- Irises rest in August, too. Beautiful as iris flowers are, they often are damaged by a late frost or gusty winds. The foliage, on the other hand, lasts most of the year and provides a marked accent in the landscape. In August, though, irises begin to brown out and wither. It's best to accommodate this natural tendency by withholding water and allowing them to die down completely. They need a rest. Don't worry; they're not dead.

- And flower beds take a beating. Heat and bright sunshine play havoc with bedding plants. It's the end of their season, and it's not worth fussing with them. It's the wrong time to fill in gaps where plants have died; the whole bed is due for replacement soon. The most you can do for your flower plants now is to remove dead flower heads in the hope that new ones will replace them. But don't expect too much.

- Most geraniums rot out in the summer because of overwatering, but if yours are still alive go easy on them until the weather cools. There's a strong temptation to help them along with liberal waterings, but that is the worst thing you can do. Don't worry about leaves fallling off. Bare stems will send out new leaves when they like the weather better. Cut back the stems halfway at the end of August. If you like, root the cut pieces in pots of perlite and vermiculite to make new plants.

- Change lawn-mowing schedules to match grass growth, just as you did last month. Reduce the interval to five days, or maybe four. Take off a small amount of new growth, about a quarter of the total height, each time. Be careful not to mow too close to the ground. You want a couple of inches of foliage to shield the soil and the roots from strong sun.

- You may get good rains in August, in which case you can turn off the automatic irrigation system. On the other hand, showers may be so unreliable that you'll have to irrigate by hand in between the time-clock applications. Only your soil probe can tell you. Remember, too, that heavy rains or repeated irrigations wash nitrogen out of the soil. You may need to put some back, in the form of ammonium sulphate.

- All hedges, but especially oleanders and privets, exhibit a new burst of energy during summer rains. It's important not to let this new growth spoil the shape of a formal hedge; give it a light trim every two weeks to keep the sides clean and tidy, and don't forget the topline. If you prefer to save yourself a lot of work and let the hedge grow the way it wants to, you don't have to worry unless it gets completely out of hand; if there's a STOP sign nearby, don't let the hedge overgrow and hide it. If foliage is pale green, give the hedge a dose of ammonium sulphate once a month.

September

In the landscaping year, September comes between harrowing summer and delightful fall. Unfortunately, September can't make up its mind; fierce heat alternates with cool spells, but cool nights give a promise of things to come. It can be a rainy month or a dry month, and it often is a windstormy month. Treat September with caution. Don't get too many ideas. It's your last chance to use the heat as an excuse to avoid hard work. There'll be plenty of opportunity for that next month.

- Whether storm clouds bring moisture or not, they invariably bring strong winds. Repair wind-damaged trees quickly. Chapter 21 will tell you how.

- A good storm may deliver a lot of water, but that doesn't mean the root zones of your plants will get it. Summer rains, rightly called gully-washers, often run off the surface instead of soaking in. Use your soil probe after every downpour to find out what's happening underground. Don't use the color of the sky as an indicator of whether to irrigate or not.

- A truly wet summer can be a real threat to the safety of your trees, too, so turn off your automatic irrigation system and water by hand. It's more work, but it's a way to save your trees. Overwatering can lead to root rot and tree loss.

- September's storms, coupled with frequent irrigations, cause citrus fruits to swell quickly. Because the skin has been baked hard by summer sun, exposed fruit often splits. This is particularly true of navel oranges, sweet oranges, and tangerines; it's not such a problem with grapefruits or lemons. To avoid attracting vinegar beetles, remove all damaged fruit from the tree and from the ground underneath. The fruit is not ripe, so you'll have to discard it. To help avoid the problem, be careful with the watering. Turn off the automatic system. Use your soil probe.

- Don't be hasty about overseeding lawns with ryegrass. There's more warm weather ahead, and it will be too much for the cool-season seed. Be patient; wait for soil temperatures of 75 degrees. Don't change horses yet.

- In fact, it's a good idea to fertilize summer lawns now. There still are several weeks of growth ahead. Every two weeks, apply a pound of ammonium sulphate for every hundred square feet of lawn and water it in well. Your lawn will green up quickly.

- If your lawn is yellow, it might also be due to a lack of iron brought on by overwatering. Check for moisture with your soil probe; if the soil's too wet, let it dry out a bit. The grass will turn green again, all by itself and at no cost to you.

- Warm weather, ample moisture, and fertilizer all lead to vigorous growth. Don't let the lawn get away from you. Keep the height at 2 inches; taller grass shades itself too much, which leads to exhaustion. You want a lawn to go into winter as strong as possible. Continue irrigating Bermudagrass until it goes dormant and turns brown naturally, usually in mid-November. Stop irrigating at this point; begin again in March.

- As soon as roses recover from summer's heat and start putting out new shoots, it's time to prune for flower production. Buds develop about 50 days after cutting the old stalks. It will be cool then, and the flowers will unfold more slowly and last longer than they do in the quickly warming spring. Because pruning stimulates growth, give each pruned plant a half-pound of ammonium sulphate and water it in well. See Chapter 24 for details.

- Oleander, privet, xylosma, Texas Ranger, and Arizona rosewood are all good candidates for an early fall pruning, if you like a shaped hedge. September is a good time, too, to take drastic measures on an old hedge that has become overgrown at the top. See Chapter 20 for details.

- September is a time to put back lost fertility. Your shrubs, trees, and vines all want to grow in the cooler temperatures, and there are several weeks of good growing weather ahead. All they need is ammonium sulphate; you scatter it on the surface at the rate of two pounds for every hundred square feet. Precede and follow with a good watering.

- But be careful about fertilizing frost-tender plants. Winter is coming, and it might come early. You don't want frost-tender plants to be actively growing when the first nip arrives in November. Citrus, bougainvillea, hibiscus, palm trees, and a few others will grow well during the next few weeks, but don't encourage them too much. If in doubt, don't apply ammonium sulphate.

- September is a good time to plant trees—even citrus trees—and shrubs, vines, palms, agaves, cacti, even Bermudagrass. It's too early for fall flowers, though; wait until October. You can get ready now by digging flower beds, if you like.

- Geraniums, like tired lawns and tired roses, can be revived as the weather cools. If they are not too far gone, cut them back to produce fresh new growth. If summer has been really hard on them, it might be best to dig them up. Resist the temptation to refill the bed with more geraniums, in case the soil has become contaminated with fungus; remember the farmer's need to rotate crops.

- September is iris-dividing time. Dig up big clumps and cut them into smaller pieces for replanting; make sure there are no grubs in the roots. Cut the fan-shaped leaves back to about 6 inches and clean away any dead stuff. If you're concerned about soil-borne diseases, wash the soil off the roots and dip them in a fungicidal solution before planting. While you're at it, examine the roots for maggots and throw the infested ones away. Plant the roots quite shallow, barely covering them with soil. Don't keep the soil too wet after planting. Irises grow out from the center, so make sure the new pieces point outward. You want them to spread, not to grow toward one another. Again, try to avoid planting in the same place every year.

- The agave snout-nosed weevil becomes active again with the return of cooler weather and invades agaves. Before it strikes, pour diluted *Diazinon* on the top of the plant, letting the liquid slowly trickle down to the leaf bases and, finallly, to the soil. It's a hit-and-miss measure, but it's worth doing. By the time you see the signs of damage, it's too late for treatment. When you discover a totally wilted plant, pull it up and dispose of all the beetles and their grubs. Don't leave them lying around to infest other plants.

- It looks like wetted toilet paper on prickly pear pads. If you don't do anything about it, your plants will be weakened for a long time; they might even die. "It" is a colony of cochineal scale insects. During biblical times, colonies were collected from wild prickly pear plants in the Mediterranean region, as they are in Mexico today, for use as a dye. If you're not interested in making your own dye, the best way to get rid of a colony is to blast it off with a strong jet of water. The scale's protective fuzz keeps insecticides from its soft body, making chemical spraying ineffective.

- It seems an unlikely time for sowing spring flowers, but sweet peas are slow growers. Sow them now. Choose a sunny spot and dig a trench 2 feet deep. Put 8 inches of steer manure in the trench, then scatter ammonium phosphate on this to give a fifty-fifty coverage. Now cover the fertilizer with 8 inches of bagged garden mulch. Finally, put 2 inches of sand on top. Keep the layers, even though doing so breaks all the rules of soil preparation. Give the trench a good soaking. Sow your seed 1 inch deep in the sand, in order to ensure good drainage for the daily watering you'll apply until the seed emerges. (Try to get the Spencer varieties of seed; they seem to do best. Not many nurseries carry them, so you may have to order from a catalog. Second best are the more readily available "heat-resistant" varieties at your local nursery.) You will still have about 4 inches of space left in your trench; fill in with leftover soil as the plants grow. Fresh roots will develop from the stems as they are covered, yielding strong plants. With all that fertility in the trench there should be no need for further fertilizing. You'll need to provide climbing support for the plants before too long; don't let them fall over as they grab one another with their tendrils. You can start with chicken wire, but it will not be strong enough for the mature plants when the wind blows; construction mesh, stood on edge, will make a good circle of support.

- If you want a fine red display from your poinsettias at Christmastime, make sure they have twelve or more hours of darkness each night for the next three or four weeks. Outdoor plants near a porch light or a street lamp will not perform nearly so well as will those that receive complete darkness. Use a large cardboard box or a light-proof cloth (a white sheet won't do) to ensure complete darkness at night. Start this operation early in September; at the very beginning of the month, give the plant a light haircut, snipping the ends of all the branches. This trimming will stimulate dozens of new shoots, and it's on new end-growth that the colorful bracts develop.

- Mexican (red) bird of paradise flowers strongly in September. During the next few weeks the flowerheads will turn to brown seed pods. Trim them off in their early stages if you don't like them, and you'll most likely get more flowering from new shoots. If you prefer to save the seeds, let them stay on the plant until they are hard and brown. Just before they split open, cut them with long stalks and hang them in a paper bag in a dry place. After a few days the pods twist open and forcibly throw the seeds out; you hear them banging away against the bag. The seeds are hard and their thick coats won't allow water in easily. If you want a quicker germination than Mother Nature allows, file a nick in the brown coat, just enough to let you see a lighter color; file the side, not the edge, so that you don't damage the embryo. Sow the seed an inch deep in a styrofoam cup of sandy soil mix, water it regularly, and keep it in a warm place. When the plant is about 4 inches tall, move it into a gallon can of the same soil mix. A little judicious fertilizing will help it along. Next summer, it will be ready to plant outside.

- There'll be a resurgence of plant pests toward the end of the month. Dichondra lawns become infested with flea beetles that scar the leaves and weaken the plant to the point of death; treat as directed in Chapter 19. Orange dog caterpillars appear on the citrus again. Pick them off if you like, but even if you ignore them the damage will be superficial. Grapeleaf skeletonizers are back. Shake the vines in the cool of an early morning and the insects will fall to the ground. (If you should come back from vacation and discover that the skeletonizers have completely eaten up your grape arbor, don't try to get it to grow back now; if you do, the plant will use up next spring's buds and next spring's energy prematurely. Just let it go into an early dry dormancy. This will give the plant a long rest, making it stronger in the spring.) Cutworms in the soil go for newly planted flowers. They've spent the summer deep down where it's cool and haven't had a feed for a long time. They come out at night, encircle the stem, and chew right through it. Plants fall over as if a miniature beaver has been at work. In the evening spray the soil surface with *Malathion*, *Diazinon*, or *Sevin* to control them.

October

October is a good month for working in the landscape. There are things to do, and the release from frequent watering gives you time to do them. The days grow shorter and cooler—mid-80s are the rule—but the sun is bright. Night temperatures in the 50s give plants a welcome respite from summer stress. This difference between day and night temperatures widens as the month progresses, encouraging those plants that survived the rigors of summer to grow again. If a shower or two washes the dust off our plants, the whole landscape looks fresh and bright. It's ready for another growth spell before cold weather arrives in early December.

- "Apply fertilizer when new leaves appear"; it's a good rule to remember, except in the fall! Be pleased that your plants are growing this month, but don't encourage them. Allow them to slow down in harmony with the gradually cooling weather.
- Harden-off tender plants; in other words, ease your plants into an early dormancy by simply letting them dry out. Of course, you mustn't dry them out so thoroughly that they die. Don't water in smaller amounts; you still have to keep the soil around roots moist. Instead, lengthen the interval between waterings. Should it rain, a distinct possibility in October, your strategy will be spoiled, but work on the assumption that it won't rain.
- Don't do heavy pruning in October. A pruning cut stimulates tender new growth, and you don't want that now. Limbs and heavy branches of trees should not be trimmed, except to repair storm damage. You want to keep the tree quiet.
- Hedges are another story. The vigorous new shoots produced by September pruning can now be lightly sheared. The first half of October is a good time to thicken up a hedge with a weekly trim.
- You can still plant some trees and shrubs in October. Junipers and pine trees, for example, will grow new roots for several more weeks, even if air temperatures cool considerably. The semi-tropicals, such as citrus, hibiscus, and palms, won't put out much root growth in cooling soil, so planting them now is a little risky. October is not a good time to set out desert trees, shrubs, or cacti.
- Nurseries often are anxious to clear their sales areas this month to make room for Christmas trees and fall gardening mate-

rials. There are bargains to be had, but be careful. Inspect the merchandise, especially the roots, carefully. If the roots are going round and round at the bottom of the container, that plant is no bargain.

- October is the time to pull out the miserable remnants of summer flowers and put in cool-season flowers. Flowers take fertility from the soil, just as any farm crop does, so it's best to renew it every time you plant afresh; Chapters 6 and 7 tell you how. Don't forget to rotate your flower crops from year to year.

- It's important to give new transplants plenty of moisture while their roots are getting established. October's days are sunny, suggesting a need for frequent watering, but temperatures are cooling and plants' needs for water actually are diminishing. Use your soil probe to tell you when to irrigate. Don't rely on an automatic sprinkler system. In fact, it's better not to sprinkle flowering plants at all; it discolors the flowers. Flood irrigate or use a drip system.

- Whether you are overseeding Bermudagrass or starting a new ryegrass lawn, the weather will be just right sometime in October. Don't panic. You'll have about three weeks of optimum conditions, and several more days when sowing is still possible. But when is the time "just right"? If you start too soon, while it's still hot, most ryegrass seed will not germinate and any that does will be weakened by competition from still-vigorous Bermudagrass. If you wait too long, the seed will germinate slowly in the cool soil and the Bermudagrass will have started to turn brown. The trick is to have the fresh green of ryegrass seedlings imperceptibly replace the fading green of Bermudagrass. A soil thermometer comes in handy now. Sow your ryegrass lawn when the soil temperature 2 inches deep falls to 75 degrees. Don't rely on last year's sowing date, and don't watch for the other guy to begin his operation. There's more time for sowing seed on a new lawn, because you don't have to consider the competition between two grasses or the gradual color replacement of one by the other. There'll be suitable weather right into mid-November, although the longer you wait the cooler the soil will become and the slower the seed will germinate. See Chapter 19 for how to prepare the soil for planting.

- If you want wildflowers in the spring, sow their seeds now. Seedlings need a shower every two weeks in order to grow strongly. If rain falls at steady intervals during the next four months, you're in good shape. If not, you'll have to water. See Chapter 18 for how to start a wildflower patch or garden.

- The first showers of fall both cool the soil and moisten it, triggering germination of a mass of dormant seeds. If we like these annuals we call them wildflowers; if we don't, we call them weeds. Control the latter before they go to seed again.

- October is the month for planting bulbs. A number of them are suitable for the desert, most originating in Africa. You can enjoy a little success with many of the Dutch bulbs, too, but not hyacinths or tulips. Several kinds of bulbs can be left in the ground all through the hot summer; they will survive, provided they are allowed to stay dry. As soon as the first winter rains fall you'll see leaf shoots of amaryllis, daffodil, narcissus, jonquil, Star-of-Bethlehem, and Leucojum. This is the signal to start watering them to keep them growing. Bulbs need to be thinned out after a couple of years; otherwise, they crowd one another and produce small blooms.

- Don't follow the "planting-depth" charts of Europe, where it's a good idea to put bulbs deep down in the soil to keep them safe from the cold. If you plant daffodils 8 inches down in the desert, they won't come up until the weather is hot; as a result, the blooms won't last long. Because you want bulbs to flower before March, plant them at half the recommended depth. Dig the planting ground deeply, and add in ammonium phosphate—or bone meal, if you are an old-time bulb person—but stay away from lots of organic matter that holds moisture; bulbs will rot if they are kept too wet. Some gardeners plant their bulbs on a two-inch layer of coarse sand to ensure good drainage. Then they fill in the soil on top of the bulb. (Don't forget it's the point that goes up; the flat part goes down. In the case of ranunculus, the "fingers" point down.) Bulbs are succulent things and live "off their hump" when they start their growth. Don't drown them with frequent irrigations. Don't let them dry out, either, once they have started growing.

- If you plant daffodil bulbs between yourself and the sun, you will only see their backs; daffodils always face the sun. You'll get a better result if you plant them thus: your back to the sun, their faces toward you.

- As soon as the weather begins to cool, there's usually a fine display of azaleas, camellias, and gardenias in the nurseries. They look lovely in their gallon cans. Shiny leaves and full buds simply call out for you to buy them. Don't fall for it. These plants have just come from cooler, more humid, less sunny places. They are growing in a soil mix high in acidic peat moss. Such plants seldom last a year in the desert. Plant them out now and they'll do fine until June or July; then they'll begin to drop their leaves and die back. If they do survive a summer, perhaps in the shade of a north wall, their buds drop before they open. You have to be a special kind of gardener to be successful with these plants in the desert.

- October is the month when older leaves turn yellow and drop. It's a normal occurrence, almost like a rehearsal for the real fall that's coming. Leaf-fall is the chief way trees get rid of unwanted chemicals; it's a neat discard. Don't worry when you see this for the first time; it seems strange that the mild weather that causes new growth also causes your plants to drop colorful leaves, but usually there's nothing wrong.

- Expect a nut-fall from your pecan tree. The first time you experience an October shedding of immature nuts you assume that something awful has happened. The ground seems covered with black nuts, and just before harvesttime! Take a look up in the tree; you'll most likely see as many nuts on the tree as on the ground, if not more. The nuts still on the tree are as green as the foliage; those are the good ones. The ones on the ground are the poorly filled ones; they're no good to the tree, so it drops them. To make sure the good nuts stay where they are and continue to fatten, give your pecan trees one last deep irrigation before harvest.
- Finally, October is a "buggy" month—so consider yourself forewarned.

November

The cooling trend continues. Days are shorter, the sun is lower in the sky, and shadows, even at midday, are longer. There's no doubt that winter is on the way. There might be a few hot days at the beginning of the month, but there's the danger that the first freeze of the season will take you—and your plants—by surprise before the end of the month.

◆ Take up systematic temperature recording. If you are determined to help frost-tender plants through a possible cold winter, you'll want to know how quickly it's getting cold. You also should know how many degrees warmer or cooler it is at your place than at the official recording station; this will help you decide whether to be complacent or concerned when a frost warning is issued.

Here's how. First, go to a hardware store or a nursery and buy a minimum-recording thermometer. It has a little metal bar on the cold side of the gauge that is moved by the column of mercury as the temperature falls; when temperatures rise again, the mercury moves away from the bar and leaves it where it rested. At any comfortable hour of the day, out you go to read last night's recorded low at your place. Mark your coldest temperature on a chart to see how it differs from that at the official recording station and from the predicted low. (On a sheet of graph paper [four squares to the inch], make the bottom line the days of the month from November 1 through January 30. On the left side mark the temperature in intervals of 5 degrees from 0 at the bottom through 90 near the top. Follow the weather reports; use one color to mark last night's actual low temperature on your chart and another to mark tomorrow night's predicted low.) You'll soon discover whether temperatures are falling steadily, whether you are colder or warmer than the official weather station, and whether the radio and television forecasts are accurate enough to be useful. If temperatures fall a few degrees each night in a regular pattern, your plants will harden off nicely and will be able to withstand the freeze when it comes. If the forecasts prove to be accurate, you can rely on them in the future and protect your plants only when you need to. If your temperatures are consistently warmer than those at the official recording station, even by a few degrees, you don't have to worry so much when they say it's going to freeze.

Hang your minimum-recording thermometer near the plants you are concerned about. Don't hang it inside a citrus tree, where it will be protected, or on a wall, where it will be warmed by residual heat after an afternoon of sunshine. If you have frost-tender plants scattered around your landscape, you'll need several thermometers. You'll be surprised how temperatures vary between an open southern aspect and a walled-in northern patio.

- Cool-season flowers and ryegrass lawns continue to grow in November, but native vegetation and warm-season plants slow down considerably. Deciduous trees and shrubs begin to turn color, a sign of beginning dormancy, and more yellow leaves drop each day. The first frost takes care of the rest. Evergreens, such as bougainvillea and citrus, will hang on to their leaves, but as they go dormant they'll show a lot of pale green or yellow. Don't worry; this is normal. The leaves will green up again when warmer temperatures return. You'll notice a color change in citrus fruits at the beginning of November, too. This is not a sign that the fruit is ripe, although tangerines, navel oranges, and lemons may be, but that falling temperatures are affecting the pigment in their rinds.

- November is not a planting month. It's a month for enjoying the results of work you did in September and October.

- In lower, warmer elevations you may be able to repair gaps in newly seeded lawns and flower beds, and don't forget to dead-head pansies, stock, calendulas, petunias, and roses.

- Be sure your ryegrass lawn is dry when you mow it. Otherwise, the machine's wheels crush soft leaves and this invites disease organisms to enter the watery tissues. Sometimes, particularly if the mower blades are dull, young seedlings are torn out of the ground. Use a catcher to gather the soft mowings; if you leave them lying around, they provide a home for diseases as they lay on wet turf. If you want your winter lawn to look great, be sure your mower blades are sharp and closely adjusted.

- Ammonium sulphate is the usual garden fertilizer, and it works very well in warm soils, but spread it on a lawn in November and nothing happens. The reason is that bacteria are dormant; they can't change ammonium to nitrate, and the grass stays sickly-looking. Try ammonium nitrate. It is stronger than ammonium sulphate, so you use less. Apply small amounts, say a pound to a hundred square feet of winter lawn, every two weeks or so.

- If you overwater flowers, and this easily happens if November is wet and you haven't adjusted the automatic sprinkler system, you can expect soil-borne fungus diseases to kill your plants. You can drench the soil with a fungicide in the early stages of such diseases to save appearances (try *Captan*, *Dyrene*, or *Benomyl*), but the important thing is to change those conditions that favor the fungus. If you irrigate less often, the soil will not stay wet and cold all the time.

- The wildflower seed you sowed in September has now turned into a carpet of young plants, provided there have been intermittent rains or you have been irrigating regularly. Keep up the watering if rain fails to appear or is insufficient. Provide the plants with nutrients, too, even though they are desert plants. Scatter half a pound of ammonium nitrate to every hundred square feet of moist soil. Then water it in, washing the caustic chemical off the leaves. Do this every two or three weeks to keep the plants growing well, but don't overdo it. Keep the foliage a good dark green, but not too dark; otherwise you'll delay flowering. Too much nitrogen might even suppress flowering altogether.

- Nurseries have plenty of chrysanthemums in November, and they are not expensive. If you buy them on the point of flowering you'll know what colors you're getting. Use them for beds, in hanging bowls, and in containers on the patio. Make splashes of winter color all over the place, but don't begin to think of chrysanthemums as permanent additions to your garden, even though they are perennials. You'll find it hardly worth your while to struggle with them through a hot summer. When the flowering is over, pull them out and replant with something more attuned to hot weather.

- If it rains before the freezes start, you'll see mud tunnels resulting from termite activity. These constructions cover the dead stalks of desert plants that dried out during the summer, climb the stalks of roses, palm trees, and saguaros, and lace the walls of buildings. Don't panic. These termites don't attack living plants. Neither do they like bright sunshine, dry desert air, or being eaten by birds. That's why they make tunnels to hide in. By the time you notice termite activity, the insects usually have gone back to their homes deep in the soil; the tunnels are empty. If the tunnels are against the foundations of your house, brush them off. You can ignore the tunnels on landscape plants. There's little point in spraying either the tunnels or the surrounding area. The desert is full of termite nests, and the darned things will surface again when the soil is warm and moist. Watch your house foundations, though; brush, brush!

- Sometimes in November you'll see neat holes, about as big around as a pencil, on the sides of ripening oranges and grapefruits. Out of the hole come a lot of little flies; very soon the hole turns brown and rots, and the fruit is finished before it's ready to eat. Many people think the insects, which are called vinegar beetles or fruit flies, make the holes, but it's not the case. They are simply attracted by the smell of damaged ripening fruit, but the bacteria they track into the sugary juice turns the juice to vinegar. Sapsuckers and thrashers make the holes. They like fruit juice as much as you do. They don't heed such warnings as scarecrows, rubber snakes, or stuffed owls. All you can do is cover your tree with a bird net.

- When is citrus fruit ripe enough to eat? You can't go by fruit color; that's determined by temperature. Tangerines are the first to be ready, then navel oranges and tangelos. Limes and lemons ripen in November, but they stay green until later in the year. Sweet oranges won't be ready until March, and grapefruits, although yellow in November, won't be at their best until April or May. But the question remains. How do you tell when your fruit is ready to eat? A simple taste test does the trick: Find a friend, give him a fruit to eat, and watch. If his lips pucker up, you have to wait a few days more; if a smile covers his face, go for the harvest.

- Citrus picking is not like apple harvesting. Pick just what you need and leave the rest on the tree for another day. The tree is the best place to store citrus fruit. (Tangerines need to be eaten during the next five or six weeks, so don't hold back once this fruit is ready to eat.)

- The desert broom is a much maligned plant. It grows so successfully on its own that it's called a weed. Admittedly, it sometimes grows where it is not wanted, from seed blown in by the wind, and it's not easy to kill with chemicals. It's hard to dig out, too, because its roots are strong and deep. Still, it's a green plant all through the heat of the summer and requires hardly any irrigation. It makes a fine specimen plant standing alone, or it can be planted to make a hedge; trim it to make it tidy. In short, it's a good arid-land plant. In November it attracts our attention. Whole female plants are bent over with the weight of tiny white flowers; the bushes appear to be frosted or covered with snow. It's an attractive sight in the fall sunshine. Now comes the criticism. There are rumors abounding that the white fluff floating in the breeze causes allergies. This is quite wrong. The stuff is too big to get up your nose, so it's impossible to breathe it into your body. Relax.

December

December's weather is unreliable. We may get rain or it may be dry and sunny. The only thing that's certain is that the days are short. For most of the month the sun rises soon after 7 and sets before 5:30. This doesn't give you time to do anything in the yard before or after work; only the weekends are left. Fortunately, there's not a lot to do. Short days and low temperatures mean plants aren't very active either.

- Have your frost protection materials handy; you may need them in a hurry. Frosts are unpredictable. Be prepared with light blankets or heavy sheets, extension cords, and low-wattage light bulbs. Frost warnings often come at the last minute—or you react to them at the last minute—and you don't want to be looking all over the place for misplaced items that you need immediately. See Chapter 9 for more.

- Some years we get to enjoy fall colors in November; some years we have to wait until December. Find out the names of those colorful plants that please you, and think of putting them into your landscape next spring. Trees that give us autumn color include locust, chinaberry, poplar, cottonwood, pistache, and ash. Peach, apricot, and pomegranate trees are colorful, too. A persimmon tree, with its orange fruit hanging at the tips of bare winter branches makes a wonderful living Christmas ornament in your landscape; be sure to plant it where you'll see it. Another "Christmassy" plant is the shrub *Photinia fraseri;* its bright new red leaves sit atop a green shrub like glowing candles. The pads of Santa Rita prickly pear turn reddish as the cold weather continues, too. Other colorful plants include the small wild poinsettia (it seeds itself far and wide), fountain grass, New Zealand flax, nandina, and hopseed bush. All have leaves that turn dark brown or purple in cold weather.

- December is not pruning time; wait for complete dormancy. People are impatient, and some love the sound of chain saws. This often leads to imprudent pruning. Don't rush the job. In the case of deciduous trees, wait until the leaves are off the tree. Then take a test snipping of a twig or two; if sap runs out the end, the tree is not completely dormant and it's not yet time to prune. In the case of palm trees, don't cut off any green fronds. In the case of tall trees, don't saw off the branches all at the same height; don't top your trees. See Chapter 21 for details.

- What happens if you prune too soon? The sap that comes out the ends of the cut branches acts like glue. Any fungus and bacteria spore blowing in the wind gets caught in it, the sap provides food for the spores, and the spore grows into the space between the bark and the wood. Your tree is now infected with either sooty canker (a fungus) or slime flux (a bacteria), and either will kill your tree. When the time is ripe, use a spray can of pruning paint to protect the cut ends from these invaders.

- Fallen leaves are money in the bank for home gardeners. They will make a beautiful soil additive when the time comes to dig a flower bed or plant a tree. All you have to do is rake them into a pile and surround that pile with stout wire so that they don't blow away. Keep the pile lightly moist, turn it when the temperature reaches 160 degrees, and beneficial bacteria will do the rest. They will decompose your unwanted leaves, as well as added kitchen vegetable scraps, weeds, and garden clippings, into a very good alternative to expensive peat moss or "mulch." With proper turnings—three or four of them—you'll get a good compost in 3–4 months.

- Don't let frost warnings frighten you into picking citrus fruit. It's true that fruit will be damaged if it is exposed to three hours of temperatures at 28 degrees or below, but the weather forecast won't tell you how long the coldest predicted temperature will last. Cover your tree and provide heat inside it, but don't pick the fruit to avoid possible damage unless the forecast is for several days of continuous freezing temperatures. If you have lots of trees and few blankets, first protect the limes, then the lemons, then the oranges, then the tangerines (you're probably eating them by now, anyway), and finally the grapefruits, which are more hardy than the others. If you feel you must pick, start with the exposed outer fruit; inside fruit is somewhat protected by the foliage. Remember that citrus fruit is better stored on the tree, all things being equal.

- Don't rely on irrigating to protect your trees from freezing. You'd have to flood the whole yard 6 inches deep to achieve your purpose, perhaps every night.

- Don't water plants with ice-cold water. This is especially true of container plants, which have a warmer soil because they are in a sheltered part of the patio or sunporch. Be especially careful with house plants. Keep your watering container full of water in the room where the plants are.

- Keep the wildflowers growing. If it doesn't rain much in December, water them occasionally. Once a week might be too often, but they are shallow-rooted and need some attention. During one of these waterings, give the plants some ammonium nitrate if their color is a little pale. Scatter it on wet soil at the rate of 1 pound to a hundred square feet and water it in well. Don't hesitate to nourish wildflowers as they grow.

- It might snow in December. Snow itself isn't all that cold, and as it melts it provides a sort of drip irrigation that soaks the soil. Snow is unwelcome only because it is heavy. It can break branches of junipers and other leafy evergreens. It's best to brush snow off your plants to save them from being bent over.
- Prickly pears are weakened by a freeze, and frozen pads tend to snap off and fall to the ground. If you are a purist, this may not bother you; this is how prickly pears grow naturally into thickets. The fallen pads easily root where they rest on the soil. If you are a tidy landscaper, however, you may want to clean up after a freeze. You can discard the fallen pieces or you can cut them cleanly into smaller bits and plant them. If you plant them right away, dust the ends with powdered sulphur to keep out fungus and bacteria. Otherwise, store the pieces in a sheltered carport or under a tree where they won't be further damaged by more frosty nights. The cut ends will scab over on their own and will be ready for planting in two or three weeks, even two or three months. Plant the pieces on a mound for good drainage; succulents easily rot in cold wet soil.
- There's not a lot of urgent work to be done in the December landscape, aside from repairing any damage caused by storms. Plan your springtime plantings, clean and sharpen tools, overhaul engines, or clean out the garden shed if you must. Then go in and sit by the fire (remember: don't spread the ashes in the garden), dream over the garden catalogs, and read a good landscaping book.

Index

References to illustrations are printed in **boldface** type.

ABOUT THE AUTHOR

George grew up in England where landscaping is a way of life—an environment that cannot fail to shape those who live in it. He went to school in the countryside and learned maintenance tasks under the supervision of the grounds manager whose philosophy was, necessarily, one of minimum care because of budget constraints.

George's understanding of appropriate landscape maintenance was strengthened during eleven years in Tanganyika, East Africa, where he worked as a Government Agricultural Officer. The harsh environment did not allow extravagant landscapes of exotic imported plants. Native plants, already there, had to do the job. Water for plant care was a luxury. Planting had to coincide with the seasonal rains. Plants had to survive the long dry season on their own, and landscaping development had to coincide with nature's unreliable cycles.

This African experience reinforced George's belief that landscaping should be determined by local conditions, not textbook definitions. Maintenance should be sparing in cost and effort, and it should assist, rather than alter, plant growth.

George has spent nearly thirty years in Arizona, first teaching landscape maintenance classes at Arizona Western College in Yuma and then serving as an Extension Agent (Urban Horticulture) in Tucson with the University of Arizona.

He has encouraged people to change their landscapes from conventional "back-east" large lawns and extensive flower beds wastefully watered to more economical desert themes using arid-land trees and shrubs that are irrigated by drip systems and don't need constant trimming and fussing over.

George's educational programs reach commercial landscape maintenance people and thousands of home-owners through talks, seminars, workshops and demonstrations, newspaper and magazine articles, radio and TV programs. He has written more than thirty Garden Guides for public distribution by the University. He contributed to the chapter on citrus in the book *Plants for Dry Climates* by Jones and Duffield, and he is the author of the popular *Desert Gardening—Fruits and Vegetables.*